Postmodern Humanism in Contemporary
Literature and Culture

About the Jacket Illustration

Rebecca Strzelec's innovative art work is created in a digital environment using Computer Aided Design. These pieces, which she describes as "wearable objects," are realized tangibly though the use of Rapid Prototyping. The object displayed on the cover is from her series entitled *Army Green Orchids*. Inspired by early botanical illustrations, the series consists of some 30 brooches that attempt to redefine the corsage. The series is designed to bring awareness to the practices surrounding commercially cultivated flowers and the increasing number of American military casualties in Iraq. "I am unable to reconcile the need for these deaths and find it hard to imagine that each individual has been given the reverence or attention he or she deserves," Strzelec writes. "To bring attention to the preciousness lost in the overwhelming numbers, I turn to color. 'Army' green speaks to military activity in general, but also to the familiar toy soldier, sold in bags by the millions. In many ways, we have created the mass-produced soldier." In this manner, Strzelec is seeking to reconcile the postmodern void through the *Army Green Orchids*.

Postmodern Humanism in Contemporary Literature and Culture

Reconciling the Void

Todd F. Davis

Kenneth Womack

First published 2006 by
PALGRAVE MACMILLAN
Houndmills, Basingstoke, Hampshire RG21 6XS and
175 Fifth Avenue, New York, N.Y. 10010
Companies and representatives throughout the world

PALGRAVE MACMILLAN is the global academic imprint of the Palgrave
Macmillan division of St. Martin's Press, LLC and of Palgrave Macmillan Ltd.
Macmillan® is a registered trademark in the United States, United Kingdom
and other countries. Palgrave is a registered trademark in the European
Union and other countries.

ISBN-13: 9781–4039–4681–2 hardback
ISBN-10: 1–4039–4681–7 hardback

This book is printed on paper suitable for recycling and made from fully
managed and sustained forest sources.

A catalogue record for this book is available from the British Library.

Library of Congress Cataloging-in-Publication Data

Davis, Todd F., 1965–
    Postmodern humanism in contemporary literature and culture :
    reconciling the void / Todd F. Davis; Kenneth Womack.
        p. cm.
    Includes bibliographical references and index.
    ISBN 1–4039–4681–7
        1. American literature—20th century—History and criticism,
    2. Postmodernism (Literature)   3. Humanism in literature.   I. Womack,
    Kenneth.   II. Title.

PS228.P68D38 2007
810.9'113—dc22   2006044298

10 9 8 7 6 5 4 3 2 1
15 14 13 12 11 10 9 8 7 6

Transferred to Digital Printing in 2010.

For Kjell Meling (1941–2005)
"We are all Viking marauders!"

Contents

Acknowledgements

We owe special debts of gratitude to the many friends and colleagues who helped make this volume possible. We are particularly grateful for the encouragement and advice of Lori Bechtel, Ervin Beck, Bruce Bode, Joyce and Harold Davis, Shelly Davis, James M. Decker, Lee Ann De Reus, Andrea Endriga, Kate Latterell, Amy Mallory-Kani, Ian Marshall, Kjell Meling, Jim Mellard, Dinty W. Moore, Rebecca Strzelec, Gary Weisel, Michael Wolfe, and Jeanine Womack. We also wish to thank our friends at Palgrave—particularly Paula Kennedy, Emily Rosser, Helen Craine, and the editorial team of Macmillan India—who helped see this volume through production.

Finally, we are indebted to several publications for granting us permission to reprint portions of our work, including *Mosaic: A Journal for the Interdisciplinary Study of Literature* for "Writing Back through the Body: Flesh and Spirit in the Work of Mary Swander"; *Style* for "Saints, Sinners, and the Dickensian Novel: The Ethics of Storytelling in John Irving's *The Cider House Rules*"; *Textual Ethos Studies—Or Locating Ethics*, edited by Anna Fåhraeus and AnnKatrin Johnson, for "David Mamet's Altered Ethics: Finding Forgiveness, or Something Like It, in *House of Games, The Spanish Prisoner*, and *State and Main*"; and *Western American Literature* for "Embracing the Fall: Reconfiguring Redemption in Jim Harrison's *The Woman Lit by Fireflies, Dalva*, and *The Road Home*."

Introduction: Necessary Negotiations

> To my fellow prisoners I say, Just because the escape
> tunnel goes on forever is no reason to stop digging.
> Stephen Dunn, "Personal"

Narrative Acts: The Task of Telling Our Stories

Humans are, if anything, meaning-making creatures. Under the constraints and demands of living in the twenty-first century, we turn time and again to the act of storytelling, to narrative constructs of our own creation, to make (or to *find*, as some might suggest) meaning. At present, given the current knowledge we possess of the animal world, it appears that humans find themselves alone in this activity, particularly suited and adept to its demands. From the earliest instances of cave drawings to the innumerable oral traditions in cultures across the world, from the oldest extant written texts to today's multiplying proliferation of narrative making in songs, films, computer games, blogs, books, poetry slams, and so on—if one thing is clear, it is that we are compelled to tell and retell our stories—to cope, to comfort, to control, to manipulate, to dominate, to heal, to make gestures toward understanding our place in the universe or, at the very least, the appearance of it.

Myriad reasons for this intensely human penchant exist, and, needless to say, we make no claim to understand all of the motivations or implications of these complex and at times baffling acts. What interests us the most as literary critics, as professors of English, as fathers and husbands and friends, is how humans deal with the condition of mortality. What we wish to examine is the manner in which a story becomes a way of reconciling the void—for the artist and for the person who enters into the work of art in a posture of partnership and collaboration. As Jim

Morrison succinctly (and now famously) put it: "No one here gets out alive." If indeed—as Mr Morrison and the biological facts of our bodies constantly remind us—we cannot continue to live forever, that despite our best efforts at prolonging the inevitable we will not get out of here alive, then how can we begin to place this experience, this thing called "life," in a context that helps us to embrace it, that helps us to further it in ways that lead toward peace and health and wholeness, instead of fragmentation and the violence of certain kinds of dissonance? In other words, with what should we fill our fleeting days of living, and how does a story fit into this way of being "present" in the world?

Questions abound as we move through the mundane moments of daily existence: How does love, or faith, or violence, figure into the ways we choose to live? How do the narratives we consume shape the way we see and interact with the world? How do these narratives encourage us to frame the stories we tell, and to what narratives beyond ourselves do we subscribe? More to the point: How do we make sense, through the act of storytelling, of these befuddling postmodern times? Can story making continue to possess not only meaning but also power and influence given the developments in philosophy and literary theory over the last several decades (that is, deconstruction and anti-essentialism)?

We need only pick up a newspaper, flip on the television, or visit a webpage to bear witness to the current state of things. War rages; AIDS spreads virulently from country to country; famine destroys hundreds of thousands of lives; epidemiologists offer dire predictions about the next flu pandemic; terrorist attacks flare and in their light each night on the news fear-mongers peddle their wares; diseases once thought to be eradicated forever resurface, resistant to antibiotics and vaccines; hurricanes, tornados, tsunamis—with growing power and frequency—recklessly destroy large swaths of the world; religious fundamentalism rears its head, convincing its followers to condemn, and, at times, even to kill in its name; intolerance of all kinds (political, social, religious) rewards its followers if they judge harshly those who do not adhere to the same central tenants and texts; technology continues to find ways to solve and then to create more problems; fossil fuels burn and burn, firing the planet in the bright light of global warming; vast numbers of species of flora and fauna walk into the darkness of extinction at a rate that staggers, sending ripples across the various ecosystems that sustain both human and animal life.

This ill-composed cacophony—made from the fabric of the harm we do to one another and to the other forms of life with which we share this planet—seems to rise in pitch and decibel with no end or solution in sight. The darkness of these times opens like an abyss, a void wracked with pain and doubt and the chilling winds of oblivion. It is this void to which we all wake—some of us choosing to ignore it utterly, others stumbling around its edges, acknowledging the horror of its implications yet turning away with a sense of powerlessness. It is this condition that our storytellers struggle with and against, their responses as vast and different and complex as any of the reactions we have as human beings.

Certain artists chronicle the present moment without comment; some despair, falling into a state of detachment, of numbness; still others celebrate with the masochistic energy of dread; and as incongruous as it may seem, some even find means for hope, for the possibility of change or transformation. In an interview, Li-Young Lee explains that because he has children, "everything's at stake. My final report to them can't be that our true human condition is homelessness and exile. Of course," he adds, "if that's what I ultimately discover, then that's what I'll report. But my hope is that someday I will be a poet of blessing and praise. I need to find my way home, and I need to get there authentically" (6). As odd as it may seem to certain factions in the world of literary scholarship, at least part of *Reconciling the Void* was born out of concerns similar to that of Lee's. We believe that literature is part of the very fabric of humanity, and, as in any ecosystem, each part impacts the whole. Because of this we wonder what role literary art might play in blessing the world to come? How what we read and celebrate in literature may affect our children, our students, our colleagues, our political leaders, and, in turn, the very shape of the world for subsequent generations? Like Lee, we wish to find a way that is authentic, one that connects literature and home, our stories to the lives we live both in and out of the classroom. What is an authentic way to respond to literature, and what might happen if we take seriously Mary Oliver's claim that "No poem is about one of us, or some of us, but is about all of us." Oliver contends that a poem "is part of a long document about the species. Every poem is about my life but also it is about your life, and a hundred thousand lives to come" (*Blue Pastures* 109). While such questions and assertions cannot be answered or defended definitively, we argue that for far too long literary critics have ignored these kinds of issues, suggesting that such matters fall outside the boundaries of academic discussion. What we offer in this study is a gesture—one possibility among many—toward the real ways artists combat the devastating forces of the contemporary landscape, ways that can be navigated by the student and scholar to great reward.

Story as Sound Bite: The Culture of Debate

As we have argued elsewhere, although postmodernity offers a proliferation of narratives that calls into question any univocal meaning based upon an essential center of reference, the rise of fundamentalist thought—be that in the political, religious, or social sphere—appears to hold sway for many, offering comfort for those who do not wish to "negotiate" meaning based upon referential slippage.[1] Increasingly, over the past decade or more, the discourse within political, religious, social, and, sadly, even intellectual spheres has been framed by the construct of duality and dichotomy—an outcome that few postmodern theorists foresaw in the 1970s and 1980s. This limiting structure of power herds all of us into the ark of intellectual and public discourse, two by two, creating a system akin to factory-farming—one which does not possess or allow for the diversity and complexity, the hybridization of human thought and action, so necessary to our health. The corrals and stanchions we find ourselves standing in are labeled conservative or liberal, Republican or Democrat, red state or blue state, patriot or traitor, modernist or post-modernist. The stories we seek to tell are reduced to nametags and sound bites. Our very movements—both physical and intellectual—are boxed in, leading to atrophy. Given the strictures of the present system, the possibility of our lives is truncated radically, and it would be our contention that art—with its potential to change the ways people think and feel and live—is often irreparably damaged when scholars and teachers attempt to make it fit into a particular theoretical box.[2]

The popular media must carry part of the blame for this polarization. Twenty-four hours a day, television doles out journalistic "debate" that has little to do with the act of listening or consideration. The nuances of daily living that flesh out any full and fulfilling picture of the contemporary landscape are seldom acknowledged by popular news. Lines are drawn clearly, albeit facilely, and the rhetoric too often is filled with violence and animosity. Generosity or trust in the exchange of ideas or perspectives seems as quaint and archaic as a novel by Charles Dickens. This is the age of the gladiatorial shouting match where nothing is resolved, where no middle ground is sought, no compromise parlayed into something greater than its opposing parts for the possibility of growth. Whether it is Bill O'Reilly on Fox or Chris Matthews on CNBC (or any of the other programs that dominate print, television, radio, and Internet media, for that matter), the format remains the same: (1) simplify the issues; (2) bring in a political leader or representative from the right and the left; (3) give each representative the scantest of time (in reality, only enough time to reel off pithy clichés and "talking points"); and (4) encourage all who are involved to shout and interrupt each other, obliterating any chance for the possibilities that dialogue might hold. Perhaps none of this would be much cause for concern if it were not for the ubiquitous nature of this kind of "news" coverage and its impact upon our educational system. Sadly, even our intellectual discourse and study have begun to take on the worst accoutrements of this model—in both universities and privately funded think tanks. We must remember that over the past 20 years the growth in programming and the variety of delivery systems (cable, digital, satellite, Internet) has multiplied at a pace few could have imagined in the first half of the twentieth century. The world we live in now seems to have materialized out of the pages of some outlandish 1930s science fiction magazine, and at present, the vast majority of people in the Western world receive their information from kinetic sources that flash with an energy and a penchant that is maddening. Needless to say, future generations are being shaped in a radical fashion by these influences, and we already can see the impact in the ways we draw lines and use theory within literary criticism.

Theory as Monolith

Theory, by its very nature, is monolithic. When Derrida, Levinas, Habermas, Lyotard, or some other renowned philosopher or theoretician maps out his or her philosophical concerns and accompanying answers to those concerns, he or she seldom attempts to build bridges toward theoretical counterparts. While they may use the work of some other philosopher who has come before them to distinguish the ways in which their own position differs, they do not offer the opposition—a "theoretical" enemy of sorts—a seat at their table, a slap on the back for a point well made, the warm embrace of solidarity. (Aren't we all trying to make sense of our journey?) In fact, it appears that Harold Bloom's Oedipal beliefs may prove more apt among theorists than the artists he wrote about in *The Anxiety of Influence: A Theory of Poetry* (1973). Theorists have become the new intellectual prophets of the day, espousing philosophical visions that help their followers see the world "the way it really is." Theory resembles science in its desire to validate itself through various forms of reason, and while we would never suggest that rational thought in and of itself is a bad thing, we do wish to point out that most humans do not think or act rationally with any consistency. Rather, humans exist as an admixture of a wide range of forces. Take a sojourn through the halls of nearly any graduate school and you are likely to find devout followers of particular genres of theory, and like any new converts, the fervor with which these graduate students espouse and argue for their particular "prophet" and theoretical "religion" is rather impressive. But how long can such fervor last? While the newly converted burn brightly with hard-edged conviction, where might they go with their disillusionment at discovering that the professor who has championed Marxist thought actually drives a Jaguar and lives in a gated community? How do they negotiate the news that a leading feminist thinker danced her way through graduate studies at a strip club? Is it similar to the way Christians must accommodate the "sins" of their spiritual leaders—hating the sin but loving the sinner? The point here is that humans are always "fallen" creatures, if we may borrow and remake for other purposes this term from Christian theology. Theory has the power to affect the ways we think and act, but ultimately, theory lives in an ideal world where ideas do not gather mud on their feet, where the range of needs and desires we have as humans do not hold sway. As Jim Harrison comments in his brief memoir, "Tracking," "Scholars can talk of 'belief systems' but the brain is welter, not a linear construct" (273).

Even more distressing is the fact that for some in this profession the idea that one's life beyond a text plays an integral role in one's reading of a text essentially invalidates the critic's interpretation. For example, recently ecocritics have come under fire because the very thing they study is the thing they love. As the ecocritic delves into Thoreau or Muir or Carson, often he or she will tell us about some lived experience—a backpacking trip, something they saw from their home in the woods— that relates to the text under consideration. Such patterns of connection are deemed by some as unprofessional and out of bounds. Michael P. Branch explains that he questions "any call to arms that would solve the problem of lightheadedness among nature writers and ecocritics by suggesting that hiking or playing music or loving the subject of study (all of which have recently become targets) constitutes a form of intellectual enfeeblement" (43). The humanities have long been plagued by a sense of insecurity when their scholarly endeavors are compared to those of the sciences. Over the past half century, we have seen the language of science borrowed by a range of literary critics; we have seen an increasing desire on the part of the academy to divorce the humanities from the very thing that comprises its essence in the first place: human experience. Human relationships not only comprise the study of literature, but they also affect it. If we agree that there are only levels or degrees of "objectivity," not some pristine place where all human concerns and desires fall away, then we should not find ourselves loosening our collars and wiping sweat from our brows when we compare the work we do in literary study with research on diabetes or cancer. (As it has been shown, even science—with its greater degree of objectivity—is not free from human concerns. What diseases are studied, what programs are funded, what populations are examined—all of these issues are far more subjective than some would care to admit.)[3]

Where once postmodern philosophers like Jean-François Lyotard believed a proliferation of narratives would flourish, leading to multiplicities—to a range of discourse that might offer the possibility for liberation and freedom—we bear witness instead to a reduction of narratives based upon the premise of polarization and an economic model—which Fredric Jameson anticipated in his writing about late capitalism—that "sells" the goods of duality to an ever-growing and ever-eager audience. Instead of a range of viewpoints that demonstrates the disparity and complexity of human perspectives, the "two-party system" of popular intellectual life dominates and dictates to the exclusion of nearly all else. This kind of thinking also encourages dichotomous ways of knowing, a black and white approach to the world that demands that we march artists into specific, opposing categories in which they have become classified and entrenched, filing them under neat titles and labels, their sole purpose as evidence that our theories function as we alleged they would. Strangely, although much postmodern theory champions the idea of multiplicity, of the constructed nature of borders and the delimiting quality of definition, many practicing critics will boldly state that certain artists are either postmodern or they are not, that certain theorists should be used to examine a literary text while others are excluded because of the categories they place them into. Like the talking heads of television debate who seldom respond to one another—instead offering opposing monologues that dismiss the far more valuable possibilities of dialogue—at present we have far too many scholars dismissing one another because theory has become the *essential* and *essentializing* text within our profession.

What we hope to offer in this book is not a dismissal of theory; it is a valuable source and a way of knowing that has been explored and highlighted in volumes too numerous to count. (In fact, we would argue that no act of interpretation can take place without some kind of theory, whether it be recognized or not.) However, the concerns and passions that drive the writing of this book—while clearly constructed upon the foundation of an amalgamation of theory[4]—have little to do with highlighting any particular theoretical perspective. What engages us in this moment is the manner in which artists and storytellers at work today create particular responses to the human condition—and how these responses, when examined with a collaborative posture that wishes to make meaning not undo it—proffer interpretative possibilities that work within as well as outside of the academy. What these artists have in common is that they believe (and we certainly agree) that their poems and stories, songs and films, are merely gestures toward the big questions that have plagued humankind in every century, and like these artists, our interpretations should not be seen as authoritative. As readers, we, too, are making gestures, working our way through these texts, trying to make meaning within a particular context that encompasses as many spheres of our lives as possible.

While such a confession on the part of the critic might have caused great consternation at one point in our profession's history—perhaps even our own personal history as literary critics—we hope that it does little to contribute to the anxieties and worries of a scholarly community already wracked with the problems of an egregious job market, a shrinking publishing industry, and a position that can only be described as perilous when we look at a broader culture that at best shakes its head at what we do and at worst ignores it completely. Even if the critic cannot speak with absolute authority, he or she does a great service—not just to the profession but also to the world of story beyond the profession. After all, as we read and interpret, as we attempt to make meaning, the possibility for connection, for community, for relationship looms before us. What binds human to human, community to community, country to country are our stories. The chasm of everyday existence can only be bridged as we listen to one another, as we judge the relative worth of differing artistic and scholarly voices, as we speak to our students, our spouses and partners, our friends about why this film or song or novel made such a difference for us.

Language Games: Acknowledging and Then Moving beyond the Imperfect

In *A Primer to Postmodernity* (1997), Joseph Natoli contends that "postmodernity has questioned the authorizing and legitimizing of both faith and reason, opting for the view that both offer stories of reality, none of which can validate a precise correspondence between themselves and what may actually be going on in reality" (15). While postmodernity clearly questions the ultimate authority and legitimacy of faith and reason—recognizing the power that resides in their stories, but contending that neither can conclusively demonstrate an absolute knowledge—postmodern dogma and doctrine cannot deny that many who dwell in the contemporary landscape continue to use both epistemological forms to help guide their way in daily living. It appears that the majority of us choose by default a middle ground between faith and reason where neither the modern nor the postmodern ultimately wins the day, and the fact that neither faith nor reason may be proved or disproved conclusively causes little consternation in the general populous. More to the point, it would appear that postmodernism's own dogmatic assertion that we cannot know "reality" in any absolute manner—a position that is difficult to dismiss on a theoretical plane—does not, then, acknowledge or highlight in the same fashion the fact that all of our endless negotiations with the demands of the human condition finally *are* based in a faith of sorts.

The difference between acknowledging the constructed system in which we live, the essential artifacts of the nonessential culture and language systems that compose our "reality," and the ways in which we must navigate the day-to-day demands of living as human beings—replete with emotional, spiritual, psychological, and physical needs—might best be illustrated by the following two poems that focus on language and the manner in which some of us approach wordplay to meet our aforementioned and all-too-human needs. The first poem, "Tattoo," examines the radical dissonance and sweeping distance between a more theoretically charged approach to linguistic signification that keeps the body's lived experience at arm's length and an approach that sees language as part of the body, rooted in our most base knowledge and physical practices.

Tattoo

> Try telling the boy who's just had his girlfriend's name
> cut into his arm that there's slippage between the signifier
> and the signified. Or better yet explain to the girl
> who watched in the mirror as the tattoo artist stitched
> the word for her father's name (on earth as in heaven)
> across her back that words aren't made of flesh and blood,
> that they don't bite the skin. Language is the animal
> we've trained to pick up the scent of meaning. It's why
> when the boy hears his father yelling at the door
> he sends the dog that he's kept hungry, that he's kicked,
> then loved, to attack the man, to show him that every word
> has a consequence, that language, when used right, hurts.

(Davis, *Some Heaven* 71)

When the poet says that "Language is the animal / we've trained to pick up the scent of meaning," he emphasizes the animate qualities of language, the fact that it is a living and ever-changing medium. In addition, it is the "scent of meaning," not meaning itself that language has been trained to pick up. Meaning—the exact, precise idea or thought we wish to communicate—may never be attainable in its most pure, Platonic sense, but the fact that we do make gestures, at times successful ones, toward communicating love or hatred or forgiveness, does suggest that the "slippage between the signifier / and the signified" may not be as important as the flawed meaning conveyed in the imperfect use of language. The second poem, "Spelling Test," acts out one of the earliest encounters many of us have with language in its written manifestation. Who among us cannot remember studying our weekly spelling words, attempting to remember if the rule is *i* before *e* or if the *f* sound is made with an *f* or a *ph*? More to the point, the initial recognition that the language we have been using—the words that our parents have spoken while reading our favorite story to us or that we have begun reading to ourselves as we try to make sense of comic books and chapter books—is dazzling and literally life-altering. Our ability to identify and enter fully into a written system of communication, comprised of individual markings that somehow coalesce to form sounds that in turn represent images and ideas that move us, that make us laugh, that frighten us, that change the way we think about our very physical existence, seems improbable, yet such "miraculous" events transpire daily as we train and instruct our children to become part of such a system.

Spelling Test

> The mother makes the boy repeat the word aloud
> three times, asks him to roll the sounds out upon
> the edges of his tongue, the much talked of tip.
> She tries to demonstrate the logic of the letters
> following in a line, how each hugs the next
> in friendship, fastens part of its own life to the life
> of its neighbor: their voices in conversation, heads
> bent out of windows, arms resting on top of fences.
>
> Together they build something bold or something
> shy, that despite their demeanor holds fast to meaning.
> The boy's hands grow tired, clinched so tightly
> white forms around the knuckles, until the word
>
> has passed, until at last he lets go, sees language
> can't be corralled. It's the lips after all—a smile,

teeth showing, tongue wet, and words slipping out
to taste every good thing we might remember.

(Davis, *Some Heaven* 90)

As this poem demonstrates, language can and does create stress as we attempt to master it. If we try to think metacognitively about language at the very same moment we attempt to use it, most of us fall miserably on our linguistic faces. The high priests and priestesses who guard the gates to language acquisition—linguists and language poets, semiologists and deconstructionists—may wish to highlight the constructed nature of language, but as we use language pragmatically in our day-to-day dealings, the best most of us can do is to try to see through language, like a window, to the thing it seeks to describe or communicate; it is the thing on the other side of language's pane of glass that we are moving toward in our relationships with one another. In *Standing by Words* (1983), Wendell Berry contends that "love makes language exact, because one loves only what one knows" (61). Building upon Berry's contention about the relationship between love and language, we argue that language is used most honestly, with the most integrity, when we are attempting to move toward someone in verbal relationship. In other words, language relies upon trust in some form of relationship when we hope to communicate with precision. One need only compare a loving parent trying to explain to his or her child about a grandparent's sickness or death to a politician explaining his or her latest fiscal plan. What might the windowpane look like in each of these examples?

Where Do We Place Our Faith: The Ethics of Trust in Literary Study

Consider how we use language in other areas of our culture. For example, in the medical professions it is crucial—often a matter of life and death—that those involved bargain in good faith with one another when speaking or writing. In such cases, there is little margin for error, and the very idea that one would "deconstruct" the language being used for medical treatment during a heart attack or some other life-threatening illness seems rather nefarious. While doctors and nurses and physicians' assistants may recognize that language is an imperfect tool, they must seek to create or construct meaning in an effort to come as close as they can to the correct interpretation of a fellow medical professional's statements.

Like these kinds of professionals, while we recognize the flawed nature of language, acknowledging the seams where the threads of words unravel in deferment, ultimately we seek connection and unity. Once we witness the ways in which a story or a film or a song may come undone, word rubbing against word in the friction of (mis)reading, we are compelled to return to the commonalities of human experience and the overarching desire for meaning and relationship that offers not only hope for the future but in many ways also serves as the loadstone in the arch that carries us across the chasm of alienation as we confront the void. It is our aspiration to treat the artists that we engage in this book in a similar fashion to the doctor who seeks to understand a patient, to make a connection that allows for communication and the possibility of healing that comes with understanding. What might happen if we begin to think of understanding and comprehension within literary studies as a form, or at the very least, a means for healing? Aren't the literary arts, at least in part, about confronting what haunts us and what plagues us?

Let us be clear: when we refer to meaning-making in these contexts, we are not talking about performing interpretative acts with the kind of "certainty" that leads to perfunctory relationships and dogmatism. As Mark Strand says of his parents' reading habits, "Both my parents were avid readers of nonfiction, pursuing information not just for enlightenment but to feel in control of a world they had little say in. Their need for certainty was proportional to their sense of doubt. If one had facts— or what passed for facts—at one's fingertips, one could not only banish uncertainty but also entertain the illusion that one lived in a fixed and static universe, in a world that was passive and predictable and from which mystery was exiled" (48). Far from seeing the universe as static and the world as passive and predictable, we are drawn to forms of story and literary art that grapple with the mystery of our existence, with the unpredictable and fleeting nature of it. Moreover, language itself, while potentially clear and lucid, may be the glass through which we see what ultimately is beyond us and beyond our comprehension. Like Emerson, we see language as a gesture not a concretized act. It seems to us as readers, as critics, as humans in relationship with others, that one of the outcomes of narrative and the interpretative acts that serve as an accomplice to narrative is the trust that is implicit in interpretation and how that trust joins us not only to the artist but also to each other.

We contend that trust should be seen as an ethical category for the study of narrative. The act of storytelling requires trust of those involved: the reader must trust the writer; the writer must trust the reader. And such a relationship ultimately spreads in a circle as we come into contact with the community of readers who have shared the experience of a particular book or film or play. Inevitably, both the writer and the reader will make mistakes; both the writer and the reader will betray each other during the act of interpretation. But if we are to come to an understanding of a given text, each party involved must forgive the other, must move beyond vengefulness or self-pity to continue to make gestures toward interpretation that bring us a little closer to shared meaning. Language is a series of negotiations rooted in a finite and imperfect system. Yet language is necessary for the creation of community, which is fundamental to the human condition.

The Many Faces of Postmodern Humanism: Why We Read What We Read

How does *reading* a particular narrative make any difference in the life of the reader? How might art hold out the possibility (or possess this possibility within itself) to change or transform a reader? How do we talk about transformation or reconciliation or consolation in the contemporary landscape, because surely we continue to turn to narrative for these gifts? And, finally, do such questions suggest that we continue to live under the precepts of modernist humanism, or has a shift occurred in certain factions, transforming humanist thought in significant ways? As Ihab Hassan passionately implores in *Paracriticisms* (1975), "I believe that an answer must go beyond our current shibboleths: disconfirmation, decreation, demystification, deconstruction, decentering, depropriation, difference, etc. Perhaps we need to go beyond Irony (as Nietzsche sometimes did), beyond the current aversion to Wholeness and Meaning, to some working faith in . . . What?" (xv).

As we have suggested elsewhere, perhaps the most significant difference between modern and postmodern humanism is the transparency of postmodern humanism. Postmodern humanism openly acknowledges that, in the absence of a "given" center of value agreed upon by all peoples, it creates a center of value, that it constructs a position that reveres all life. Unlike historic Western European discourse that first placed value on human life because of its belief that humanity was created in the image of God, postmodernism feigns no assurance that "truth" may be founded on the knowledge of providence or science or any other grand narrative that wishes to establish itself as the essence or center on which discourse may be grounded. The differences between modern and postmodern humanism finally boil down to the issue of essence: one believes in a fixed, essential reference point while the other, dismissing this notion, offers only an operational essentialism, a working faith in the preservation of all forms of life, not just human life (Davis, *Kurt Vonnegut's Crusade* 32).

With the increasingly fast-paced devastation of life on this planet—whether such devastation is caused by terrorist attacks, sanctioned wars, environmental catastrophe, and so on—we are confronted by the void that exists beneath the surface play of language and culture, a void that grows out of our limitations as mortal, finite creatures who struggle to make meaning in our individual, embedded contexts. "The effete nature of postmodern literary theory," David Kirby observes, is "as hopelessly out of touch with both reality and literature as was Lenin with real-life economics." Whether one agrees or disagrees with Kirby's bold pronouncement, little argument can be made about the ways in which literary theory and the practice of literary criticism increasingly have become professionalized. Few undergraduates, let alone laypersons, can pick up an essay from these fields and work their way through the dense and often formidable language. Where, then, shall we turn for help in discerning how certain texts are shaping us, and why do we have such strong feelings toward one story as opposed to another?

As our title suggests, the idea of reconciling the void—the locus of our sociocultural disillusionment and despair in an increasingly uncertain world—refers to explicit artistic attempts to represent the ways in which human beings seek out meaning, hope, and community in spite of the void's immutable shadow. In this sense, the act of reconciliation does not connote any sort of triumph over the void. If postmodern theory and philosophy have taught us nothing else, we understand intuitively that we cannot eclipse the void's reach in any absolute sense. Instead, we draw upon the notion of reconciliation to highlight the ways in which human beings continue to negotiate the void, to find means of coping with our limitations in the face of philosophical, spiritual, and biological desires and needs. Hence, we will investigate a variety of artists and cultural artifacts that attempt to address humanity's struggle to derive hope and meaning in a postmodern landscape beset by ethical contradictions and vexing moral dilemmas that offer no clear resolution.

This volume also finds its origins in our desire to explore the intersections among critical theory, interpretive practice, and pedagogy. Do we, as scholars and professors, have an obligation to our students and other readers to connect the study of a story with the lives that such persons pursue beyond the walls of the classroom? As one student commented after a lecture on deconstruction and Lyotard's contention that the grand narratives that served as the structure for twentieth-century culture have collapsed into multiple narratives, "If there's nothing at the center, no foundation for it to rest on, then what's holding it all up? And if nothing's holding it up, then why should I try to help fix what's wrong with this place anyway?" While many theorists and critics have acknowledged that the shift from modernism to postmodernism would not take place without tension and anxiety, what can be done to help this particular student understand that a single paradigm fixed to an essentialist tradition is not the only paradigm that might offer hope or meaning for living? Indeed, how do the scholars or professors who profess such theory participate in loving relationships? What are their lives like as parents or sons or daughters, and how do they reconcile their scholarly or professional ideas with their personal lives? What is the role of political activism for the contemporary professoriate, and how do they negotiate ethics or morality given their philosophical proclivities? Lisa Ruddick suggests that "since September 11th, many scholars have discovered that the challenge of meeting their traumatized students on some shared human ground has evoked some of the most meaningful encounters of their teaching lives" (B7).

Far too often, students are asked to walk with a professor or scholar to the edge of a story, to the edge of a theoretical idea embedded in that story, and then to peer over that edge, looking down into the abyss of certain postmodern ideas. Sadly, many students are left tottering, their fall inevitable. And what do they fall into? For some, the fall lands them in the pit of practicality. The course and the content introduced become a game to be mastered, a set of jargon to be memorized. These students perform admirably on the graded evaluations that the course demands. Others, often students truly invested in the act of learning and not merely the acquisition of a degree or a grade, fall into the void itself, unable to see how what they do will make any difference whatsoever. In this despondency, the act of reading means nothing; the interaction between their lives with their friends or siblings or parents or lovers means nothing—like a story that turns back upon itself in exhausting self-reference. If postmodernity demonstrates that all of our relations and all of our stories are merely constructs built upon the many backs of language, and language itself has no final foundation, what difference do our actions make? Why not join in the free play that Lyotard suggests in his mid-career work?

As cultural critics, we are especially concerned about how the act of reading and the act of living intersect. We do not wish for our students merely to play the game of school, to memorize difficult concepts and vocabulary only to regurgitate them upon an examination. Instead, we hope that our students will not forsake the important philosophical and artistic ideas and ideals created by contemporary artists and postmodern thinkers. We wish to make these ideas real and accessible to our students by bridging the act of reading with the act of living. In *Reconciling the Void*, we will highlight the emerging gaps between literary scholarship and the reading experience itself. In addition to drawing upon the teachings of cultural and literary theory, we will, as Hassan called for so many years ago, demonstrate the provisional answers that we all live by daily in response to the deconstruction that much of postmodern philosophy has wrought.

The artists and their works that represent the focus of *Reconciling the Void* clearly do not shy away from events and characters that raise interesting, provocative, and frequently moving questions of an ethical or spiritual nature. Although postmodernism calls into question the very idea of a unified, essential subject, this study usefully reveals the ways in which the postmodern subject nonetheless lives pragmatically as if some of the grand narratives of the past remain firmly intact. When we speak of love or hate in our relationships—of the oppression of racism or the liberating freedom of tolerance—we do so using a modernist model of the individual subject. Via a form of postmodern humanism—and despite the claims of many postmodern theorists—a variety of contemporary storytellers continue to memorialize the manner in which we seek to posit essence or value in our lives. In *Reconciling the Void*, we hope to offer an innovative critical analysis of their stories and the ways in which they impact our lives, as well as of the evolving nature of our understanding of the ethical possibilities of a postmodern humanism.

Part I Into this World: Body and Spirit in Contemporary Literature

1

Embracing the Fall: Reconfiguring Redemption in Jim Harrison's *The Woman Lit by Fireflies, Dalva,* and *The Road Home*

> When despair for the world grows in me and I wake in
> the night at the least sound in fear of what my life and
> my children's lives may be, I go and lie down where the
> wood drake rests in his beauty on the water, and the
> great heron feeds. I come into the peace of wild
> things . . . I rest in the grace of the world, and am free.
>
> Wendell Berry, "The Peace of Wild Things"

> Every shred and ounce of nature equals mortality. We
> must not stand up to this but absorb it.
>
> Jim Harrison, *The Road Home*

In much of his poetry and fiction, Jim Harrison works against the broader cultural ethic of dualism, frequently presenting us with characters in the midst of life-altering struggles that in some way relate to an unhealthy participation in the structures of American life.[1] Harrison's critique of those structures cannot be characterized as facile, however; nor should we assume that his characters or Harrison himself have managed to divorce themselves completely from the broader cultural influences that all too often lead not only to personal crisis but to a larger environmental predicament that mirrors our spiritual malaise. Standing on the precipice of an ecological void, Harrison's characters attempt to transcend their own malaise by engaging nature on its most primal levels.

In *Wolf* (1971), his first novel, Harrison chronicles the midlife crisis of Swanson, a man who enters the deep forests of the Huron Mountains in Michigan's Upper Peninsula in an attempt to make sense of his life. This structure—a man in middle life facing the existential dilemma of his own mortality and finding, if not answers, a form of consolation in the

3

natural landscape—surfaces time and again in Harrison's work. In subsequent volumes such as *Legends of the Fall* (1979), *Warlock* (1981), and *Sundog* (1984), for example, Harrison describes the encounters of men who have become estranged from their place in the natural order and who return to the wilderness to rediscover and reconnect with what might best be called a sacred attentiveness. Some critics accuse Harrison of an exclusive male focus, a gender bias that imitates the work of writers like Hemingway, their male characters striding into the forest to be healed by the touch of moss and fern, the play of a fish at the end of a line. When we look more closely at Harrison's body of work, however, we begin to see the influence of what he describes as "the female umbrella" under which he grew up. In "First Person Female," Harrison suggests that writing in the voice of a woman has saved him from death by "drugs and booze" because "manliness in our culture can paint you into a corner" (101). Deeply connected to dreams, Harrison often remarks that Dalva is his twin, and their separation at birth—a Jungian notion later taken up by James Hillman—represents a more fluid idea about gender, one that transcends simple ideas about biology and accounts for Harrison's remarkable passion for his female narrators.

The extraordinary way of seeing the world that Harrison returns to in so many of his poems and novels—a not so distant relation to Emerson's notion of transcendence—is not gender exclusive in Harrison's conception. Rather, this attentiveness allows Harrison's characters to open their minds—regardless of gender—to the radiant life that exists beyond the borders of their cities, to see how all living things are interconnected. Time and again, Harrison depicts the lives of men and, in later works such as *Dalva* (1988), *The Woman Lit by Fireflies* (1990), and *The Road Home* (1998), women in whom a conversion experience transpires, allowing each character to live again with a fuller sense of what life may encompass. Such spiritual transformation does not come easily, however, and, although Harrison's work is informed by an early love for Romantic poets such as John Keats, his response to the present crisis in the environment stays far afield of the naïve pastoralism of which Lawrence Buell writes in *The Environmental Imagination* (1995). Seldom, if ever, can Harrison's protagonists leave behind the trappings of the "civilized" world, and, in Harrison's fictive universe, nature does not warmly open its arms to nurture and guide a character toward final answers. Harrison takes great care to present both the beauty and danger inherent in nature; each of his characters must work to survive such encounters, whether it be a confrontation with a bear or the need to find shelter and water for a night. For Harrison, establishing a sense of relationship with nature represents the possibility of redemption into a different way of perceiving the world around us, not into some mystically untouched locale where we are no longer tormented by the limitations of our mortality.

In *Nature's Kindred Spirits* (1994), James I. McClintock contends that "to re-inhabit a place, one must have an ecological perspective that affirms interconnectedness and acknowledges limits, a perspective that extends beyond the intellectual to an ethical and spiritual vision" (114). In many cases, Harrison's natural philosophy centers precisely upon the "limits" of our humanity, on the margins of our mortality. In *The Woman Lit by Fireflies* (1990), Harrison depicts the struggles of Clare, a middle-aged woman who has been dominated by her husband Donald, a man who long ago abandoned the leftist politics of his youth to pursue with an inspired fervor the spoils of business. As Clare flees into an Iowa cornfield and spends the night in a farmer's woodlot, Harrison seeks to expose the hypocrisy of contemporary life. Through Clare's story, he critiques the accoutrements of a civilized world that attempts to hide its vacant and morally bankrupt activities with cocktail chatter and elaborate banquets; through Donald's actions, Harrison discloses the deadly consequences of our desire to control and manipulate others by creating systems of classification that leave us with truncated views of life. By examining the relationship between Clare and Donald in light of ideas about wilderness and its transformative power, Harrison's own ethic of transcendent nature and its significant role as a kind of religious experience becomes evident.

Harrison's first religious impulse found its origins in fundamentalist Christianity. "Between 14 and 15, I was a passionate Baptist preacher," says Harrison. "And I was president of the Bible Club, champion Bible whiz kid. But it didn't last very long" (Reilly 2). After he "jumped from Jesus to John Keats in three days" ("Man" 28), Harrison channeled his religious energy into an art that seeks to illuminate the natural world. He refrains, however, from eschewing his evangelical zeal or his desire to communicate a moral vision. As he comments to Kathleen Stocking, "without moral vision there is no future. Without vision you die" (73). Harrison's vision, then, is one that demands that we see ourselves as part of the natural order, one that admonishes us to make note of the tree we sit under, the stream that flows through the field, the brilliant light of the firefly that hovers around our head. In "Poetry as Survival," Harrison writes that "the natural world has been a substitute for religion, or a religion of another sort" in his life (373). This reverence for the environment translates into a literal conversion experience in *The*

Woman Lit by Fireflies. Considering Harrison's own fervent belief in the transcendent power of nature, Clare's journey might usefully be interpreted as a rebirth into a new life precipitated by a religious encounter with what is wild and unbound in the landscape.

In "'Natty Bummpo Wants Tobacco': Jim Harrison's Wilderness," John Rohrkemper observes that Harrison "knows the natural landscape in detail, and, more importantly, he understands and reveres its spirit" (20). Perhaps no other characteristic distinguishes Clare from her husband more distinctly than her reverence for life, for the spirit of not only the landscape but all that lives within the landscape. As Clare's story begins, she is plagued by migraine headaches, seemingly precipitated by her husband's presence and, more specifically, his ideas about the world. Driving home from a visit with their daughter Laurel, Clare is subjected to one of Donald's tapes that plays the "witless drone of a weekly financial lecture sent from New York City" (177). Lost in a reverie about financial domination, Donald's worldview does not allow him to take in the life that flashes by the windows of his Audi 5000, but Clare, despite the waves of pain that sweep across her vision, notices the beauty of the "dense green wall" of early August corn that lines the roadside. As they pull over at a rest stop for Donald to call his broker, Clare has a revelation about her husband and their relationship, which she has been contemplating as she approaches her 50th birthday: "Donald didn't feel really good about making money unless others were losing theirs" (179). This understanding of such a crucial element in Donald's personality permits Clare to perceive how his response to her also has little to do with knowing his wife or winning her affection but has everything to do with taking her as his own so that others cannot have her. For Donald, the notion of human relationship has little to do with *knowing* and everything to do with *controlling*. His world, in short, is a world of possession.[2]

Speaking about contemporary American culture in *Fables and Distances* (1996), John Haines contends that "what is missing, and for some time now, is delight, that sense of delight in discovery that renews everything and keeps the world fresh" (126). In an interview in *Brick*, Harrison furthers Haines' notion of delight when he connects it to the idea of liberation. "It's very liberating sometimes to just walk off the porch, climb the fence, disappear," Harrison explains in reference to Clare's decision to leave Donald (20). In *The Woman Lit by Fireflies*, Donald cannot experience the delight of which Haines speaks or the liberation that Harrison refers to because he does not wish to know anyone or anything on a deeper level. Instead, he hopes merely to classify that with which he comes in contact; he would rather focus his attention upon his impressive stock portfolio, his well-heeled circle of friends, and his trophy wife than upon the world that lives and breathes beneath the surface of his topical observations. In a moment of illumination, Clare describes the basic difference between herself and her husband: "I want to evoke life and he wants to dominate it" (236). But Clare will never have the opportunity to evoke life fully while she is in the company of Donald. For this reason, while Donald speaks with his broker at the rest stop, Clare begins her spiritual journey away from the world of concrete and steel into the lush green and gold world of an August cornfield by crawling on her hands and knees.

Such a move exemplifies Clare's awakening to the presentness inherent in all of nature.[3] Having in the past visited a clinic in Arizona in hopes of ridding herself of her migraines, Clare is given the *Tao Te Ching* to read and is surprised when a fellow patient, an elderly farmer named Frank, assures her that the "'secrets' of the book might save them" (201). During the course of her sojourn in the Iowa wilderness, Clare returns again to a particular passage in the *Tao*: "Thus whoever is stiff and inflexible / is a disciple of death" (205). In *The Tree* (1983), John Fowles describes a similar phenomenon, contending that moments of stasis, brought about by our desire to classify, are the true destroyers of nature: "There is something in the nature of nature, in its presentness, its seeming transience, its creative ferment and hidden potential, that corresponds very closely with the wild, or green man, in our psyches," he writes. "And it is a something that disappears as soon as it is relegated to an automatic pastness, a status of merely classifiable *thing*" (51). After the deaths of her best friend Zilpha and her dog Sammy, both victims of cancer, Clare has no defense against Donald's invading perceptions of the world, and she labors hard to hold onto Zilpha and Sammy rather than accept their deaths (and, in turn, her own mortality) as part of the natural order. In short, Zilpha struggles with the ever-shifting presentness of life, a condition that inevitably changes from moment to moment and includes both birth and death, times of fertility and barrenness: "Goddamn but her mind was so exhausted with trying to hold the world together," Harrison writes. "Tired of being the living glue for herself, as if she let go, great pieces of her life would shatter and fall off in mockery of the apocalypse" (225).

But no apocalypse occurs as Clare spends the night outdoors. Rather, Harrison describes her transformation as a spiritual reawakening. *The Woman Lit by Fireflies* essentially involves one woman's attempt to shed the skin of her present life to begin again. Beyond the sterile environs of finance and crumbling marriages, Clare finds a world that Harrison describes in numinous terms: "The green wall of the cornfield behind the Welcome Center became luminous and of surpassing loveliness" (182). As she walks into the midst of the field and eventually into a thicket next to a stream, though, Harrison never allows us to think that Clare might somehow become one with the landscape, an earth mother who will never return to the urban cities of her past. Clare's past and future are held within the borders of the contemporary; she may recognize her connection to the natural order—even feel it more deeply—but there can be no ultimate dissolution of the world that remains beyond this Iowa cornfield. This wilderness, nonetheless, presents her with a space for a kind of learning that she can find nowhere else, a moment in which her other interests—all rather cosmopolitan—join with her observations and experiences of a greener world, allowing for the possibility of transformation. As Max Oelschlaeger writes in *The Idea of Wilderness* (1991), "Perhaps modern people cannot go home again, since at least ten thousand years of cultural history separate us from intuitive awareness of the *Magna Mater*, the natural, organic process including soil and sun that created *Homo Sapiens* and all other life-forms on earth. But wild nature," he concludes, "still offers opportunity for contemplative encounters, occasions for human beings to reflect on life and cosmos, on meaning and significance that transcends the culturally relative categories of modern existence" (2). Harrison suggests that the only way to forge such a relationship with nature is through exposure of some sort—perhaps even a night in a woodlot next to a field of corn. In an interview, he contends that we need to spend time doing "nothing"—walking for hours along a remote region of Lake Superior, for example—and in doing nothing, we will discover "emptiness, of course, isn't empty" (*Brick* 22). "You're not going to get an epiphany every day," Harrison explains, "but sometimes you never get the epiphany unless you have some open space, where your mind and body are at moving rest" (22). Because Harrison believes that there is an ancient or primal connection—that we are part and parcel of nature—he does not dismiss the kind of revelation that may occur when a person enters the landscape with an awareness, a desire, for insight or healing. This is not, however, the only influence on Harrison—or Clare for that matter. In the same interview, Harrison confesses that in addition to "a lot of walking in remote areas," he also uses Mozart and Rilke (20)—an experience that prefigures Clare's own experience of such writers as Albert Camus.

Resting in the thicket after her "inadvertent baptism" in the muddy waters of a stream, Clare imagines conversations with her daughter

Laurel and remembers sessions with her therapist Dr. Roth. In these talks, she considers the various indiscretions and acts of kindness she has committed over the course of her life, and we learn that she "lacked the solace of a religion" (214). Yet, Clare also does not accept easily the "responsibility of freedom" that she reads about in Camus' novels. Conflicted and depressed by the barriers of her friend's death and her marriage, Clare builds a shelter for the night and waits out a thunderstorm. She thinks about the childhood prayer that she learned in Sunday school and how it "lacked a great deal in terms of assurance" (214). Still covered with the dry mud of her natural sanctification, she makes her way toward the sound of a farmer's irrigation system, where she bathes in the nude, letting the "breeze dry her off" (228). Casting off the constructed mores of American culture and childhood Christianity with her clothes, Clare begins to accept Zilpha's death and her own mortality. Being "lost" in this field in Iowa represents a letting go of absolute order, something that she cannot do easily, yet essential to her ultimate transformation. Clare even wonders to herself if she "might be like a patient from an asylum, using a cornstalk as a scepter, and saying, 'As of today I'm giving up control of the entire world and all of its inhabitants'" (235).

For Harrison, Clare's willingness to be "lost" is a healthy and fundamental step in her recovery, a mark of her progress toward a deeper connection with the natural world and, in turn, with her self. Harrison's notion of the natural world finds its roots in the vision of John Muir, the most noted and influential naturalist and conservationist in American history. As J. Baird Callicott notes in *Beyond the Land Ethic: More Essays in Environmental Philosophy* (1999), Muir's moral vision was informed by both an evolutionary and an ecological worldview. Callicott explains that "Darwin had unseated from his self-appointed throne the creature Muir sometimes sarcastically called 'lord man' and reduced him to but a 'small part' of creation, and the likes of H. C. Cowles, S. A. Forbes, and F. E. Clements would soon validate Muir's intuition that there exists a unity and completeness—if not in the cosmos or universe at large, certainly in terrestrial nature—to which each creature, no matter how small, functionally contributes" (325). Harrison's characters celebrate a vision of terrestrial nature that is remarkably similar to Muir's. Transformed over the course of Harrison's fictions, they come to see all life—flora or fauna, human or animal—as part of the natural world. For Clare, the initial realization of this fact leads to her own self-healing and later to her projection of the self's role as an element of terrestrial nature.

In his essay "Passacaglia on Getting Lost," Harrison contends that "getting lost is to sense the 'animus' of nature" (215), and, accordingly, as Clare settles into the bed she has made under her cornstalk shelter, she feels like she is "sinking into the ground, into a point well past sleep . . . the green odor transmitting a sense she belonged to the earth as much as any other living thing" (237).[4] Harrison reinforces the idea that Clare belongs to the earth, that she can sense its "animus," when he depicts her in the act of stirring from her deep sleep, waking to the light of "countless thousands of fireflies," their "yellow lines of light everywhere" (239). In an interview with Edward C. Reilly, Harrison remarks that in writing this passage the "old myths" surface because they are "true of human experiences" (158). As with Fowles, Harrison seems to believe that our psyches possess some latent, primal connection to the things of the earth. Such an experience—a form of sanctification that occurs via the spirit of the earth—might usefully be referred to as a kind of natural grace. Freya Mathews contends that deep ecology approaches the question of meaningfulness by emphasizing not only the thesis of intrinsic value, but also by exploring the idea that human self-realization finds its origins in a sense of ecological consciousness: "When the universe is viewed under the aspect of a self-realizing system," Mathews explains, "then the relation in which it stands to me, when I am viewed as a self, is the equally holistic one of ecological interconnectedness: its selfhood conditions mine, my selfhood conditions its" (142–3). Many of Harrison's protagonists evolve toward a similar perspective as they establish a sense of connection with their surroundings, an experience that often yields its own form of natural grace. In their interaction with various natural places and with the animal and plant life that populate them, Harrison's characters grow more aware of their own material position as *animals*, as living creatures within a particular ecosystem. During such epiphanies, they discover a deeper relationship with their surroundings, understanding more fully what Mathews describes as their selfhood being conditioned by the local, material world, while at the same time shaping and altering the local, material world in which they live.

In *The Woman Lit by Fireflies*, Clare's moment of natural grace involves the absolution of her transgressions by the glow of the fireflies' sacred light: "Quite suddenly she felt blessed without thinking whether or not she deserved it," Harrison writes. "She went back to her nest, lay down and wept for a few minutes, then watched a firefly hovering barely a foot above her head" (239). As if to highlight Clare's redemption, Harrison tells us that she wakes at first light to the song of birds and feels as if "she were *within*" them. In many ways, Clare has become a part of this place, this earth that she inhabits. Turning away from any ideology that the only creatures with souls are human, Clare glimpses the sacred in all living things. After being blessed in this way, she prays, "*All souls will be taken, including the souls of fireflies*" (239). While her consecration into the church of the green world does not excuse her from the terrible freedom that she will face in going forward, it does offer her some sense of solace and a new beginning. In Harrison's vision, life must continue to be a mystery and a struggle, and thus he tells us that "Clare felt a little lost but then she always had, and supposed easily that it was the condition of life" (247).

Via a passage from Robert Duncan's *Roots and Branches* (1969), a book of poems that Clare's lover tellingly gives to her in the novella, Harrison reminds us that "Robin Hood in the greenwood outside / Christendom faces peril as if it were a friend" (213). As with his protagonist in *The Woman Lit by Fireflies*, Harrison chooses to live "in the greenwood outside Christendom," and like Clare, who discovers she has slept with a snake in her lost garden by the stream, Harrison embraces the fall and our mortal position within it. William H. Roberson remarks that "death in Harrison's work emphasizes life. Life is all there is, all that is offered; it should therefore be made meaningful and purposeful" (29). Perhaps the conviction that we should not look for something beyond life, that we should embrace the presentness of the moment as a sacred thing, lies at the root of Harrison's most consuming character, Dalva. The namesake of one novel and a central figure in Harrison's prodigious *The Road Home*, Dalva, more than any other fictional creation, tormented Harrison in her making. As he explains to Reilly, "*Dalva* fucking near killed me. By the time I finished *Dalva*, I had an old thyroid inflammation and both my eardrums were broken because I had had different kinds of flu and viruses, and I ignored them totally until I was about dead" (115). Having to divest himself of his own personality to write Dalva into existence, Harrison says that he followed the words of Zen master Dashimaru—"You must concentrate and consecrate yourself wholly to each day as though a fire were raging in your hair" (*Just Before Dark* 286). To become one with his character, to write in her voice—a technique closely akin to method acting and one for which Harrison sought the advice of his old friend, the actor Jack Nicholson— Harrison says that he had to "totally abnegate my own personality to become her" (Stocking 74–5).[5] In the process, Harrison wrote two novels of enormous strength whose power resides, as with *The Woman Lit by Fireflies*, in the crisis of a middle-aged woman and her coming to terms with a landscape that in many ways owns her, that offers both comfort and potential harm.

Harrison's philosophical approach to nature in these two novels, however, demonstrates a movement beyond the individual redemption we have examined in *The Woman Lit by Fireflies*. While this shift from the microcosmic to the macrocosmic may be due in part to the limitations of form—a novella certainly does not afford the writer with the same potential expansiveness as a novel—it also signifies Harrison's far-reaching meditation upon the connections that he sees between all forms of life, upon what some might refer to as a kind of deep ecology. In an interview with Jonathan Miles, Harrison divulges his own particular understanding of reality and his place in the scheme of things by relating a conversation that led him to an epiphany of sorts. "This strange Hasidic scholar I know named Neal Claremont, a brilliant young man, said to me one day: 'Don't you really think that reality is the accretion of the perceptions of all creatures?' I said, Jesus Christ, that's a monster statement. But of course it's true," Harrison reflects, "and what a marvelous thing to say. I don't think I'm any more important than a dog or a cat. It's become alien to my nature—that sort of self-importance that is so egregious."[6] The notion that a human being is no more important than a dog or a cat, than any other living thing on earth, certainly presents a radical shift from the Enlightenment and, later, modernist thought in the Western world. Yet such a shift places Harrison—at least in part—in line with Oelschlaeger's description of one of the fundamental concepts of "deep ecology." According to Oelschlaeger, "Deep ecology is committed to an explicitly ecocentric orientation where humankind is understood as a part of rather than apart from wild nature" (302). In other words, this way of looking at the world conceives of the system of nature as something of which humankind is only one part, neither above nor below any other living thing. We do not wish to misrepresent Harrison as a deep ecologist, however. Such a gesture would not only limit any larger understanding of this author's knotty and delightfully unexpected work, but also misconstrue the relationship between the ways that humans actually live their lives on a daily basis and their inherent conflicts with the constructs of ideology and theory. Far too complex and recalcitrant an individual to be reduced to a single descriptor, Harrison does not subscribe to any specific ideological position when approaching environmental issues. In a characteristic turn, in the same interview, Harrison humorously rants that "we're nature, too. It's that schizophrenia that you often see in the environmental movement—on the dweebish side of the environmental movement—that wants to save something. Well, save yourself too, asshole, on the way, or you won't have anything to save anyway." In a gesture toward saving Dalva and redeeming several generations of the Northridge family, Harrison walks the line between individual and communal redemption, between care for the earth that births all life and the human lives that move forward into situations and structures that often destroy both the land and those who inhabit it.

Over the course of *Dalva* and *The Road Home*, Harrison presents Dalva's return to her family's farm in northwest Nebraska as the turning point in her life. The story begins as Dalva, who is 45, tells us that she has journeyed back and forth between remote areas of the globe and some of its largest cities. "All my moves had been radical—New York City and Los Angeles had alternated with remote regions of Montana, Minnesota, Michigan, and Nebraska," she writes. "There had been short unsuccessful attempts to live in foreign countries—France, England, Mexico, Brazil—but I was so thoroughly an American that my home-sickness led to a premature return" (*Dalva* 73). What actually precipitates such moves, according to Reilly, are the ghosts of Dalva's father—killed in the Korean War—and her half-brother and father of her son, Duane Stone Horse, who committed suicide by riding his buckskin horse into the Gulf Stream (116). While Reilly is correct that the specters of these two men haunt Dalva, pushing her away from her family and their Nebraska homestead, so many other ghosts also move beneath the current of her grief.[7] During a week in which Duane's mother Rachel rides with Dalva as she explores some of the first Northridge family sites, Rachel introduces Dalva to the Oglala word, "Hanblecheyapi." She explains that it means a rite of lament, "a period where you expressed all your anguish, then received a new vision of life to keep you going" (249). Clearly, Dalva laments the loss of her father and her half-broth-er; these are the two men she has loved the most. But to focus on these losses to the exclusion of all else does not account for the novel's epi-graph, nor its constant refrain that we are the accretion of all that has come before us, that our present reality represents the accumulation of all that has ever lived and all that will live long after our own deaths.

Harrison begins *Dalva* with the austere epigraph: "We loved the earth but could not stay." Here is the loss that Dalva laments, that drives her to cry out, "Goddamn the world who gives me no father and no son. No husband" (268). Dalva's rage strikes to the heart of our mortal condition—the complexity and brevity of the life we lead in the moments we have upon this earth. It also speaks to Dalva's own imminent death, her struggle to come to terms not only with the deaths of her loved ones, but with her own mortality—a loss of oneself to the earth that ulti-mately will hold us all. In the same way, the original Northridge feels this loss when he watches the native people that he has lived among decimated by government actions, when he contemplates the Christian faith he no longer finds tenable, and when he remembers the Eastern landscape that he has left behind in his push West to search for some form of home. Indelibly linked to such losses, however, is the love that empowers both Dalva and her ancestors and allows them to cope, to survive, and, at times, to transcend. At the crux of these losses, Harrison envisions the Northridge family's continued wonder and amazement at the bounty of the earth and its ability to heal those who truly attend to it. In this way, Harrison asserts his belief that because we are part of the created order—organisms whose lives are sustained by the earth and what grows upon it as well as creatures whose bodies potentially will give back to the earth—we must increase our awareness of its cycles, its ecosystems, its flora and fauna as well as our understanding of our rela-tionship and place in those cycles and systems. As Peter Quigley sug-gests, the idea that an environmental narrative should focus on the local and material finds its strength in our revaluation of the relation-ship between human and nonhuman agents—historically defined in Western culture in vertical terms—as horizontal. Such an idea is espe-cially important for Harrison, who consistently questions any ideologi-cal position that maintains that we are somehow *other* than nature or superior to other forms of life that exist within it.

Interestingly, the original title for *The Road Home* was *Earthdiver*, "a Native American term for 'someone who belongs to the earth'" (Reilly 115). This idea first surfaces in *Dalva* when Northridge writes in his jour-nal, dated 13 May 1871, that the Sioux refer to him as "earthdiver": "I was called thus because I am forever digging holes and inspecting the root systems of trees to determine their hardiness in certain soils," Northridge explains (*Dalva* 124). Although the reference might have been too subtle for some readers, *Earthdiver* is the more telling of the two choices. Indeed, both *Dalva* and *The Road Home* explore the inter-generational "root systems" of the Northridge family as well as their spiritual attachment to this place on earth; both dig into the soil that brings forth the fruit of a family history so tenuous that many of its secrets have been buried in a room dug deep beneath the Northridge home, the bodies of Sioux warriors and the remains of murdered cavalry officers entombed but never forgotten.

Early in the novel, we witness the power of the natural landscape in Dalva's life. Burdened with her family's secrets and the realization that those secrets were in part responsible for her having a son with a man she did not suspect was her half-brother, Dalva lives on the West coast, taking solace in the seascape: "It was barely light and there was a warm stiff breeze mixed with the odor of salt water, juniper, eucalyptus, oleander, palm," she writes. "The ocean was rumpled and gray. I think I stayed here this long because of the trees and the ocean. One year when I was having particularly intense problems I sat here for an hour at daylight and an hour at twilight. The landscape helped me to let the problems float out through the top of my head, through my skin, and into the air," she concludes (*Dalva* 17). Yet this is not Dalva's *home*. Rather, this landscape serves as a salve for her wounds, offering some form of solace but never a true working out of the Hanblecheyapi. For Dalva to receive a "new vision of life," she journeys back to Nebraska where she finally comes to terms with the lives of her ancestors and ultimately meets the son whom she has never known. Of course, in Harrison's world, such events cannot be separated from the place in which they transpire, and because of this the most dramatic and telling trials leading to Dalva's spiritual renewal are firmly situated in the Nebraska countryside.

In *Dakota: A Spiritual Geography* (1993), Kathleen Norris asserts that "the high plains, the beginning of the desert West, often act as a crucible for those who inhabit them. Like Jacob's angel, the region requires that you wrestle with it before it bestows a blessing" (1). Indeed, like Jacob wrestling the angel, Dalva struggles physically and spiritually with the turning force of her own life and her connection to the past. Over the course of the book, she is buffeted by many storms—the Northridge family's legacy on the plains of Nebraska, their relationship to the indigenous peoples of the region, and, perhaps most importantly, the family's potential future that resides within Dalva's estranged son Nelse. In *Imagining the Earth* (1985), John Elder suggests that our culture too often ignores the idea "that human beings may be nourished by tapping the nutrients of the past" and that "the problem is not so much that of a present tyrannized by an overbearing past as it is an impoverishment, a lack of significant *connectedness* with our legacy from 'the dead'" (31). Through a series of events, Dalva slowly releases the pain caused by her disconnection with the past, a pain described by Dalva as a "knot, a lump of coal beneath my breastbone" (*Dalva* 266) that travels "upward from my stomach to my heart to my throat and into my head and back down for another circle" (268). Dalva's pain presides over her life because she has not yet accepted the ever-present condition of mortality—its grave costs, its inevitability—and seems unwilling or unable to release the dead she carries with her. Her relationship with her father John Wesley Northridge III and her half-brother Duane is not the kind of healthy, nourishing relationship to which Elder refers. Instead, Dalva's wanderings, her constant need to be on the move, appear to represent a form of denial, a conviction that the deaths of these two men in some way went against the natural order.

Dalva's first step in reconciling these deaths occurs when she has a symbolic and unexpected baptism in a place of significance to both her father and her half-brother. On a ride near one of the creeks that runs through the Northridge family land, which pools to form a swimming hole, Dalva's fury and frustration crest in her cursing of God. Still bewildered and plagued by events more than 30 years in her past, she goes as far as to ask the red-winged blackbirds who perch on the bobbing heads of cattail, "What kind of fucking world is this?" (268). Her incredulity at the circumstances of the natural order burns in her, but at the sight of deep water her horse Peach plunges forward—immersing rider and horse at once—then makes a circle to Duane's tipi ring where the white skull of a deer hangs. As if this cleansing by water was not enough, Dalva sheds her clothes and, like Peach, begins to roll in the sand and dust. "I stood up laughing as Peach watched me, then I got back down and rolled in the sand again" she tells us. "It was so wonderful I wondered why I had never done it before. I rolled over and over and down the bank and back into the water" (268). The result of this baptism by the elements of water and earth mark the beginning of Dalva's journey *home*. As she explains, "When I lay stretched out on the damp and smelly horse blanket I realized that my stomachache was gone and with it the pain beneath my breastbone and in my throat and head" (268).

While her encounter with the very earth that her family has worked and walked upon for more than a century and a half is symbolic; it also demonstrates the necessity of the particular, the tangible. Such actions confirm the power of what is concrete or material over the ethereal quality of abstraction. As Berry suggests, in *Life Is a Miracle: An Essay Against Modern Superstition* (2000), "abstraction alone is merely dead" (136). If Dalva allows her idea of home and its relationship to death—particularly the deaths of her father and half-brother—to remain mere abstraction, never acted out in some specific, physical form, then their power over her in many ways relegates her to a living death, a stagnation where nothing new may take place. By showing her anger toward God and, subsequently, acting out a physical ritual of rebirth with the *magna mater*, Dalva breaks the chains of stasis that have gripped her life for several decades and experiences some degree of healing. Not long after this encounter, she tells us that "I had begun not to drift, aware that I had been acting out effects rather than causing anything new. It was as if I had made my decision, gradual as it was, to come home" (*Dalva* 292). By not simply "acting out effects," Dalva begins to create, establishing a new way of life not only important to herself but to the Northridge homestead and its surrounding country. Perhaps the clearest indication that Dalva is becoming part of the community occurs when she decides to accept a position counseling bankrupt farm families from the region, a hopeful act of potential renewal and regeneration.

Dalva completes her Hanblecheyapi, however, with two subsequent events that Harrison links in his use of imagery and action. The first transpires several days after Dalva's baptism as she drives through the Oglala and Buffalo Gap National Grasslands. Overcome with rage as she witnesses "the Sioux equivalent of the Warsaw Ghetto," Dalva's righteous anger at the Native American holocaust causes her to drive recklessly around "three campers with Iowa licenses" and eventually lands her in a ditch. Leaving her car, she walks into an ocean of grass where she comes to the realization that she can no longer keep the souls of the dead in the basement of her spirit or in the literal basement of the Northridge home:

> All that had just happened disappeared into the density of green with abruptness: "What I am trying to do is trade in a dead lover for a live son. I'll throw in a dead father with the dead lover and their souls I have kept in the basement perhaps. Even if I don't get to see the son I have to let the others go. The world around me and the world of people looks immense and solid but it is more fragile than lark or pheasant eggs, women eggs, anyone's last heartbeat. I'm a crazy woman. Why didn't I do this long ago? I'm forty-five and there's still a weeping girl in my stomach. I'm still in the arms of dead men—first Father then Duane." (293)

In the midst of the plains' grasses, green and gold heads blowing with the movement of the wind, Dalva finally understands what may truly heal her, recognizing that she must accept the fragility of existence. She sees that the world which seems "immense and solid" rests precariously at the edge of death, and the only recourse to such a reality is found in her acceptance of this fact.

Armed with the knowledge and conviction gained in her grassland revelation, Dalva makes her way back to the farm where she moves into the dark recesses of the subbasement dug beneath the family root cellar.

Blacksnakes squirm across the floor toward the light of the lantern she carries, and she comments that her "only irrational feeling was that I was in some way by this act releasing the souls of Duane and my father" (297). Although irrational, Dalva's desire to see the room where her family hid its secrets of both murder and preservation in many ways is linked to the souls of Duane and her father. Dalva tells us that she sits in the room where skeletons of warriors and cavalry officers lie "for a full hour in the state that perhaps approached a prayer without words, not thinking about anything except what I was looking at" (298). And what she looks at, quite simply, is the assembling of her family's history, no distinction made between the natural world and the human world. Around her, placed with great care, are the artifacts of the people, indigenous and immigrant, who lived in this place, the detritus of their existence made from the world they inhabited and precious to their understanding of it:

> The rest of the room was full of tagged and labeled artifacts from tribes of the Great Basin: braided sweet grass, otter-skin collars, fur bands of mountain lions, badger skins—Northridge's clan, Crow bustles of eagle and hawk feathers, painted buffalo heads, kit-fox wrist loops, grizzly-claw necklaces, turtle rattles, horned ermine bonnets, rolled ermine tails, coup sticks and three medicine bags, painted buffalo hides, a full golden eagle into which a Crow holy man's head had fit into the rib cage, buffalo horn bonnets, ravens, otter-skin-wrapped lances, rattlesnake-skin wrapped ceremonial bows, mountain-lion sashes, bearskin belts. (298)

Dalva's lengthy description of the contents of this room demonstrates the same kind of attention to detail. Her litany emphasizes an important conviction displayed in much of Harrison's work: that we belong to the earth, and all that we have to show for our lives here is what we literally make of it.

After her hour of prayer, Dalva tells us that she has been released: "My father and Duane seemed to be with me, then went away as did the weeping girl I had felt in my chest," Dalva writes. "She went out an upstairs window where she had sat watching the summer morning, the descent of the moon" (298). And in this way, Dalva concludes her Hanblecheyapi. A few hours after the sacred ceremony in the basement, Dalva steps out from her shower and notices "that all the photos on the dresser failed to cause any heaviness in my chest. They were men and smiling, all quite as dead as I would be some day" (299). Death no longer haunts Dalva. She acknowledges its place, the way it connects all living things, but she will not allow the past to destroy her present anymore. As if to reinforce such a notion, she closes her story by describing her reunion with her son. Looking together at the photos of his father, she and Nelse hear the hired hand Lundquist playing his violin as the rest of the family prepares a cookout: "The music came from Lundquist who was wandering around in the groves of lilacs, among the gravestones, then back into the yard, playing his miniature violin, as if he were at the same time serenading the living and the dead. We went down to join them" (324).

In the thirty-fourth and final section of his long poem *Geo-Bestiary*, Harrison suggests that the true power of story is certainly more than "the harsh and quizzical / chatter with which we all get by" (7–8). Rather, story finds its spiritual and physical strength when it begins to acknowledge what nature is, how reality is no more and no less than all of the perceptions of living things that comprise the universe, and when, as in the end of *Dalva*, it "joins" us with the past and the future to form a sacred circle rooted in the rhythms of the natural world. As Harrison's poem concludes,

> if she or he passes by and the need
> is felt we hear the music that transcends all fear,
> and sometimes the simpler songs that greet sunrise,
> rain or twilight. Here I am.
> They sing what and where they are. (9–13)

This is our solace—what buoys Dalva and her family, allows them to endure the past; what consecrates Clare in the open field as water from the farmer's irrigation washes over her, taking her to a new place in her life: we tell our stories, connecting with the past and the future, in the hope that we may survive.

2

Writing Back through the Body: The Communion of Flesh and Spirit in the Work of Mary Swander

> How surprised we are to find we live here,
> Here within our bodies.
>
> Eric Pankey, "Santo Spirito"

> Woman must write her self: must write about women
> and bring women to writing from which they have
> been driven away as violently as from their bodies.
>
> Hélène Cixous, "The Laugh of the Medusa"

I.

The desire or, more accurately, the need to write back through the body pulses beneath the lines of Mary Swander's poetry and prose. From her first book of poems, *Succession* (1979), to her most recent memoir, *The Desert Pilgrim: En Route to Mysticism and Miracles* (2003), Swander has made every effort to write and rewrite her way back through the flesh, the body she claims and which claims her, shaping not only the patterns of her life but her emotional and spiritual center as well. Her Catholic heritage, her life as a citizen of the rural Midwest, her struggles with environmental illness and other physical maladies, and her particular feminist vision coalesce in her work in ways that not only challenge the dominant views of illness and the body that harbors it, but also the traditional Western conception of the soul and the paths we may choose to understand better the relationship between body and soul, flesh and spirit. For Swander, writing the body represents her last, best hope for establishing a living, breathing present in the face of a blinding, uncertain future.

Many feminist writers have worked to expose and critique the patriarchal prison-house of language and its accompanying ideologies and the-
ologies. Much of this critique focuses upon the harmful and degrading
vision for women's bodies bound up in the crass dichotomies of *virgin*
and *whore, mother* and *prostitute*. This razor-edged turn from beatific beauty to demonized object of lust leaves no space for the range of emotions
and physical attributes that a woman may possess. Such objectification
encourages in women the idea of abandonment: the leaving of one's
body behind to be ravaged or used by its cultural counterparts but never to be known or explored in its integrative whole. To acquiesce to such
pressures, although fully human and understandable, tells a tragic story
of loss and the perpetuation of a sickness that not only poisons the individual but also the ecosystems in which we live, the environments that
we help to create and sustain with our behaviors and beliefs. At the root
of such abusive models is a profound ignorance about what comprises
the act of human *being*. In "The Laugh of the Medusa," Hélène Cixous
explains that "by writing her *self*, woman will return to the body which
has been more than confiscated from her, which has been turned into
the uncanny stranger on display" (337–8). To look at the self, embedded
in the body, as somehow separate, set upon a pedestal for the world to
goggle and use as it sees fit is to undo the intricate webbing of flesh and
spirit, to rend one from the other in an act so destructive that what
remains is hardly recognizable. The outcome, of course, is to make the
other less than whole, to take away her very *being*, because implicit in
the word *being* is the idea of activity not stagnation. When we objectify
another, we first tear from his or her person any true sense of the active
self and all of the prospects and conundrums such activity implies. With
mobility comes the possibility for change, for difference, for potential
beyond the present. When we objectify, we paint our limited idea of that
person upon the page of utility, capturing her as a one- or two-dimensional object, holding her in a stagnant world, fixed in the present where
the many dimensions of her person are denied, cut off from their sources
to slowly vanish in a sadistic act of attrition. In such acts of denial, the
threat of death lurks; we rob the other of any possibility beyond the lie
we have created. For this reason, Cixous cries out to the woman artist,
imploring her to "write your self . . . Your body must be heard" (338).

This fundamental cry to write the body into existence becomes that
much more poignant for Swander because not only is she marginalized
as a woman artist but also as a person who has struggled with an ongoing battle against physical pain and its crippling effects. While at one

time in the not so distant past, disease and physical defects were considered as the sign of moral imperfection, the result of some "sin" in the person's life, our contemporary view, although a bit more enlightened, still does not make much room for images or stories of those who struggle with disease or handicap. As Nancy Mairs, a poet and essayist who lives with the debilitating effects of multiple sclerosis, explains, "Physical imperfection, even freed of moral disapprobation, still defies and violates the ideal, especially for women, whose confinement in their bodies as objects of desire is far from over" (*Plain Text* 16). Despite, or perhaps because of these forces, Swander struggles mightily to rework and rewrite our culture's traditional ideas about the body, placing her own body in a matrilineal line that she seeks to recover in the stories she tells about her great grandmother, her grandmother, and her mother.

In *Carnal Acts* (1990), Mairs contends that the pervasive dichotomy between body and soul, flesh and spirit is reflected in our naming of these ideas as separate entities and in our hierarchical privileging of one over the other. In the Western world, Mairs explains, we say "I have a body," rather than "I am a body," and in doing so we "widen the rift between the self and the body," making it possible to "treat our bodies as subordinates, inferior in moral status" (84). To say one *has* a body suggests an act of ownership. In a cultural landscape that increasingly encourages us to believe that we may possess virtually anything we want and in turn to discard what we no longer desire, this is a truly frightening prospect. To *be* a body demands that we acknowledge the ways in which we are rooted in the physical world, to examine how our very flesh shapes the ways we think and act, and to understand that there is no *returning* or *discarding* the bodies we have been born into for a refund or an exchange. As a poet, playwright, essayist, and editor, Swander continually explores the multifaceted dimensions of this crass and often unhealthy dichotomy, insisting that not only does she *have* a body, but she *is* a body—inseparable from it.

The title of her third book of poems, *Heaven-and-Earth House* (1994), names this way of seeing most clearly. Our body houses both heaven and Earth; the mind and soul are bound up in the flesh that must be fed, the body that must be allowed to sleep and rest. In their research, the scientific community increasingly demonstrates the vital connections between one's psyche and one's physical well-being; the heaven of our emotions and intellect can rule the earth that is our body with either despair or hope. Out of this metaphoric and physical relationship, Swander writes about the epiphanies she experiences while driving her dead mother's body back to her home to be buried, about a pygmy goat who by giving birth will make someone rich in the "salvation of [her] vast girth" (*Heaven* 12), about a Russian Orthodox monk named Father Sergei who tells her "to look to [her] own ancestors for icons" (*Desert Pilgrim* 192).[1] In story after story and image after image, Swander illuminates the potential healing found beyond the stifling and stagnate world of dichotomy. Indeed, for Swander there truly is salvation in the vast girth of a pygmy goat; her mother's dead body does offer the potential for renewal as she listens to the voices of relatives, both alive and dead, speaking to her as she drives across Iowa; by making her ancestors icons, as Father Sergei suggests, Swander heals herself physically and spiritually. While Swander insists that neither science nor faith can describe exclusively her own particular path, she celebrates the fact that the language she uses and the stories she tells are born from the flesh that supports her and makes it possible for her to move through this world, to gather the experiences that will be translated later on to the page. And on the printed page, instead of claiming that language controls or defines such experiences—making a sensible road map of what is too often inexplicable in her life—Swander acknowledges that her books are mere gestures toward the mystery of her existence.[2] Swander's writing should be seen as an act of subversion, a demand, as Cixous called for, that we recognize the fullness of both her body and spirit and the way these forces in tandem shape the telling of her story.

II.

Swander's concern for the coils of life—body and soul, soil and culture, one wrapped around another and then another—is evident even in her earliest writing. In *Succession*, Swander makes use of reoccurring images of connection, many of them drawn from the Catholic faith of her Iowa childhood. While she did not embrace the Catholic religion of her parents and grandparents, she understands its deep hold on her. In the book's third and final section, "Let Down the Nets," she transforms the theological idea of transubstantiation so that it may encompass more than the wafer and the wine, more than the body and blood of Christ. In the poem "Song," Swander describes her vigil beside her mother's deathbed. It is a scene of stark, tragic images: wicks burning down through the diseased body, lungs filling and draining, "green mold boring a hole through the bread" of her mother's flesh. But as the poem ends, there is a release from the slow deterioration and the pain of death's conclusion. Tongues ring inside bells, "tongues inside your body when I was there" (48), Swander writes. Like the Holy Spirit that

Swander had been taught about in her catechism, these tongues sing of a resurrection. But not the ghostly resurrection of the soul as preached by her priest. Like the communion wafer that becomes the flesh of Christ in transubstantiation, Swander mystically resurrects the body of her mother with images of an earthly communion. We are told that "the moon, rising over your bed, was a host. / And your body was eaten" (48). Similarly, in the poem "In a Dream," the ghostly spirit of her mother is remade in Swander's own flesh; her ethereal Irish ancestors swim through time and space into the river of the speaker's corporeal body, "like water through gills, / sifting, settling" (42). Swander's mystical vision allows her both to welcome and become one with her deceased mother, for the flesh of the mother's frame to be remade in the daughter's. In the ecstatic moment, Swander collapses the distance between the speaker and the reader as well by shifting to the second person. She tells the reader that in death *you* will feel:

> her bones in your lungs,
> her whole body growing
> inside yours, pulling
> you downward to a
> pillow, a bed of coral. (42)

Like Adrienne Rich diving into the wreck to recover a matrilineal past from the sea, Swander's own movement through the water, allowing her mother to pull her down to a bed of coral where her maternal ancestors reside, presents us with the dominant theme of the book: Here is our need and desire for connection in all its eclectic dimensions—to place, to people, to custom, to the very act of *being* which cannot occur without acknowledging the body that holds us. This is the stuff of life knit into bones and flesh; this is the call to come to the altar of both body and soul, to take and eat of one another and ourselves.

Like Rich, Swander wishes to explode the patriarchal ideas of duality in order to move toward a healthier understanding of who we are in relation to each other and the earth. She contends that "collaboration is a female concept," that "women are used to working together and sharing tasks co-operatively" ("Crossing the Borders" 127). The Catholicism Swander was introduced to as a child would have body and soul struggle against one another for dominion; there was no model of collaborative, co-operative interaction, of a unified and holistic correspondence between the two. Instead, in the church of her youth, she witnessed the denigration of the flesh; it was named as the workshop of the devil where lust and the desires of the physical body might damn the soul for all eternity. Swander's own religious journey took her far from these notions, and, as she says in an interview, "I think I can now finally sort out my spirituality from my religion and the flaws of a patriarchal structure" (129).

Swander's approach to seeing flesh and spirit as one—not in some holy competition for eternity but as so deeply immersed in one another as to make it impossible to speak about the one without the other—is aligned closely with the teachings of certain ancient mystics as well as with fellow contemporary author, agrarian Wendell Berry. In his essay "Christianity and the Survival of Creation," collected in *Sex, Economy, Freedom and Community* (1993), Berry argues that the dichotomy that plagues Swander, and so many other orthodox Christians, finds its roots in a radical misreading of the creation story. Berry explains that this dualism manifests itself in several ways: "as a cleavage, a radical discontinuity, between Creator and creature, spirit and matter, religion and nature, religion and economy, worship and work, and so on" (105). Berry believes that such dualistic thinking may be the single "most destructive disease that afflicts us" and that its most fundamental form is "the dualism of body and soul" (105). This harmful dualism, Berry explains, is a result of a misreading of the Genesis creation story. Instead of the popular interpretation, which would make us believe that a human equals "body + soul," Berry claims that "God did not make a body and put a soul into it, like a letter into an envelope. He formed man of dust; then, by breathing His breath into it, He made the dust live. The dust, formed as man and made to live, did not *embody* a soul; it *became* a soul" (106). Thus, the dust of the earth is just as valuable as the breath of the creator in Berry's cosmology; without one or the other, no soul exists; there is no human *being*. Poet and translator Stephen Mitchell corroborates this strong sense of human *being* as comprised of flesh and spirit in his own translation of the creation story: "the Lord formed man from the dust of the ground and blew into his nostrils the breath of life," Mitchell writes, "and the man became a living being" (129).[3]

Swander embraces much of what Berry and Mitchell suggest in their interpretations of the creation myth. The epigraph she chooses for *Succession* is particularly telling in this matter, offering yet another metaphor or analogy for the relationship between body and soul. Drawing from the world of science, Swander quotes Lewis Thomas's *The Lives of a Cell* (1974): "There are some creatures that do not seem to die at all; they simply vanish totally into their own progeny," Thomas writes. "Single cells do this. The cell becomes two, then four, and so on, and after a while the last trace is gone." While the last trace may be gone, it has not ceased to exist. These former cells live and breathe in the being that stands in the world now—in this time and in this place. In such a transference, something of the original lives on, and *Succession*'s penultimate poem extends this idea, joining the speaker not only with her Irish grandmothers but with the earth itself in an act of transcendence:

> The tides, the full moon, a tangle
> of yarn, pulling me in, cell by cell,
> My flesh unraveling, all revealing
> Marks gone: scars, face, fingerprints,
> My whole body the shore by dawn. (49)

In this physical rapture, the speaker's soul neither leaves her body, nor does her body leave her soul. Both are subsumed into the earth's frame, "cell by cell," to become part and parcel of the world. In her "unraveling," her individual being vanishes, but it is not lost. Like Whitman, Swander also suggests that our end is only a new beginning, a different kind of transcendence that does not allow our souls to finally break free of their earthly vessel but rather liberates us to move more boldly into the material world. At the conclusion of *Song of Myself*, Whitman gives himself over to the earth: "I bequeath myself to the dirt to grow from the grass I love, / If you want me again look for me under your bootsoles" (89). In the dirt, in the grass, upon the shore at dawn, Whitman and Swander both call us to join with the universe's way of *being*, not to depart to some far-removed heaven.

Swander's second volume of poetry builds upon this idea of reverence for the earth and for the connection of our human *being* with it. Using a line from the Old Testament book of Job for its epigraph—"Speak to the Earth and it will teach thee"—*Driving the Body Back* (1986) recounts the story of a woman who must take her mother's corpse across Iowa so that she may deliver it into the ground where the rest of her family resides. In doing so, the earth and those it holds speak to her. Over the course of the journey, they reassure her that upon her death "there's enough room at least / for you and me" (81). The narrative of *Driving the Body Back* has antecedents in Swander's own life. As she explains in an interview, "My mother died when I was twenty-three years old. I had the job of driving her body across the state of Iowa for burial in our family cemetery. Just as I was about to start this journey, my godmother appeared on my doorstep, as all good godmothers are supposed to do" (125). Over the course of the trip, her godmother narrates many of her relatives' deathbed stories while Swander's mother's body, wrapped in a blanket and roped to a cot in the back of her station wagon, rides along with them. As with her previous collection, the theme of connection and succession links many of the stories in *Driving the Body Back*, and this idea of connection is most often tied to a deep and abiding knowledge of the world we inhabit. Such knowledge may include ways of sowing and reaping; butchering and gleaning; the names of birds, the plants they eat, the trees where they roost; even the knowledge of how we should treat the bodies of the dead who remind us of our own mortality and ultimate connection back to the body of the earth. Jim is the first relative to speak, and he relates to us how he became a butcher, how he learned this trade, the ways it shaped his understanding of not only the bodies he worked with but his own body. The most stunning moment in his monologue occurs when he describes what happens to the body at death, how it fattens,

> opens, the blood drains,
> the hide peels from the skull,
> the pink tongue turning purple,
> split in two like a piece
> of pine, the one clean hole
> in the forehead drawing
> the darkness in. He told
> how the fat is scraped off,
> rolled into a ball and
> hung from a tree in late
> fall for the birds,
> how the fields close,
> the pheasants gleaning
> the few last seeds,
> how the earth turns under,
> then an explosion of wings
> flies up in front of your face. (8–9)

As in *Succession*, Swander does not see death as an ethereal release; rather, any kind of release that may occur remains rooted in the earth. The fat of death becomes the food for those who still live. The life seemingly gone, explodes with wings, flying up in a new body. Yes, there is release at death, but such release is only the relinquishing of our bodies so they may move even deeper into the physical world, becoming yet again a physical part of the whole.

Another example of Swander's emphasis on the acquisition of knowledge about the lives that reside around us, that may envelop us if we will acquiesce to them, appears in Ed's monologue. Ed knows his birds, their songs, their coloring, and their movements and behaviors. He knows his butterflies, encouraging the young to join in their winged procession. In "Summers," the poet tells us, "Ed paid every kid / in town a nickel for each butterfly named. / Monarchs, admirals, swallow tails, / sulphurs and skippers, we dashed around the cemetery and railroad cut / with jars and nets" (62). And this connection to the earth's body and the bodies that it supports emphasizes how our minds—what they examine, what they learn about—may join with the physical world beyond our finite and too often truncated existence. Even the priest who comes to bless the dead body of the poet's mother intuits how the soul and spirit are connected to the physical life once grounded in the body. Father Grieving, who oversees miracles at the Grotto of the Redemption, tells the poet about how healing began there, how the first woman rose from her wheelchair at the Shrine of the Virgin. And the poet reveals to us that this is the place where the town doctor sends those whom science can no longer help. Swander writes that "he felt a light spread / through his bones, / his muscles, move out of his skin, / filling the shrine" (46–7). The miraculous in Swander's world does not fall like rain from some intangible realm beyond; instead it emanates from within the body, moving over bone and muscle, out through the skin, to touch another's body, to move deeper into the body to heal it. "Where does the soul begin and where does the body end?" Swander's poems seem to ask over and over. What is life everlasting when the priest feels compelled to sprinkle "holy water / on us, circles the car, / blessing the body in the back" (55). Yes, even in death, Swander suggests, the body deserves the blessing that water will bring, the way it will help it to decompose, its cells joining with the soil. Is there anything more sacred than this?

III.

Swander explains in an interview that part of her urgency to write the stories that comprise *Driving the Body Back* was born out of her own battle to survive. "I was deathly ill myself when I wrote that book," Swander remarks, "and had a little bargain with God going to please just let me live long enough to finish my second book of poetry" (125). In *The Alchemy of Illness* (1993), Kat Duff asserts that "illness is the simple though painful reminder that we are not the masters of our bodies or our lives" (59). Such a point is not lost on Swander. "Illness and injury have been a constant for me since the age of 15," she notes. "I've made it through severe and deadly situations—multiple car accidents and near-death experiences" (128). Born to a farming family in Manning, Iowa, during the height of pesticide and DDT use, Swander's own existence is marked by what was written on her cells while growing in her mother's womb. As she explains in a conversation, "The very land my family was a part of, that fed them, also shaped and fed me as I grew, leading to chemical sensitivity issues that marked not only my body, but my siblings' bodies as well." Such a claim, which at one time might have been disputed by an industry whose very existence was based upon convincing farmers and consumers that there were no harmful effects from such products, now seems commonplace. Yet in the name of agricultural production, we continue to use and experiment with insecticides and pesticides, a fact that forced Swander to take refuge in the Amish and Mennonite community of Kalona, Iowa, where she raises her own food organically and writes out of a physical and spiritual experience of commitment to peace and plain living, learning to feed herself from the land she works with her own hands, learning to worship again with people whose faith helps her to reconsider her own abandoned Catholicism. Swander's more holistic approach to living— which includes the act of writing—is an affirmative response to Rich's call for women to think and act outside of the traditional patterns of objective, rational thought. "I am convinced that 'there are ways of thinking that we don't yet know about,'" Rich writes. "We have by no means yet explored or understood our biological grounding, the miracle and paradox of the female body and its spiritual and political meanings" (*Of Woman Born* 290).

Swander's life among the Amish—the subject of her first memoir, *Out of This World* (1995), as well as many of the poems in her third volume, *Heaven-and-Earth House*—highlights another way of knowing. As we move ever forward into a world driven by technology, we become increasingly ignorant of the ways we depend upon the earth and the plants and creatures that comprise the ecosystems we live in that help sustain our very way of life. As Swander explains, "Losing my health has made me question not only the goodness of doctors, but every principle, every custom and mode of behavior I once took for granted. It made me critical of the whole American way of life, and thrown me back to a more primitive existence" (*Out of This World* 107). It is interesting that Swander describes such a way of life as "more primitive." And, of course, in a world where many spend a majority of their working day in cyberspace, it may very well look like a form of regression. But moving backward, in this case, represents a healthy step forward in the recovery of a more complete or holistic means of human living. In *A Plain Life: Walking My Belief* (2000), Scott Savage offers a compelling example of how technology cuts us off from the natural rhythms of the world. After spending an afternoon observing cars and trucks racing here and there on a highway in Ohio, Savage writes, "I think how violent cars are when you experience them from the outside. Inside, all is comfy and smoothly serene, just like in television commercials, but out here there's a lot of noise and the feeling that the world is being slammed to pieces by all those tires" (76–7). This violence—which so many of us live with, virtually numb to its presence—disrupts the relationship between mind and body by pushing us deeper into the intellectual world of ideas and further away from the physical world of the body. In a car or truck, we are not able to pay attention to an individual tree or flower, to the track of an animal, in the same manner as we might if we were on foot. Isolated by the machinations of speed, we travel with the noise of the radio, the wind ripping through open windows, and the roar of other vehicles passing us. We are unable to hear the whippoorwill's call or listen to aspen leaves as they quake in the wind. So much is lost in the isolation of modern means, and, while Swander's most pressing cause for her move to Kalona to live among the Amish may be attributed to her environmental illness, it was not the only reason. She confesses that she "came to Fairview School to also find balance and reawaken myself to a life of simplicity" (95). This life of simplicity is most often discovered or rediscovered in menial tasks, using one's hands and arms and legs in acts of physical labor. "In my childhood rural Midwest," Swander explains, "you found your place in the world through your hands" (*Out of This World* 49).

Not surprisingly, Swander has continually searched the world with her hands. As a massage therapist, she used her hands to help heal others, to bring their bodies in line with their emotions, moving muscles and tendons, stretching ligaments, releasing toxin from the body. This vocation allowed her to perceive the complex relationship between body and psyche. She explains that she "loved the physical and emotional release" that such contact with the human body provided, how it enabled her to see "that the human body is a work of art" (54). "In my Catholic upbringing," Swander writes, "I'd been taught that the human body is a temple of the Holy Spirit. At that time, the phrase was used almost solely to deter us from 'the sins of the flesh,' but years later, it came close to capturing the reverence I felt for the people I touched.

Through contact with so many bodies, I could sense the presence of something deeper, more mystical" (*Out of This World* 55). In many of the poems in *Heaven-and-Earth House*, we find the speaker working with her hands as both an act of discovery and recovery: in the garden during a drought trying to deal with insects, praising the endurance of okra, asking it to teach her the secret of its stalks ("Ode to Okra" 33); in the coop, a rooster charging her shin, as she takes a duck, beginning the process of slitting sternum to anus, loosening and plucking feathers, asking it to forget, to forgive ("Stay Still, Duck" 40); in the barnyard, penning a doe against a woodpile, hugging her, feeding her oatmeal and beans by hand, smoothing her fur ("Take Two" 43). When humans have such experiences, an inevitable shift occurs. A physical and intellectual connection is made. We can no longer ignore how the food that rests upon our plate came to be there; we must begin to consider what sacrifices, what kinds of physical and emotional energy have been spent in bringing this sustenance to our mouths. Swander's own writing might be described best as liturgical. In her praise for the natural world, of which she is a part, there is a ritual established, a road map by which others might move toward a deeper understanding of the ground that supports their feet, of the life that is taken to sustain their own lives. In such moments, Swander claims that "what I was experiencing was rare and wonderful, nonreligious but surely divine, linking me to whatever it is that links all spirit, all flesh. I was graced. I was blessed. I was lost but now found" (*Out of This World* 70).

In *The Barn at the End of the World: The Apprenticeship of a Quaker, Buddhist Shepherd*, Mary Rose O'Reilley laments that the classic texts of spiritual autobiography too often suppress the body and the created world. "To be a spiritual person, do you have to climb out of your body?" she asks (xii). O'Reilley's answer to her own question seems apropos for Swander's work as well: "It's a long climb and not worth the trouble" (xii). I do not wish to suggest, however, that Swander's more holistic perspective came easily to her, that the decision not to climb out of the body was natural. Her journey toward such ideas and perspectives is marked by the pain of physical ailment, by the loss of faith and then a return to a new understanding of faith. As she notes in *Desert Pilgrim*, "Belief in science was the official creed in my family" (67), and because of this Swander's own relationship first with the Catholic church and later with the mystics was filled with disease. It is Swander's relationship with the things of this world, her varied experiences with the flora and fauna that surround her in Kalona, that begin to break down barriers that objective, scientific thought first established in her life.

In "Dear Diary," collected in *Heaven-and-Earth House*, these two ways of knowing come into direct conflict. While in the hospital for more tests, the poet considers medical science's worth and its claims in relation to her growing intuitive knowledge, comparing her own dilemma and what science can tell her about it with the migration of the monarch butterfly: "Some say it's all scientific, that once you record / the facts: wind shift, temperature dip, you can predict their coming" (62). But knowing how little the scientific community has been able to discern about what plagues her own body and the pain that rattles through it, Swander insists that this may not be the best or most complete way to discern the monarch's migration. "No one's ever explained / why they come back to that precise elm near the pond," she points out. "And who but me can sense the exact moment / their legs cling to branches, their bodies mimicking / bark, needles, leaves?" (62–3). In this reverie that pushes the boundaries of mysticism, the poet suggests that there is a faculty within her body that connects in some way to the "consciousness" the monarch possesses. Like these butterflies who eat "milkweed, that toxic weed that kills / birds on first bite," like the viceroy who "falls in line, / spreading its Halloween wings, the perfect / costume" (63), the poet *feels* the monarch's movements, *senses* when they begin to pump their wings, when they must land for rest and sustenance. And it is in this way she intuits that someone on her hospital ward will "light for the last time, fold in, a house of cards" (63). As the poem concludes, Swander brings these worlds—the scientific and the intuitive, the medical and the spiritual—into stark contrast. She and her fellow patients are instructed to record their scores: "fever, racing pulse, drop in weight from the start" (63), and, as she tells her diary about such objective measurements, "I notice these / things, and more. My body has no secrets" (63). But where are we led if our bodies hold "no secrets"? Is this a step toward some kind of earthly nirvana? Will our suffering rise like the early morning mist when the last secret is revealed?

Perhaps this is one of the most interesting points that Swander makes about the knowledge of the body: writing back through the body, bridging the gap between flesh and spirit does not necessarily culminate in some New Age epiphany where pain flies from the one who suffers like so many birds taking to the sky, nor are all dilemmas healed by this knowledge, this love. While the miraculous does indeed occur in Swander's life—her attending physicians did not think she would walk again—she nonetheless challenges herself and her readers to acknowledge that miracles do not always come in the form we fervently desire. In *Desert Pilgrim*, Swander brings together many of the stories that comprise her volumes of poetry and initial memoir. In this book, we are given an extended account of her mother's death: how Swander took a leave from her undergraduate studies to nurse her mother in a motel south of Iowa City; how at this time in Swander's life she believed in the sanctity and ultimate authority of science. "I believed in modern medicine throughout my youth," she confesses. "I believed bigger was better. I believed in experimentation, surgery, radiation, and chemotherapy" (71). Swander continued to believe even after her mother's three-year battle with cancer finally had failed. In *The Alchemy of Illness*, Duff contends that "in the secular world of modern medicine, we try desperately to rescue ourselves from the grasp of the Unknowable. Doctors have supplanted the gods" (46). While Duff perceives this concept as an existential constraint—ignoring the positive advances that the medical community has introduced in the fight against so many diseases and debilitating conditions—she perceptively underscores the absence of the "unknowable" in science.

Significantly, the act of naming, which enjoys a fundamental role in the treatment of disease, finds its origins in the modern notion that in naming a thing we can in some way control it. In *The Wounded Storyteller: Body, Illness, and Ethics* (1995), Arthur W. Frank argues that the modern approach to illness finds its basis and form of expression in a medical world where doctors are trained to diagnose, to name a disease or condition. By designating such a disorder, we assert that we know it in some manner, and in knowing it, we may come to control and ultimately destroy it. While this linguistic strategy helps us to move forward in the treatment of disease, even leading to cures in some cases, other conditions exist that we can hardly begin to comprehend. Frank argues that modernity's medical narrative once succeeded in trumping virtually every other narrative in existence: "The story told by the physician becomes the one against which others are ultimately judged true or false, useful or not," he explains (5). As Frank astutely observes, though, "the capacity for telling one's own story [has been] reclaimed" as we shift from the modern to the postmodern. In the contemporary setting— although medical science obviously remains extremely valuable in working toward cures and treatments for a variety of health issues—we recognize that in naming a disease we do not control, understand, or speak to its every facet. We bridge the modern and postmodern worlds of medicine and humanity when we no longer assume that a person's story of illness is secondary to the narrative that a physician might offer; instead, the patient's own story begins to assume a primary role in the equation—equal, if not greater than, the significance of medical prerogatives (Frank 7).

Swander's own journey through the medical community—with her mother's illness as well as her own—ultimately exposes this glaring weakness. Despite the many medical tests she endured and later chronicled in her poems and memoirs, Swander's physicians could not resolve the pain that plagued her, and because of this failure, Swander writes, "I stopped believing" (*Desert Pilgrim* 71). *Desert Pilgrim*'s creation is found at the nexus of her lost faith in medical science, her struggle to believe in something beyond the rational and its seemingly objective abilities of science to heal, and her own ongoing negotiations with chronic pain and suffering. Struck in her car by a drunken college student one evening on her way home from the university, Swander ruptures a disk and has a hole punched in the spinal cord. The extent of the injury, however, is misdiagnosed and later grows worse when a flu virus settles into the spinal cord, creating central cord syndrome and transverse myelitis, a condition similar to polio. In the throes of crippling pain, Swander finds her condition so debilitating that she takes a leave of absence from the university to go to New Mexico as a visiting writer. *Desert Pilgrim* seeks to chronicle Swander's own pilgrimage through pain, while examining how suffering shapes us. Swander contends that "at its best, suffering opens the heart to others' suffering and produces love and compassion—what we all long for from each other but find so hard to both give and find. The love for our fellow humans seems inevitably to work its way 'down' toward all other living creatures and 'up' to find its full force in the love of God or a higher power" (23). Swander's notions of suffering, and the potential good that may come from it, are grounded in the philosophy that we have highlighted in so much of her work: We should not seek to escape from our physical bodies, or condemn them as a weaker vessel that our spirits, our intellect, and our emotions must tolerate. Our bodies—where much physical suffering takes place—help us to discover new ways of thinking spiritually, intellectually, and emotionally.

When Swander heads to New Mexico—with a graduate student driving her across the country because she is not physically able—she does so with some degree of skepticism. After encountering Father Sergei and meeting Lu, a *curandera* or herbal healer, Swander is confronted with her own tenuous desire to hold back from such unorthodox ways of thinking about body and soul, flesh and spirit. As is often the case with spiritual autobiography, the writer slowly demonstrates how one moves from one level to another, progressing in stages, not arriving at some destination all at once. In fact, in Swander's case, the very idea of a final destination appears antithetical to her spiritual vision. Her faith is always in process combining the past with the present. In *The Nature of Suffering and the Goals of Medicine* (1991), Eric J. Cassell concurs when he argues that "the personal meaning of a disease and its treatment arise from the past as well as the present" (38). Not surprisingly, Swander structures *Desert Pilgrim* with this notion in mind. We consistently move back and forth from the past—her mother's death, her own previous struggles with illness—and the present—where she grapples with not only her physical pain but also with the possibility that physical pain and spiritual well-being may be connected in some way she has yet to consider. "Healing is a process of looking back," Swander writes, "of finding the things in the past that have been significant to you. That mean the most" (319). Ultimately, Swander is led—by her discussions with Father Sergei and the healing herbs that Lu offers—to a vision of ultimate connection, one in which her body and spirit play an equal role, neither dominating, each nurturing the other. "I learned to have faith in the unfolding of these events, the unwinding of lives," Swander explains. "All forces, all of nature became closer to my consciousness: Brother Sun, Sister Moon, Sister Water, Brother Fire, Sister Mother Earth, Sister Bodily Death. I tried to forgive, and I learned to play—to realize the spark of life in the rosebush, the zucchini plant, the horsetail herb" (320).[4]

It is this idea of connection—the seeds of which we witness in Swander's earliest poems—that undergirds all of her work. She sees herself as a healer, her writing no different in this regard than her previous work as a massage therapist or hypnotherapist, and because of this desire to heal, Swander admits that while she "may have been a writer if I hadn't gone through all of this pain . . . I wouldn't be as good of a writer. I wouldn't have had the life experience to understand loss. Loss allows for spiritual growth and opens a writer to an exploration of deeper thoughts and emotions" ("Interview" 128–9). Any discourse between flesh and spirit must account for loss. As we age, our bodies inevitably break down; we experience a loss of physical capacity, no longer able to accomplish the feats of our childhood or teen years. Whether we will experience a physical condition as extreme as Swander's is not important; her writing nonetheless helps us to heal the division between body and soul, to understand how these two facets of our being work together as one grows and the other diminishes. If these two elements are actually one, entwined in ways that are ultimately unknowable, then loss itself may help us begin to negotiate the natural order of things and to gain insight into that order. Like the novelist Madison Smartt Bell—who in his essay "The Story of the Days of Creation" explains that the Hermetic version of the Genesis account suggests that "matter is alive and full of potential to liberate the soul," that "the fall into the body is expressed as a falling in love" (29)—Swander's body, with all its maladies and accompanying difficulties, actually liberates her spiritually. Following Rich's urging in *Blood, Bread, and Poetry*, Swander "reconnect(s) our thinking and speaking with the body" (213). As Father Sergei says in one of his last sermons before his death, there is no need to fear such loss. He proclaims that his brothers and sisters should be happy not saddened by the prospect of his death. "It's the natural cycle of life," Sergei explains. "We rejoice when babies are born. In death, that baby has come full circle. We should rejoice when the adult dies and makes room for another baby to be born. It's the cycle, the cycle that we must become attuned to, that we must never forget we are an integral part of" (326). In this way, Swander's poetry and prose are an act of praise and rejoicing, a continual pilgrimage toward a greater understanding of how she is connected to her flesh, to her spirit. In pointing toward a reconciliation between flesh and spirit, Swander proclaims, like her spiritual mentors, that her human *being* is connected to a larger living organism and that she is blessed by its making, of which she is a part.

3

Always Becoming: The Nature of Transcendence in the Poetry of Mary Oliver

> I become a transparent eyeball. I am nothing. I see all.
> The currents of the Universal Being circulate through
> me; I am part or particle of God.
>
> Ralph Waldo Emerson, "Nature"

> The god of today is rampant and drenched. His arms
> spread, bearing moist pastures; his fingers spread, fin-
> gering the shore. He is time's live skin; he burgeons up
> from day like any tree. His legs spread crossing the
> heavens, flicking hugely, and flashing and arcing
> around the earth toward night.
>
> Annie Dillard, *Holy the Firm*

> By morning / I had vanished at least a dozen times /
> into something better.
>
> Mary Oliver, "Sleeping in the Forest"

The desire to transcend one's position in the world, to move beyond the limited and limiting moorings of the physical self, serves as the essential foundation for transcendental ideas and the narratives of quest-ing found in numerous religious and philosophical traditions around the world. While this desire clearly functions in the nineteenth-century writ-ings and teachings of Ralph Waldo Emerson and later in those of Margaret Fuller, Henry David Thoreau, and, perhaps most memorably, in the poetry of Walt Whitman, little scholarly attention has been paid to this same impulse in the work of some of contemporary poetry's most noted authors. While the bulwark of contemporary literary theory ignores or is blind to this particular domain, who upon reading the poetry of James Wright can deny the desire for transcendence that permeates nearly every line and stanza of his work? For instance, in "Trying to Pray" the speaker says that he has "left [his] body behind [him], crying / in its dark thorns," and in "A Blessing"—perhaps Wright's most famous poem—the speaker confesses that he yearns to step out of his body, to "break / into blossom" as a horse nuzzles his hand in the middle of a Minnesota pasture. In the same way, Galway Kinnell's poetry is filled with images of a movement out of the self and into another— and, ultimately, into a different state of consciousness that the other may afford him. In Kinnell's "The Bear," the speaker's perspective merges with the animal he has hunted and killed. Having cut the animal open and crawled inside to survive the brutal weather, the very flesh that has sustained him through this Arctic night now carries him outside of his former life as he lumbers away on the tundra—somehow part bear and part man. Similarly, in "The Gray Heron," Kinnell tells us that the heron has watched him, has waited "to see if I would go / or change into something else." It is this changing into something else—an act at once spiritual and physical—that Mary Oliver seeks after in so many of her writings, as well as in her life beyond the text, and it is this self-same act— mystical and unaccounted for by so much of contemporary theory—that must be examined and taken seriously if we are to grapple with the profound influence Oliver's art has over her considerable audience and the work of contemporary poetry's future generations.

A direct philosophical descendent of Emerson, Oliver has won both the Pulitzer Prize and the National Book Award. And since the publication of her first book of poems, *No Voyage* (1963), she has steadily amassed a body of work whose tone and subject matter are marked by a constant quest for the joining of the material and the spiritual, for a movement deeper into the self and ultimately outward into communion with the broader world. Despite her critical and popular success, however, Oliver's work has received, at best, a lukewarm response from the scholarly community.[1] In " 'Keep Looking': Mary Oliver's Emersonian Project," Mark Johnson argues convincingly that scholars inevitably are befuddled by Oliver's devotion to Emersonian ideas, and despite their best efforts to categorize her as an "environmentalist or feminist or post-post-modernist," Oliver's work keeps slipping out from beneath the noose of theory and interpretation, away from the straightjacket of ideology, to become something else, something that resists definition because of its allegiance to what Emerson called the "ever-present now." Like Whitman, who boldly asserted that to contradict oneself was of no concern or consequence, Oliver's work slips out from the straightjacket of prescription and insists that, like life itself, there can be no label or doctrine that describes and, thus, circumscribes the work of a life.[2] "In the tradition of those folk who think everything looks like a nail because they have only a hammer," Johnson explains, "some critics cannot recognize a Romantic and hastily provide her with fig leaves for her 'quaint' naïveté" (78).

While we agree with Johnson's assessment of Oliver as Romantic, we would only add that her decision to follow the path of Emerson, Fuller, Thoreau, and Whitman is informed by the breadth of historical, cultural, and artistic events in the twentieth century. Unlike Emerson and his contemporaries, Oliver must account for two world wars; the atrocity of the Holocaust; the creation and use of the atomic bomb; first-, second-, and third-wave feminism; the gay movement; the globalization of American thought and economic practice; abstract impressionism; nihilism; fabulism; and a myriad of other cultural, historical, and artistic events and movements that comprise the twentieth century up to the present moment. Of course, we would do well to note that one of Oliver's favorite poets, the Romantic John Keats, also lived during a turbulent political era, which was plagued with the ravages of disease and the malaise of empire-building. Perhaps the tenants of Romanticism are not as incompatible with the current epoch as some have suggested. In other words, while Oliver's poetry at every turn betrays her as a contemporary transcendental thinker, the nature of her decision to pursue such values comes about in a radically different fashion than that of her nineteenth-century forebears. Like Jim Harrison's and Mary Swander's penchant for differing forms of redemption, Oliver represents that segment of the arts in a postmodern world which remains affirmative, open to spiritual questing and contemplation, dedicated to communicating with a kind of language that, despite its limitations, presents itself as a means for making gestures at the infinite, nonlinguistic world of nature.

In *Blue Pastures*, Oliver acknowledges Whitman's profound influence upon her own conception of what a poem is and what a poem might become. "I learned from Whitman that the poem is a temple," Oliver explains, "—or a green field—a place to enter, and in which to feel" (15). The act and artifact of poetry rests solidly at the center of what Oliver perceives to be sacred or spiritual. For Oliver, the poem is a temple where the artist goes to worship, a green place that holds the possibility of entering the domain of emotion. Similar to John Elder, who claims in *Reading the Mountains of Home* that "we enter a poem and vanish into the wilderness" (217), Oliver's conception of poem-making includes the notion of wilderness as both physical and emotional/spiritual. For example, in her poem "Some Herons," Oliver conflates the realms of prosody and religion through the act of metaphor. "A blue preacher / flew toward the swamp," she writes, and "on the leafy banks, / an old Chinese poet, / hunched in the white gown of his wings, / was waiting" (*New and Selected Poems, Volume One* 81). After the preacher (a great blue heron) makes his difficult landing, we are told that the eyes of the poet (a great white heron) flared, "just as a poet's eyes / are said to do" (81). One heron, representing one modality of consciousness, feeds off the other heron, representing another modality of consciousness. The relationship that the two birds enter into is symbiotic, and as the poem concludes both birds come to the water where their reflections multiply the effect of this kind of relationship in much the same manner that a poem multiplies or makes accessible the layers of meaning hidden within its rhythms and images.

To even speak about the idea of an animal transcendence that we might have access to through the concurrent acts of living within an awareness of the natural world and making art out of that awareness suggests a faith in a dimension beyond the province of contemporary science. As Elder claims, "Poetry, like faith, depends upon the substance of things hoped for and illuminates the evidence of things not seen" (217). At every turn, Oliver uses poetry to explore her faith and her faith to create her poetry. In her essay "Staying Alive," Oliver interrupts herself to say boldly, in italics, "*I believe everything has a soul*" (*Blue Pastures* 63), and her conception of a soul—although it shares some commonalities with Wendell Berry's notion of the soul as described in "Christianity and the Survival of Creation"[2]—continues to shift and grow as the poet struggles to comprehend this thing we have named the "soul." In her poem "Some Questions You Might Ask," Oliver considers the soul and who or what may possess it:

> Is the soul solid, like iron?
> Or is it tender and breakable, like
> the wings of a moth in the beak of the owl?
> Who has it, and who doesn't? (*New and Selected Poems,*
> *Volume One* 65)

Although many religious traditions make reference to the soul, most do not offer a way to define it. The spiritual dimension of our being tends to slip away into the abstract, into the suggestive realm of metaphor or the allusive world of theology. Notice that in this poem Oliver is doing neither. When she asks if the soul is solid like iron or breakable like the wings of a moth, she begins to establish through the use of simile the ways the soul might literally take on both spiritual and physical characteristics. She continues this line of thinking when she wonders if it has a shape like an iceberg or the eye of a hummingbird. The soul grows ever more animate as the poem concludes when the poet considers whether the soul has "one lung, like the snake and the scallop." Perhaps most radically—when we take into consideration the dominant conception in the Western world of the soul as ethereal and belonging only to humankind— Oliver asks why she should have a soul and not the anteater or the camel or the maple trees or the blue iris. Her litany continues, and the poem does not close with a statement of fact about what the soul is or is not or even who might possess it; instead, Oliver allows the poem to drift toward indeterminacy by posing yet another question about the possibility of the grass having a soul as well—a clear allusion to Whitman telling his readers to look for him beneath their feet.

The question of the soul and its relation to transcendence permeates much of Oliver's work and may be noted across the breadth of her career. In a more recent poem, "Bone," published in *Why I Wake Early* (2004) and collected in the second volume of her *New and Selected Poems*, Oliver bluntly states at the outset that she is "always trying to figure out / what the soul is, / and where hidden, / and what shape—" (72). As the poem begins, the poet discovers the ear bone of a pilot whale on the beach, and in considering the ear bone believes she may be coming closer to understanding the soul—its shape and hiding place. Yet the poem's resolution does not lead us to any certainties about it because, as Oliver reminds us, to "sift it down / into fractions, and facts" is not the role we are meant to play. "What the soul is, also / I believe I will never quite know," Oliver confesses. "Though I play at the edges of knowing, / truly I know / our part is not knowing" (73). Instead, she suggests, as does her practice of walking on the shore or in the woods each morning to "find" her poems, that our task, our obligation as creatures in this grand creation, is "looking, and touching, and loving" (74). Rather than seek definitive, static meaning—to intellectually grasp the idea of the soul as if we could wrest it from its place in the order of things and make it our own—Oliver encourages us to "play" at the edges of knowing and then to turn to the business of devotion and love—neither of which requires an absolute knowledge. At the heart of this approach to the miracle of the world, the miracle of naming life, is humility. Oliver does not possess the hubris to claim that she understands the boundaries or shapes of the soul; rather, with faith, she makes gestures toward the idea of the soul as well as toward the physical world in which she believes the soul resides. For this reason, it seems only natural that she would look for the soul beyond the finite boundaries of the human, to believe fervently that the soul knows no borders outside of the life that sustains it and makes it possible.

Even the concept of life, however, is not so easily defined for Oliver. In a rare moment of anger, Oliver says to those she sarcastically calls the "wise ones," "you live your life your way and leave me alone" ("Some Things, Say the Wise Ones," *New and Selected Poems, Volume Two* 89). What provokes her wrath is the idea that there are those who claim to have some kind of absolute knowledge of what we may call or deem "life" and what may be regarded as merely inanimate, unfeeling, and indefensible, thus expendable. The poet agrees that we can easily say cows and starfish and roses are living things because "they die, after all." Water proves far more difficult and allusive for Oliver to define—"so many living things in it"—and she cannot understand how anyone could write off this elemental source as inanimate, un-living. Her crowning blow, however, rests firmly in the rocks she holds in her hand: granite, pyrite, schist. Certainly, most would pass over these stones we quarry daily, the rocks we toss aside with no regard for how they might hold life within their framework or how they establish the very structure of a planet many would claim is a living thing. Oliver suggests—in the act of poem-making—that the stones may only be asleep, that indeed we cannot know how life is generated, how these stones may speak one day. Oliver does not wish to have a scientific discussion about this matter either, because, although she respects what science may help us to understand and appreciate, she knows science—with its abeyance to objectivity—cannot imagine what it cannot know. If the very rocks are deemed animate, perhaps even sentient, imagine what reverence might be bequeathed to them and to all those who stand and live upon them.

In this way, Oliver follows a set of precepts similar to those of novelist John Fowles who, in *The Tree* (1983), explains that he has three principles for approaching nature so that he may enter fully into a relationship with it: "One is that knowing it fully is an art as well as a science. The second is that the heart of this art lies in our own personal nature and its relationship to other nature; never in nature as a collection of 'things' outside of us. The last is that this kind of knowledge, or relationship, is not reproducible by any other means—by painting, by photography, by words, by science itself" (73). While Oliver would likely agree that such a relationship is not reproducible, she nonetheless makes gesture after gesture toward, if not reproducing, offering a partial record of her relationship with nature through the act of writing poems. As she explains in *Blue Pastures*, "I did not think of language as the means to self-description. I thought of it as the door—a thousand opening doors!—past myself. I thought of it as the means to notice, to contemplate, to praise, and, *thus*, to come into power" (67). This idea of moving past one's self—indelibly linked to Emerson's notions of transcendence, although arguably taking a path exterior to the self instead of deeper into the interior as he might have had it—might best be described as a way of being lost that brings greater enlightenment, greater contact with the world as itself, not as a projection of our myriad selves.

"Perhaps getting lost temporarily destroys the acquisitive sense," Jim Harrison writes in *Just Before Dark*. "We tend to look at earth as an elaborate system out of which we may draw useful information. We 'profit' from nature—that is the taught system" (263). Fowles suggests that this acquisitive sense owes much to the burgeoning field of science in the nineteenth century: "the most harmful change brought about by Victorian science in our attitude to nature lies in the demand that our relation with it must be purposive, industrious, always seeking greater knowledge" (33). In being lost, this penchant for acquisition, for industrious purposefulness, ultimately must fail. If we are able to rest in the moment of not knowing precisely where we are and where we are going, the world around us may open in new and surprising ways. What happens when we stray from the given paths into places humans have not chosen but rather animals have created through the patterns of their own lives? What is different about our experience when we leave the marked trail to follow a deer's path or to lay underneath the arms of a hemlock where deer bed down during heavy snows? When we begin to move outside the forms and structures, the taxonomies of human knowledge, to look more closely at structures formed by other forms of life, what happens to us? (Note: Instead of saying what do we "gain" from such moments, we are asking what transpires, what takes place, what "happens"—neither for gain nor for good, simply for what *is* in that given moment.)

While Oliver does not write or speak of getting "lost" in the literal sense of not knowing where one is on the map, of not being sure which way home is or where the car is parked, she does appear to stress the importance of getting lost metaphorically, of losing one's self in the landscape, in the lives of the animals and trees and plants that populate the landscape, of losing one's self to become, as fully as possible, part of another—part of something outside of ourselves. In her poem, "The

Delight of Being Lost," Pattiann Rogers reflects on the possibilities of being a living thing "solely as the unrecorded, passing / moments of themselves, to have no name or place but breath" (67). This notion of being "lost" may come closest to Oliver's poetic and spiritual principle: in the movement away from self and into another, in the shedding of the weight of ego and the skin with which it dresses itself, a deeper understanding, acceptance, and connection may be established. Such ways of *being* combat the idea of *using* nature for profit. As Harrison contends, "we should encourage ourselves to be a whale, a woman, a plant or planet, a lake, the night sky" (*Just Before Dark* 265). Perhaps with this new perspective we might come to the same conclusion as the Chippewa Indian who explained to Harrison that "every tree was different from every other tree" (264). Science works through generalization to name species; poetry works through particularity to demonstrate that, for example, this particular pignut hickory is unlike any other pignut hickory, or, as Fowles claims, "All nature, like all humanity, is made of minor exceptions, of entities that in some way, however scientifically disregardable, do not conform to the general rule" (72).

With this idea in mind, as we read Oliver's poetry we begin to perceive that although she names many species with a knowledge that betrays her life-long study of the field (a portion of the way science teaches us to "know"), she never allows the general rule of study (the dictatorial ways of taxonomy) to blind her to the specific and varied directions of each life she encounters. In "The Bleeding-Heart," for example, Oliver tells us that she knows "a bleeding-heart plant that has thrived for sixty years if not more, and has never missed a spring without rising and spreading itself into a glossy bush" (*New and Selected Poems, Volume Two* 61). She then shifts her attention away from the plant for a moment and addresses the reader, asking if such a phenomenon, such a life, does not deserve our consideration, because, after all, "most things that are important, have you noticed, lack a certain neatness?" (61). And herein lies the double-bind of much of the practice of art and science: to know, to generalize, to create taxonomies that allow for the accumulation of knowledge and the necessary connections between different kinds of knowledge, we must excise or ignore entire parts of the life before us that we wish to study; yet in the specificity of art, in the attention we pay to the differences between two New York asters, for instance, there is the chance to lose or miss entirely the broader picture that affords a long view of the myriad correlations between not only the two asters but other flowers of the same genus. Perhaps the genius in Oliver's poetry is built upon the manner in which she approaches the individual while never losing sight of broader connections. At the root of her vision—the individual always in contact with the whole—is the belief that all things are imbued with a soul and that all souls are in some way joined.

Vicki Graham argues that Oliver's desire and ability to take on the body of another, to lose oneself in another's being, might best be studied or described by using Walter Benjamin's theory of the mimetic faculty. While empathetic mimicry—whether physical or mental or both—assists Oliver's dissolution of her self into another, it does not acknowledge or account for the very real spiritual element that Oliver speaks of with passion and sincerity. It is not simply that Oliver peers longingly at a fellow creature, studying its every movement, imagining herself doing the same movements, living the same life, and, thus, becoming—at least empathetically—the other. Mere mimicry does little to describe the nuances of the spiritual and physical transformation Oliver not only desires but achieves, at least linguistically, in her poetry. What Oliver seeks are "the prayers that are made / out of grass" (*New and Selected Poems, Volume Two* 91) or, as she describes it in "The Soul at Last," the "Lord's terrifying kindness" came upon her like "a thousand spider webs woven together, or a small handful of aspen leaves, with their silver backs shimmering" (*New and Selected Poems, Volume Two* 94). These moments of ecstatic epiphanies that lead her out of the solitary and finite existence of the self and into a communion with the saints of the flora and fauna that surround her life are at all times spiritual journeys that Oliver often attributes to some higher power. Oliver is insistent that there is a spiritual bridge of sorts that only the imagination may open, that the imagination may be the key to the soul itself, which we share with the earth and everything that lives upon it; and by walking across this bridge—a neo-transcendentalist finding her way to one of those moments that Emerson would describe as offering a more complete knowledge of the manner in which all things are part and particle of God—Oliver joins with other living things, is part of their livelihood, not through mimicry, but through some kind of transmogrification that language and metaphor and spirit help her to realize.

Oliver contends that "it is one of the perils of our so-called civilized age that we do not yet acknowledge enough, or cherish enough, this connection between soul and landscape" (*Long Life* 91). In *Dakota: A Spiritual Geography*, Kathleen Norris does exactly what Oliver calls for: she demonstrates the correlation between a physical space and everything that particular space holds and the way the soul develops in that space, the spiritual and emotional ways of *being* such spaces shape. It should be no surprise that the parables and sacred stories within many religious traditions most often are comprised of metaphors drawn from weather patterns, growing cycles, and the flora and fauna of the region in which the religious tradition is first established. A great deal may be lost in translation when such stories are blithely transferred to a radically different physical landscape, and perhaps this is one of the weaknesses of contemporary religious faith in America: we are a transient people, often not connected to any landscape, carrying little or no knowledge of its spiritual or physical geography, of its stories and the roots of those stories that spread beneath the soil.

For this reason, Oliver's poetry insists that we notice what is around us. If there is any single driving characteristic of Oliver's poetry, it is her assertion that we must take note of the tree limb above our head, of the shrub that blossoms at our elbow, of the animal track in the grass at our feet. As she says in "Mindful," "Every day / I see or I hear / something / that more or less / kills me / with delight, / that leaves me / like a needle / in the haystack / of light. / It is what I was born for— / to look, to listen, / to lose myself / inside this soft world—" (*New and Selected Poems, Volume Two* 90). This personal delight which Oliver revels in, however, is neither meant to be exclusionary nor particular to herself. "The poem in which the reader does not feel himself or herself a participant is a lecture," Oliver explains, "listened to from an uncomfortable chair, in a stuffy room, inside a building" (*Winter Hours* 25). Because of this, Oliver claims that her poems "invite the reader to want to do something beyond merely receiving beauty, and to configure in his or her own mind what that might be" (*Winter Hours* 25). In her poem about the celebrated poet Stanley Kunitz, and his renowned gardens in Provincetown, Massachusetts—where Oliver and he make their residence—she explains how in earlier years she was misled in thinking that Kunitz was in some way like Merlin, a wizard bringing forth growth, new life, the very thunder like "moist pages." Kunitz partakes of the same delight that Oliver relishes as he cultivates the many plants that populate the landscape he cares for. This sense of delight actually comes about because of time spent "on his knees, / cutting away the diseased, the superfluous, / coaxing the new, / knowing that the hour of fulfillment / is buried in years of patience— / yet willing to labor like that / on the mortal wheel" (*New and Selected Poems, Volume One* 118). Magic and wizardry give ground to the labor we all might participate in, Oliver argues in this poem, and the mortal wheel upon which we all turn begets yet other life and still more varied lives, and in the turning— both the transformation of one life into another, the decay of our bodies back into the earth where something else will take root, grow from us—it is in these actions that the dissolution of the self occurs. In the recognition that identity is always multiple—constructed from the entirety of all that lives with us in any particular culture or ecosystem—Oliver joins the mystical, the ecological, and the postmodern.

In "The Pragmatic Mysticism of Mary Oliver," Laird Christensen contends that Oliver's poetry demonstrates the ways in which postmodern theory and ecology, although seemingly incompatible, may present a pragmatic bridge to a healthier understanding of the self in relation to the other. When we consider the systems in which we all participate—from the micro-world of the subatomic to the macro-world of the interconnected ecosystems that comprise our planet—according to Christensen, "there is no longer any possibility of an *independent* self, at least in conventional terms" (136). In this way, Oliver's desire to transcend the traditional idea of the self, to become part of the other—through the lives of animals or trees or plants—reflects the realization that in many ways we are at all times part of a system of life that swirls around and through us, creating a form of diffusion that has implications for not only how we treat ourselves, but how all of our actions eventually impact watersheds, prairies, forests, etc., and in turn come back to impact us once again. In "By the Wild-Haired Corn," Oliver is insistent in her firm conviction that "everything will be everything else, / by and by" (*Long Life* 95). Similarly, Oliver claims that "all things are meltable, and replaceable. Not at this moment, but soon enough, we are lambs and we are leaves, and we are stars, and the shining, mysterious pond water itself" (*Winter Hours* 23).[3] The implication that we will all eventually transform into something else is indelibly linked to Oliver's understanding of the soul. In "Have You Ever Tried to Enter the Long Black Branches," Oliver contends that "the soul, after all, is only a window, / and the opening of the window no more difficult / than the wakening from a little sleep" (*New and Selected Poems, Volume Two* 142). The traditional view of the soul within Judeo-Christian doctrine stresses individuality and self-containment. Relationship or association of the soul to another soul or to God seems to be shaped by this idea of autonomy. Such notions have no place in Oliver's cosmology; instead, she uses the window as a metaphor for the soul—something we can look out of, something that can be opened, something that allows for movement both in and out of the self.

This perspective, as Oliver admits, makes her "sister to the dreamy-hearted dog who thinks only small thoughts; and to the green tree who thinks, perhaps, no thoughts at all, as well as to Rumi, and St. Francis"

(*Long Life* 90). As a sister to all of this, perhaps Oliver departs from the company of Emerson, for in Emerson there seems to be a greater concern with the individual self and with the journey of the individual self toward transcendence than with connection for its own sake. In other words, Oliver's transformation into the other has less to do with a reaching after "salvation" and more to do with its state of being and the way in which this state of being represents the health of the entire system. As Oliver moves away from the more self-interested desires of Emerson, she writes toward the realization that we can only achieve transcendence when we begin to realize that we are already at all times a part of the other, that the boundaries we see between the dog and the tree and the pond and the child are artificial boundaries we have created for our own purposes—purposes often linked to unhealthy materialist ambitions. "I am one of those who has no trouble imagining the sentient lives of trees, of their leaves in some fashion communicating or of the massy trunks and heavy branches knowing it is I who have come," Oliver confesses, "as I always come, each morning, to walk beneath them, glad to be alive and glad to be there" (*Winter Hours* 15). To be in the presence of other forms of life, to be absorbed into them through empathy, through recognition, through imagination, and, ultimately, through something beyond language, something beyond the rational world of science or the dogma of theology, is Oliver's daily task and the initiatory impulse behind her poetry. "I stood willingly and gladly in the characters of everything—other people, trees, clouds. And this is what I learned," Oliver writes, "that the world's *otherness* is antidote to confusion—that standing *within* this otherness—the beauty and the mystery of the world, out in the fields or deep inside books—can re-dignify the worst-stung heart" (*Blue Pastures* 64). And it is in disconnection—a way of seeing and living in the world that is encouraged in a multiplicity of ways—that the heart is stung. Transcendence, which Oliver seeks after and shares with her readers, is the salve, the blessing, for that stung heart, and such a salve may only be found in the constant and vigilant task of making note of connection, of recognizing and celebrating the manner in which we share the same being.

In "A Blessing," collected in *Twelve Moons*, Oliver speaks of "the man in the tree, a rough amorphous pope," who makes the sign of the benediction over her as she walks through a pasture. The blessing to which the poem's title refers, as in so many of Oliver's poems, is the blessing from "father, mother, friends, / from dogs and strangers" and from "what turns / on the wheel of what cannot be defined / in the leaves, in the darkness" (75). In *Blue Pastures*, Oliver names that "wheel" when she tells us that "Nature, the total of all of us, is the "wheel" that drives our world; those who ride it willingly might yet catch a glimpse of a dazzling, even a spiritual restfulness, while those who are unwilling simply to hang on, who insist that the world must be piloted by man for his own benefit, will be dragged around and around all the same, gathering dust but no joy" (*Blue Pastures* 92). Oliver and her poetry, in its constant attempt to render the ways that transcendence might take place, wishes only joy for all of the world, an uncommon literary stance in the postmodern landscape, but one to which many find themselves drawn.

Part II Story and Possibility: Narrative Mapping as Ethical Construct

4

Saints, Sinners, and the Dickensian Novel: The Ethics of Storytelling in John Irving's *The Cider House Rules*

> The intention of a novel by Charles Dickens is to move you emotionally, not intellectually; and it is by emotional means that Dickens intends to influence you socially.
>
> John Irving, "The King of the Novel"

In his novels, John Irving continues to experiment with a narrative voice that seeks to thwart deliberately his readers' expectations, to upset our notions of conventionality, and to blur the boundaries that linger between good and evil, right and wrong. From the life-affirming presence of the "good, smart bears" in *The Hotel New Hampshire* (1981) and Owen Meany's shrill voice of reason in *A Prayer for Owen Meany* (1989) to the convoluted sexual politics of *The 158-Pound Marriage* (1974) and the conspicuous proximity of the "Under Toad" and the tragedy of the Ellen Jamesians in *The World According to Garp* (1978), Irving adorns his fictions with a host of ethical signifiers that challenge readers at every turn throughout his labyrinthine, deliberately Dickensian fictions. Irving makes little secret of his affinity for Dickens and in particular for the Victorian writer's eye for complexity of narrative and literary character. In "King of the Novel," Irving writes that "Dickens was abundant and magnificent with description, with the atmosphere surrounding everything—and with the tactile, with every detail that was terrifying or viscerally *felt*" (364). As with Dickens, because Irving loads his own narratives with considerable detail and description, he makes it virtually impossible for readers to render facile ethical decisions in the face of so much information about a given character's humanity. Irving self-consciously adopts the literary form of the Dickensian novel—with its multiplicity of characters, its narrative mass, its overt sense of sentimentality, and its generic intersec-

tions with such modes as the detective story—as the forum for constructing the fictions that intentionally challenge his readers' value systems. As an artist who has written movingly about the possibilities for
redemption in a fragmented world, Irving chooses the narrative form of
the Dickensian novel as an explicitly ethical move.

The essential formulation of the Dickensian novel as a narrative form
finds its origins in Dickens's dynamic approach to literary character. In
Poetic Justice: The Literary Imagination and Public Life (1995), Martha C.
Nussbaum remarks that Dickens endows his characters with "physical
and moral attributes that make it possible for us to distinguish every
one from every other. We are made to attend to their ways of moving
and talking, the shapes of their bodies, the expressions on their faces,
the sentiments of their hearts. The inner life of each is displayed as having psychological depth and complexity," she adds, and "we see that as
humans they share certain common problems and common hopes"
(27). Yet Dickens's characters are far more than mere vessels of transport
for the essential elements of genuine human behavior. The effectiveness
of Dickens's characters as human representations lies in their peculiar
lack of ethical certainty, in their capacity for mimicking the elusive qualities that often define human nature. Dickens's "characters do not so
much re-create actual individuals as re-create the reactions to actual individuals, and particularly the difficulties and dilemmas," Brian Rosenberg
writes in *Little Dorrit's Shadows: Character and Contradiction in Dickens*
(1996); "his doubts about the potential for understanding others capture a nearly universal uncertainty, and his struggle to make sense of
conflicting, unreliable pieces of information mirrors a struggle we under-
go daily. Shunning the rounded and definite, he leaves the reader,"
Rosenberg continues, "like many of the figures in his novels, always contending with the elusive and irreconcilable" (30).

As a literary model, the Dickensian novel provides the narrative structure for Irving's own ethics of storytelling. In *The Cider House Rules*
(1985), Irving avails himself of many of the Dickensian form's classic
narratological elements, including its intentionally conflicted mélange
of characters, its intricate layering of plots, its penchant for the detective story, and even its frequent depiction of orphans, the occupants of
society's most innocent and vulnerable stations. *The Cider House Rules*
also affords Irving with a venue for challenging our assumptions, fears,
and prejudices about abortion, the most fractious of social issues. Rather
than merely rendering an overt decision about the ethics of abortion,
Irving, using the Dickensian mode of characterization, chooses to confront his readers with detailed, fully realized visions of the complications

and uncertainties that comprise the human condition.[1] Despite Irving's careful and deliberately indeterminate depiction of human nature in his novel, Carol C. Harter and James R. Thompson argue that as a polemic *The Cider House Rules* "is seriously flawed," and because "Irving's 'correct political vision' sometimes distorts the book's larger theme—the problematical nature of personal and social 'rules'—the difficulties with Irving's new fiction are considerable" (134).[2] Yet Harter and Thompson's critique of *The Cider House Rules* neglects to allow for the tremendous import of Irving's ethics of storytelling in the novel. As an essentially Dickensian novelist, Irving simply refuses to permit his readers to resort to easy and obvious decisions about either his own ethos or the ethical systems of his characters. With its variegated landscape of humanity— and the elusiveness and uncertainty that genuine humanity necessarily entails—the Dickensian novel functions in *The Cider House Rules* as the ethical vehicle via which Irving challenges his readers to consider the abortion debate from a host of vantage points, rather than merely adopting a "correct political vision."

In *Ethics, Evil, and Fiction* (1997), Colin McGinn writes that "the fictional world is really the ideal world in which to go on ethical expeditions: it is safe, convenient, inconsequential, and expressly designed for our exploration and delight" (177). Irving's own approach to storytelling—his technique as well as his understanding of its purposes— demonstrates the ethical force of the narrative act as he conceives it. "Art has an *aesthetic* responsibility to be entertaining," Irving argues. "The writer's responsibility is to take hard stuff and make it as accessible as the stuff can be made" ("An Interview" 186). In contrast to the contemporary direction of much poststructuralist literary criticism, however, Irving does not mean to suggest that those narratives that entertain are somehow less serious or less ethically challenging. On the contrary—as Dickens's Victorian-era canon and Irving's late twentieth-century *oeuvre* seem to demonstrate—to entertain one's readers is to capture their hearts and minds in such a way that draws them into the lives of characters who populate stories that truly matter within the larger narrative of our shared humanity. "John Irving belongs to a small group of American writers," Terrence Des Pres suggests in *Writing into the World* (1991), "whose work has inspired respect for the plainest of reasons—these people write a kind of fiction useful, as genuine art must always be useful, to spiritual need" (102). In his attempt to entertain and enlighten readers, as Irving creates texts rich with the vibrancy and contrariness of existence, he portrays not only our "spiritual need" but also ways of coping with that need. In fact, the very form of Irving's storytelling seems to suggest a means for coping spiritually, for it offers a process that brings no final answers but invites us to take part in an unforgettable journey. As he tells his story, Irving moves his readers beyond the present moment in the text into a deep history of both the characters in the story and the communities in which they live; he compels his readers to wrestle with the same ethical dilemmas that the story's characters must confront; he causes us to see and feel the joy, anger, and sorrow that inevitably visits itself upon the saints and sinners who populate the landscape of his fiction. Like the wrestler he was—indeed, he *is*—Irving deliberately weaves his tales into the emotional lives of his readers. Snaking his characters' arms and legs around one another, he leaves us in the most improbable and compromising positions: entwined on the mat of his story, struggling not to be pinned by the weight of the lives we enter vicariously.

How, then, does Irving achieve this kind of connection with his readers, and why do the characters within Irving's fictional world remain vivid in the minds of both his devoted popular readership and the literati? Writing against the grain of much contemporary artistic practice, Irving grounds his achievement in his use of the particular and his consistent desire for the subject of his fictions to be recognizable in the world beyond the text.[3] In his published interviews and memoirs, Irving laments the shift in contemporary fiction away from the actual world in which we live toward the world of metafiction. In a 1979 interview, Irving addresses the debate taking place during that era between John Gardner and William Gass about the "necessity or irrelevancy of art's allegiance to morality": "Gardner has been very careless about a number of things he's said, so it's easier to pick on Gardner than it is to pick on Gass," Irving explains; "on the other hand, it seems to me that Gardner has tried to say a lot more about literature than Gass, and I have to admire him for that. I'd also have to agree with Gardner that literature should be a sign of life rather than a celebration of death," Irving concludes, "and if a novel doesn't address itself to something of human value, I don't see much worth in it" ("An Interview" 187). Irving's insistence that the novel as a literary form should address "something of human value" continues to determine many of his narrative practices, especially his use of the particular.[4] By chronicling several major and minor characters' histories in his novels with an uncanny precision and attentiveness, Irving creates an ethical construct that for the purposes of this chapter we shall refer to as "characterscape."

While novelists must in some manner establish character for their readers, not all writers agree about its import or the techniques necessary to produce it. In *Find You the Virtue: Ethics, Image, and Desire in Literature*

(1987), Irving Massey contends that the ethics of particularity, the ability to see the individual rather than the universal, illustrates the folly in ideas of repetition and categorization: "Things just do not repeat themselves, unless we are passive to them: if they exist for us fully, we do not experience them under the aspect of sameness or uniformity. Categories have something of the fraud about them" (34).[5] The ability to see human events and experiences for what they are, to be fully attentive to their originality, is a central concept in Irving's creation of characterscape.[6] To understand more fully the notion of characterscape, it should be noted that this construct does not differ significantly from the creation of character in terms of technique, but it does differ radically in terms of intention. As with the creation of character, characterscape requires the description of specific incidents that reflect the inner life of a given character's personhood; fundamental elements of anatomy, dress, physical movements, professional habits, and the like must be foregrounded for readers. In contrast with mere characterization, however, characterscape operates upon a scale of grand proportion. This is not to say that a given character is necessarily grandiose or ethical in his or her own right; on the contrary, in *The Cider House Rules* Irving borrows from Dickens by making an orphan of diminutive and humble stature a central figure in the action of his novel. Instead, the concept of proportion relates to the amount of narrative space used to create a vivid rendering of a particular character. This process might best be compared to William Least Heat-Moon's appropriation of landscape in *PrairyErth: A Deep Map* (1991). The subtitle of Heat-Moon's opus underscores the issue at hand: we must examine what lies within the deeper structures of the world that we inhabit to understand fully what lives before our eyes. By probing beneath the surface of Chase County, Kansas, and viewing it from nearly every imaginable position, Heat-Moon confronts his readers with a mental image that transcends landscape; it is as if the writer has found a way not only to transform the two-dimensional art of words on the printed page into a three-dimensional representation, but also has discovered a vehicle to transport readers into other dimensions that fuse the physical and the spiritual, the animal and the human into a single landscape.

As with Heat-Moon's work of creative nonfiction, Irving's fictional-world characterscapes offer multidimensional perspectives. Certainly, *The Cider House Rules* might be told more succinctly if we were not presented first with the history of St. Cloud's—including such ephemeral facts as to how the town's name acquired an apostrophe—and then with the history of Wilbur Larch and his circuitous journey into medicine and the practice of abortion. Yet if such material were excised, the novel's range would

be radically truncated and Larch's complicated motivations for performing abortions would not be fully realized. Characterscape demands that
many of the issues and incidents to which we are not privy in our workaday lives beyond the confines of the text—especially such wonderful artifice as *The Cider House Rules'* epilogue that permits us not only to see the
past, but also the past in the context of the future—be presented in such
a way that our understanding of the fictional persons that we encounter
as we consume the story expands voluminously toward an ethical illumination of far-reaching consequence. Of course, not all readers will
accept the invitation to enter fully into Irving's fictive world, but because
of its narrative mass the sheer number of hours that such storytelling
requires makes possible this kind of revelatory relationship.

By carefully and expansively layering his presentation of character,
Irving satisfies his own demand that philosophical issues be subservient
to the ways in which people live. Characterscape functions as Irving's
central ethic: the physical world of human activity—which he attempts
to make as vibrantly alive as possible—must never be lost in a philosophical debate about notions of right and wrong. As with William
Carlos Williams, Irving dismisses the abstract and embraces the physical.
In *The Call of Stories: Teaching and the Moral Imagination* (1989), Robert
Coles explains that Williams's "repeated call to arms, the well-known
phrase 'no ideas but in things,' is a prelude to distinctions he kept making between poetry and life; between ideas and action; between the
abstract and the concrete; between theory and practice; and not least,
between art and conduct" (193). In a similar fashion, Irving also proclaims adamantly that fiction must originate in the concrete and the
physical as opposed to the philosophical, and he offers a litany of com-
plaints against those novels that seem more about a particular ideology
than about the lives that transpire within a given text: "I guess another
way to put this," explains Irving, "is that I don't like to see a *thesis* about
life, or people, disguised as a novel. I don't think the greatest novels of
our time or any other time *are* theses. Great novels succeed much better
when they are broad expressions or portraits than when they confine
themselves to the singularity of an idea" ("An Interview" 195).

Although *The Cider House Rules* has been both criticized and lauded as
an "idea" book, one that crusades for a singular position on the abortion issue, we would do well to note the author's own account of the
novel's genesis: "I wanted to write an orphan novel. It was a year before
abortion entered the story," Irving remarks, "but it made perfect sense.
In the early part of the century, what doctor would be most sympathetic to performing abortions but a doctor who delivered unwanted babies,

then cared for them in an orphanage?" (Fein 25). Repeating his litany in an interview with Alison Freeland—"a novel is not single-issue politics, or if it is, it's not a novel" (140)—Irving derides those critics who read *The Cider House Rules* in terms of a single political vision. This narrowness of vision, of course, demonstrates precisely the problem with Harter and Thompson's critique of the novel as "polemic." While Irving admits that *The Cider House Rules* is perhaps his first polemical novel, Harter and Thompson's understanding of Irving's use of the polemic fails to account for the significance of the characterscapes that undergird Irving's fictions. Undoubtedly, Irving proffers a novel that sets forth an argument of great controversy, but, as is his practice elsewhere, the lives of his characters and the events that transpire remain too broad and various to represent a single, essentialist position within the abortion debate. Irving's confession that the novel has a polemic quality merely asserts the reality that the historic stage upon which his players strut has for its backdrop an orphanage where, in the words of Larch, some babies and some mothers are "delivered." Arguing that this notion functions as the political vision of the novel neglects the character motivations and histories of both Wilbur Larch and Homer Wells. While Larch indeed crusades in covert and overt ways for the right of women to choose, he remains in the novel but as one character among many whose past seems to compromise his ideological position in the present. The same may be said of Homer as he grapples with his role in performing abortions, as well as of the many different women who receive abortions during the course of the novel and their markedly different motivations for seeking out such a dramatic and final solution. In his review of *The Cider House Rules*, Benjamin DeMott contends that the value of Irving's novel lies in its treatment of abortion as a subject rooted both in our collective past and in the heterogeneous ways in which we live in the present. Irving's approach to this subject actually demonstrates the impossibility of rendering a facile ethical decision when confronted with such a divisive issue. In "an age ill at ease with the notion that art can have a subject" (25), DeMott praises Irving for his awareness of human relationships where abstract philosophies and political ideologies play themselves out. "Irving draws the readers close in the space of his imagination," says DeMott, "to an understanding of essential links, commonalties—even unities—between factions now seething with hatred for each other" (1).

For this reason, Irving focuses significant time and energy upon narrating intricate accounts of numerous characters' lives. In *The Cider House Rules*, Irving offers detailed histories not only of the novel's two main characters, Wilbur Larch and Homer Wells, but also of Melony, Wally Worthington, and Candy Kendall, among others. In "The King of the Novel," John Irving observes that "you cannot encounter the prisons in Dickens's novels and ever again feel completely self-righteous about prisoners being where they belong; you cannot encounter a lawyer of Mr. Jaggers's terrifying ambiguity and ever again put yourself willingly in a lawyer's hands—Jaggers, although only a minor character in *Great Expectations*, may be our literature's greatest indictment of living by abstract rules" (349). The same might be said of Irving's own depiction of abortion and the figure of Wilbur Larch, obstetrician and abortionist, in *The Cider House Rules*. Like Dickens, Irving derides the notion of living by abstract rules, and in the person of Larch he begins his assault upon the "rules" that govern the concept of abortion.

Although his associates at the orphanage refer to him as St. Larch, Irving makes it perfectly clear that Larch's sainthood comes with a price. Upon Larch's admission to and imminent departure for medical school, Larch's father purchases for Wilbur an evening with a local prostitute, Mrs. Eames. This rather embarrassing evening of sexual initiation concludes with Wilbur dressing in the glow of a cigar being smoked by Mrs. Eames's daughter, who enters unannounced while Wilbur drowses in post-coital bliss. What Larch seems to take from this experience—in addition to gonorrhea, which he studies in bacteriology at the Harvard Medical School—is a substantial measure of remorse. Wilbur compounds his guilty conscience through a series of events that bring Mrs. Eames and her daughter back into his life. While working as a young intern at the South End Branch of the Boston Lying-In, Larch treats Mrs. Eames, whom he discovers has been taking an aborticide that leaves her organs in a state of "fragile jelly." After six days of Larch's care, Mrs. Eames dies, and in the ensuing autopsy Larch learns from the pathologist that she has expired as a result of scurvy. A day later, as it only happens in the fabulistic world of Dickens and Irving, where coincidences are indispensable to the connective tissue of characterscape, Mrs. Eames's daughter visits Larch. She shows him the aborticide that her mother ingested—a "French Lunar Solution" said to restore "Female Monthly Regularity!" (57)—and asks him to perform an abortion for her: "I ain't quick! I ain't *quick*, I said!" she screams at Larch (59). But the consequences of the procedure frighten Larch and he hesitates. A week later Larch finds her beaten and in a grave condition after receiving an abortion at the shady clinic known only as "Off Harrison." He discovers a note pinned to her battered body: "DOCTOR LARCH—SHIT OR GET OFF THE POT!" (60). As like her mother only days before, Mrs.

Eames's daughter also dies in the care of Larch, but her death prompts him to visit "Off Harrison" and confront the abortionist who runs the clinic, an elderly woman known locally as Mrs. Santa Claus. This scene allows readers to see the tools of abortion, and, along with Larch, to be shocked by the awful conditions and misguided methods under which illegal abortions are conducted. This experience also serves as the catalyst for Larch's ultimate role as an abortionist in the novel. In short, the kinds of metaphorical gifts that Mrs. Claus delivers challenge Larch to seek a practical and immediate solution for such women in need as Mrs. Eames and her daughter—a solution generated out of the pragmatics of physical circumstance as opposed to legalistic ideology.

With each horrific incident, Irving adds one more layer to Larch's characterscape, but, in so doing, Irving refuses to render any overt value judgments and offers nothing more than the precarious elements of human storytelling. Although abortion clearly lies at the center of these passages, Irving carefully avoids entering into a philosophical debate about when life actually begins or whose rights must be protected. Irving eschews any theological discussion that might affect the actions of his characters or the manner in which readers might interpret those actions. Interestingly, Larch's decision seems to spring from his understanding of his own fallibility, his own fallen nature. Through his interaction with Mrs. Eames and her daughter he recognizes the culpability of his own conduct as well as that of a society that tacitly condones the creation of orphans, prostitutes, and unwanted pregnancies. In a particularly telling moment of reflection, Larch contemplates the peculiar interrelationship between celibacy and moral condemnation:

> On his mind was Mrs. Eames's daughter's last puff of cigar breath in his face as he bent over her before she died—reminding him, of course, of the night he needed her puffing cigar to find his clothes. If pride was a sin, thought Dr. Larch, the greatest sin was moral pride. He had slept with someone's mother and dressed himself in the light of her daughter's cigar. He could quite comfortably abstain from having sex for the rest of his life, but how could he ever condemn another person for having sex? (61)

Larch's unspoken vow of celibacy and his assumption of sainthood, like the disorderly nature of all genuinely human activity, finds its roots in interpersonal relationships, and in his relationships with women, Larch continually falters. As with his addiction to ether—which begins as a practical remedy to the gonorrhea he contracts from Mrs. Eames and later becomes a means for both relaxing and, perhaps, escaping temporarily from his guilt—his response to abortion represents the actions of a pragmatic doctor doing the practical things necessary for his patients and the community in which he lives. After denying Mrs. Eames's daughter an abortion, he never again pauses to consider the legal or ethical ramifications of abortion when faced with a mother in need. Instead, as Larch explains in *A Brief History of St. Cloud's*, "Here in St. Cloud's we would waste our limited energy and our limited imagination by regarding the sordid *facts* of life as if they were problems" (34). For Larch, pragmatism reigns; because the "sordid *facts* of life" can never be changed, one's moral position must never be lorded over the physical needs of another.[7] Later within the very same chapter, "The Lord's Work," in which he offers his first pronouncement of celibacy and his confession that moral pride amounts to the worst of sins, Larch reaffirms this notion in the precise language of the earlier passage. In this manner, the saint of both orphans and mothers establishes a mantra that allows him to carry on with his duties:

> Later, when he would have occasion to doubt himself, he would force himself to remember: he had slept with someone's mother and dressed himself in the light of her daughter's cigar. He could quite comfortably abstain from having sex for the rest of his life, but how could he ever condemn another person for having sex? He would remember, too, what he *hadn't* done for Mrs. Eames's daughter, and what that had cost. He would deliver babies. He would deliver mothers, too. (75)

Yet the most significant test of Larch's resolve comes not with the first abortion he performs for the young girl he rescues from "Off Harrison" or the subsequent requests by others in the neighborhood community who find themselves in similar straits, but from a wealthy family, the Channing-Peabodys of Boston, who spent their summers in Portland, Maine. Larch had gone to Maine to apply for a position in obstetrics, escaping from Boston where he "had become, in the view of the erring, the sanctuary to which to flee" (69). Larch ostensibly visits the Channing-Peabodys's palatial mansion for what he assumes will be a dinner party. Neither poor nor downtrodden like the women who sought out Larch in South Boston, the Channing-Peabodys prove insufferable in their moral superiority and presumption that their money can relieve them of any set of unpleasant or undesired circumstances. Despite such arrogance, Larch still cannot bring himself to pass judgment upon

Missy, the woman in need of his services. Instead of refusing the Channing-Peabodys, he insists that the young man responsible for impregnating Missy be sent in to watch the procedure—and, as Larch hopes, the young man vomits all over himself. Additionally, taking the money with which the Channing-Peabodys attempt to "buy" his services and his silence, Larch chooses to distribute it among the servants who help him perform the abortion as well as among those others who work throughout the great house. Such a scene, particularly important in the creation of Larch's own characterscape, demonstrates his ethical determination to refuse to judge the woman in need of his care. While Larch indeed passes judgment upon those characters who seem to stand in supposed moral superiority over Missy for becoming pregnant and over him for becoming a doctor who would perform abortions, he will not deny any woman, in this instance Missy, whom he clearly sees as a victim.

By availing himself of the ethos of characterscape, Irving establishes the motivations and the ideology of Larch, a man who claims to do both "the Lord's work and the Devil's work."[8] He further complicates our understanding of Larch as both a saint and a sinner by introducing the figure of Homer Wells, the eternal orphan who becomes a surrogate son for Larch as well as his professional successor. Homer's presence in the frame of Irving's story exemplifies the ethics of characterscape by illustrating the marked importance of human interrelationships in the construction of characterscape. Just as a landscape artist needs a horizon and a sky, a foreground and a background to capture properly the spirit of a place, the writer who hopes to achieve a fully articulated portrait of a character must place the person in close relation to another character of consequence within a given narrative. While Irving devotes the bulk of *The Cider House Rules'* narrative space to Homer's story, the orphan would not achieve his full semblance of personhood without the character of Larch to bring him into bas-relief.

As the boy whose adoption never comes to pass, Homer undergoes a trial by fire of sorts that consists of several horribly fantastic adoptive experiences, including in one instance his "buggering" by a sibling and in another case the death of his new parents in a thunderous rushing flood of logs and water on a camping expedition. As he inevitably returns to St. Cloud's, he develops a special relationship, unique and full of mutual love, with Larch. Because Homer grows to the age of "usefulness," as Larch calls it, while still residing at St. Cloud's, Larch initiates him into the world of the orphanage, first as a caregiver and later as an obstetrician. For example, Larch assigns Homer the nightly task of reading works by Dickens and Brontë to the orphans in both the girls' and boys' divisions.[9] In this capacity, Homer develops a relationship with another "older" orphan, Melony, who, like himself, has yet to be adopted successfully. Melony functions as the first female character to affect Homer's understanding of the world of sexuality and trust. As with Larch, Homer's feelings about abortion, sex, and procreation become fundamentally altered by his relations with women. In the Dickensian tradition of a penchant for the detective story, Melony's character provides Irving with the means for availing himself of the generic conventions of the detective mode to trace one of the principal desires of many orphans: to know the identity of their parents and to know who loves them. Melony's menacing attitude toward her undiscovered parents, as well as her promise to Homer that she will perform fellatio upon him if he locates the records of her parents' identity in Larch's office, inaugurates the quirky commitment that exists between Melony and Homer. Although her first investigation as Irving's de facto detective fails because Larch makes it a practice not to maintain adoption records, Melony searches for love in the person of Homer, whom she coerces into a promise that, in the fleeting world of St. Cloud's, must inevitably be broken:

> "If I stay, you'll stay—is that what you're saying?" Melony asked him. Is that what I mean? thought Homer Wells. But Melony, as usual, gave him no time to think. "Promise me you'll stay as long as I stay, Sunshine," Melony said. She moved closer to him; she took his hand and opened his fingers and put his index finger in her mouth. (105)

While Homer and Melony develop a sexual relationship, even a loving relationship of sorts, Homer ultimately breaks his commitment to Melony when he goes to live at Heart's Rock upon the invitation of Wally Worthington and Candy Kendall.

Irving later reintroduces the Dickensian detective story after Melony searches for Homer and finally confronts him in the Worthington's orchard. In addition to immediately recognizing Angel as Homer and Candy's son, Irving's orphan *cum* detective later succeeds in finding Homer, despite her untimely death, when her cadaver tracks Homer to St. Cloud's and metaphorically unravels his secret identity as Dr. F. Stone. While Irving employs the detective mode to entertain his readers with suspense—as with the detective story that undergirds the latter third of *A Widow for One Year* (1998)—the ethics of storytelling insists that Irving employs Melony's investigation to establish a layer in Homer's characterscape that will eventually contribute to his return to St. Cloud's as

Larch's replacement. While Melony's detective tale allows Irving to establish the gravity of Homer's betrayal of her, as well as that of his subsequent betrayal of Wally Worthington, it also affects the manner in which he sees the "sins" of others. As with Larch's convoluted relationships with women in *The Cider House Rules*, Homer's broken promise to Melony and his secret love for Candy teach him to see life's variegated shades of meaning, to understand the foibles of human interaction, and to recognize that a legalistic approach to "rules" never reveals the full complexity of any situation.

Yet for Homer such a lesson comes slowly. To this end, Irving offers three extraordinary scenes that demonstrate Homer's exceptional compassion, his devotion to the delivery of babies and their mothers. The first encounter takes place when Homer is relatively young but old enough to have been instructed by Larch to be of some "use." Because of orphan Fuzzy Stone's coughing and the noise the machines make that help Fuzzy breathe, on certain nights Homer roams the halls of the orphanage, often seeking out the baby room or the mothers' room. On this particular night, while standing in the mothers' room, a mysterious pregnant woman asks Homer if he would, at his age, leave the orphanage with a family who wishes to adopt him. He replies that he would not. Of course, the woman asks this question because she wants to be reassured that her baby will find an adoptive home and be cared for in ways she cannot offer. Homer does not sense this at first, however, and despite several attempts on the mother's part to elicit a "yes" from Homer, he seems fixed in his opinion that St. Cloud's is the only home he will ever know. The mother begins to cry and asks Homer if he wishes to be of "use" and touch her pregnant belly:

> "No one but me ever put a hand on me, to feel that baby. No one wanted to put his ear against it and listen," the woman said. "You shouldn't have a baby if there's no one who wants to feel it kick, or listen to it move." (87–8)

The woman asks Homer again if he wishes to be of use and suggests that he "sleep right here" where the baby rests beneath her stomach. Homer feigns sleep until the woman's water breaks. After the birth of the child, Homer plays a game with himself. Because of his "nighttime vigil with his face upon the mother's jumping belly" he hopes to recognize her child. This incident profoundly affects the way Homer looks at not only the women who come to St. Cloud's to be delivered of some of their problems—"Importantly, Homer knew they did not look delivered of *all* their problems when they left. No one he had seen looked more miserable than those women" (30)—but also the way that he looks at their pregnant bellies, the potential lives that will either be aborted or delivered by the hands of St. Larch. Because of his sympathetic vigil upon the belly of this mother, Homer cannot bring himself to believe what Larch preaches about abortion. At the same time, because of his relationship with Larch he cannot condemn his "father's" actions either.[10]

Shortly before his departure to Heart's Rock, Homer experiences an epiphany of sorts about his own right to choose what he will believe regarding abortion. In this second scene, Homer examines a fetus that bled to death during a failed delivery performed by Larch:

> Homer felt there was nothing as simple as anyone's fault involved; it was not Larch's fault—Larch did what he believed in. If Wilbur Larch was a saint to Nurse Angela and to Nurse Edna, he was both a saint and a father to Homer Wells. Larch knew what he was doing—and for whom. But that quick and not-quick stuff: it didn't work for Homer Wells. You can *call* it a fetus, or an embryo, or the products of conception, thought Homer Wells, but whatever you call it, it's alive. And whatever you do to it, Homer thought—and whatever you call what you do—you're killing it. . . . Let Larch call it whatever he wants, thought Homer Wells. It's his choice—if it's a fetus, to him, that's fine. It's a baby to me, thought Homer Wells. If Larch has a choice, I have a choice, too. (169)

Later at Heart's Rock, after Candy becomes pregnant and mentions a trip to St. Cloud's for a possible abortion, Homer—motivated by his intense convictions about the sanctity of human life—tells her that "it's my baby, too" (386), that he also bears responsibility for the life that they created together and in which he wishes to participate. Unlike Larch, who in his later years withdraws more deeply into his ether addiction and his medical routine because he believes that "love was certainly not safe—not ever" (381), Homer self-consciously shares his love with others and cannot imagine a life without Candy or his newly conceived baby. Because he believes that Wally died in the war, Homer avoids confronting his guilt over the love he has shared with Candy or his betrayal of his best friend. Soon after the birth of Angel—baptized symbolically by a drop of Larch's sweat as he delivers him—the news that Wally has been found alive tests Homer's love for Candy, Wally, and Angel. Yet Homer's real challenge comes 15 years later, shortly after the death of Larch by an accidental ether overdose.

In the third scene, Irving—using relational characterscape in conjunction with the Dickensian grand style of convergence—assembles all of the characters who have affected Homer's life most profoundly. In the novel's final chapter, aptly entitled "Breaking the Rules," Homer faces multiple, nearly simultaneous decisions regarding various "rules" of ethical behavior. The impact of these decisions upon those characters that he loves and lives with make these issues especially difficult. As the title of the chapter intimates, Homer will "break the rules," and, in so doing, he will come to understand that ethical law cannot be approached legalistically, a point that Irving underscores via his own method of storytelling. While certain rules once governed Homer's silence about his love for Candy and their true relationship to one another and their son Angel, in the end Homer recognizes—courtesy of Melony's recognition of the child's lineage—that the truth must be told. Similarly, such remarkably human situations force Homer to contemplate the possibility that certain abstract rules cannot be reconciled with the practical, physical needs of the moment, and that human suffering cannot be judged or sacrificed to legalism. As the foreman of the orchard for the last 15 years, moreover, Homer bears the responsibility for posting "the cider house rules." At times, the fact that the work crew does not follow the rules bothers Homer. In a conversation with Mr. Rose, however, Homer begins to realize that the ways in which people live together in a human community actually govern the "rules"; those rules established by forces outside the community cannot produce this same effect. Mr. Rose explains, for example, that within the black community of migrant workers who live at the orchard during harvest there emerge unwritten rules engendered from human relationships that have nothing to do with Homer's rules. Yet, Homer cannot bring himself fully to accept the relational as well as contextual aspects of ethical rules; he finds it difficult to comprehend that those rules imposed from without "never asked" but "told" (429)—a fact that itself explains the ineffectiveness of legalistic codes in contrast with ethical rules.[11]

Ultimately, Homer's decision to perform an abortion for Rose Rose, Mr. Rose's pregnant daughter and Angel's first love, alters his perspective about the procedure, but Homer does not reach this decision easily. A few weeks before Rose Rose's crisis, Homer writes to Larch to refuse his invitation to come to St. Cloud's and replace St. Larch in the operation at the orphanage. As he writes in his laconic, numbered letter to Larch:

1. I AM NOT A DOCTOR.
2. I BELIEVE THE FETUS HAS A SOUL.
3. I'M SORRY. (513)

In short, Homer refuses to break the "rules" that govern the practice of medicine. He also feels that he cannot perform an abortion because of an ethical belief in the sanctity of the human soul. At the same time, he regrets these decisions because of his loyalty and love for his "father," St. Larch. While both his belief in the sanctity of the human soul and his conviction that the fetus is fully human remain static, Homer, when faced with Larch's untimely death and his own status as the only person available to perform a safe abortion on Rose Rose, simply cannot refuse his patient's wish to abort her pregnancy. Although Irving depicts Homer's first abortion as representative of the most extreme and awful form of conception—Rose Rose has been impregnated by her own father, breaking *all* of the rules—Homer nevertheless believes as strongly in the sanctity of Rose Rose's fetus as he would in the sanctity of any other fetus conceived under less ethically challenging circumstances. As he confesses to Candy, Homer finds abortion problematic, for he considers it tantamount to "killing" a human being:

> "I'm a little nervous," Homer admitted to Candy. "It's certainly not a matter of technique, and I've got everything I need—I know I can do it. It's just that, to me, it is a living human being. I can't describe to you what it feels like—just to hold the curette, for example. When living tissue is touched, it responds—somehow," Homer said, but Candy cut him off. (533–4)

Homer's decision to perform the abortion illustrates the ethical imperative embodied by Irving's act of storytelling. Clearly, *The Cider House Rules* should not be read as a novel that finally embraces the act of abortion. Homer's own belief system radically contradicts such a conclusion. The novel demonstrates the conflicted nature of human dealings and the inadequacy of legalism as a means for responding to our most pressing needs. While Homer decides to assume the constructed identity that Larch invents for him—as Dr. F. Stone, a missionary obstetrician newly arrived from India—Homer recognizes that he cannot deny strangers what he would give freely to those he loves and those he knows: "Because he knew now that he couldn't play God in the worst sense; if he could operate on Rose Rose, how could he refuse to help a stranger? How could he refuse anyone? Only a god makes that kind of decision. I'll just give them what they want, he thought. An orphan or an abortion" (535). For Homer, then, rules do not account for the fact that we are all saints and all sinners, rather than being one or the other. Legalism offers no true, compassionate, or humane answers to the abortion issue because it operates from the abstract, not from the tangible. Irving's ethics of storytelling makes all too clear that the ways our lives intersect and the impossible decisions that the business of living forces us to make cannot be handled under a single system of rules. In Irving's fictive universe—and, indeed, in our own corporeal world—only the sanctity of individual choice in relation to human community can determine the system of ethical values that governs our lives.

In this manner, Irving's appropriation of the Dickensian form establishes—especially through its use of extensive narratological and characterological detail—an ethics of particularity in which a multiperspectival history comes to bear upon our understanding of a given narrative situation. The Dickensian novel as a literary model demands that we see the ethical dimensions of the lives represented in the text as something that ethical "rules"—whether they be the rules that dictate life in a cider house or rules that govern a promise between orphans—cannot adequately address. Using the abidingly fractious issue of abortion as the background for his story of an orphanage, Irving refuses to conclude his novel with any facile statement either for or against abortion. Rather, as a storyteller he insists that any genuine contemplation about the abortion issue must take place within the context of human relationships, and, as a disciple of Dickens, he paints characterscapes of such layered detail that we see the conflicted nature of human resolution. Only by providing his readership with fully realized portraits of humanity can Irving construct an adequate fictional tableau for narrating the moral dilemmas that trouble our society and the ways that we live now. As with Dickens, Irving intuitively recognizes that readers "want catharsis, they want to be stretched and tested, they want to be frightened and come through it, they want to be scared, taken out of their familiar surroundings—intellectual, visceral, spiritual—and to be reexposed to things" ("An Interview" 187). In *The Cider House Rules*, Irving offers precisely such an ethically complex and conflicted narrative. While some form of judgment must inevitably be rendered in the novel, clearly Homer's decision to return to St. Cloud's as Dr. F. Stone is not motivated by any "rule" about the goodness of abortion or the absolute belief that women must have a choice in the matter. As with Dr. Larch's initial decision to perform an abortion, Homer's return to St. Cloud's and all that it entails finds its origins in his genuinely human relationships with women— with Candy and Melony and Rose Rose—not out of any ideologically pure ethic. By delivering his compelling narratives and vast characterscapes through the artifice of the Dickensian novel, Irving narrates the equally captivating and convoluted stories of our own lives.

5
Curses and Blessings: Identity and Essentialism in the Work of Sherman Alexie

What is an Indian?

Sherman Alexie, "One Good Man"

In the Great American Indian novel, when it is finally written, all of the white people will be Indians and all of the Indians will be ghosts.

Sherman Alexie, "How to Write the Great
American Indian Novel"

If Indian literature can't be read by the average 12-year-old kid living on the reservation, what the hell good is it?

Sherman Alexie, "Crossroads: A Conversation
with Sherman Alexie"

She knew Indians were obsessed with authenticity. Colonized, genocided, exiled, Indians formed their identities by questioning the identities of other Indians. Self-hating, self-doubting, Indians turned their tribes into nationalistic sects.

Sherman Alexie, "The Search Engine"

How does or should the white reader/critic interpret work by the indigenous writer? How, as middle-class, Caucasian, English professors, do we (literally the two writers who have written the book that rests in your hands or upon the table in front of you) engage with the world that Sherman Alexie chronicles in his poems, fiction, and films? If a person has never set foot upon a reservation, if a person has never had a close

70

friendship with a Native American, how can he or she enter into the imaginative landscapes created by Indian authors?

We must confess that, as young boys, we played cowboys and Indians, a not uncommon activity among the male youth of America. And, as we make this unorthodox scholarly confession, we would add that during our make-believe playtime often we wished to be the Indians—*not the cowboys*. We ultimately hoped the Indians and the cowboys could be friends, but if the whites tried to do what they had done in the murky history we were being taught in school or were witnessing in some of the movies we watched, we hoped that in our backyards the Indians would get the best of the cowboys, that our subdivisions would be reclaimed by forest or prairie or desert, and that Indians would once again roam the land, their buffalo brought back by the Ghost Dance.

The pendulum between peace and violence swung with irregularity in our own imagined childhood worlds (and likely continues to do so to this day when we encounter the rare Western at the movie theater). As the products of traditional public school educations, we knew little of Native American cultures, and what we did know was often romanticized or made more primitive or simply rushed through with embarrassed backward glances. When we were children, the main source for understanding these people and their cultures was Hollywood: the Lone Ranger and Tonto, countless John Wayne movies, the occasional appearance of a tribal character on *Bonanza* or *The Wild Wild West*—(and these characters were too often played by white people in red make-up without a trace of irony). In spite of or because of these kitsch sources, we were drawn toward idealized notions of Native culture. For a range of reasons, we identified with Native Americans who appeared to have so much to offer but were not only ignored but destroyed in numbers that sounded surreal, simply ungraspable. The few friendships we had with Native Americans, mostly in college, started to disrupt the weight of misinformation. Yet the Pottawatomie, Navajo, and Sioux we did know were often disconnected from their past, struggling at times to regain some sense of continuity and at other times merely wanting to move forward in history without looking back.

Needless to say, neither of us would argue that today we've reached some plain of enlightenment. The simple fact is: we haven't. Far from it. We can't even claim that we're scholars in Native American studies. Yes, in our personal study and appreciation of native culture, we graduated from the dreck of television westerns to the photography of Edward Curtis, and, yes, we have dabbled in the study of different tribal myth traditions, different tribal ways of life based upon geography, topography, weather patterns, and so on. And, yes, we are readers of such native writers as Louise Erdrich, N. Scott Momaday, James Welch, Linda Hogan, Joy Harjo, Maurice Kenny, Diane Glancy, and Leslie Marmon Silko. But to feign some absolute or complete knowledge, some high level of expertise, would be nothing more than a sham. We are merely literary scholars who have been drawn to the writings of some Indian authors, and to one in particular, Sherman Alexie. And, in the case of Alexie, drawn is too subtle, too understated a word. Since Alexie's first book, *The Business of Fancydancing* (1992), we've held our collective breath—boys waiting for the next edition of their favorite comic book, for the release of their favorite band's latest album. Tension and excitement build as we wait to see what Alexie may do next in his acts of storytelling. We're groupies whose professional lives—whose scholarly pursuits—overlap with their human interests, their passion for not only the pyrotechnics of Alexie's stories, but also his approach to living with one foot in tradition and the other in the postmodern world. In other words, we're scholars who also happen to be fans.

But why do we offer this preamble? What does Alexie possess that cracks the shimmering surface of the professionalism so many of our colleagues call for in their literary scholarship, of at the very least the feigned distance that scholars usually hold from the subject of their study? After all, doesn't literature always have a foothold in the world beyond the text, either as a source or a potential subject for altered action? Intellectually, we would like to believe that all literature has some connection to the world beyond the text and, thus, has the potential to find chinks in our professional armor; but emotionally, spiritually, when we approach certain texts—whether they be the reflections of a Jewish Holocaust survivor, the poems of a peace activist, the stories of a writer who may have lived on welfare or been addicted to drugs and recovered at least in part through his or her art—context makes a difference. Quite simply: storytelling is human in its orientation and its perspective. The place that the artist works from, or out of, *does* play a role in our reception of a text, in our valuation of a given writer.[1] This is not to say that all literary and formal aesthetic values vanish into the ether, either. In Alexie's case, we would argue that his aesthetic mastery of the short fictional form merely burns brighter in the wind of his particular subject matter, his particular background, or writerly context. Perhaps another reason we are drawn to his work and why we include this chapter in this book is the fact that much of his storytelling—both formally and in terms of its content—has to do with recognizing the kinds of contradictions we've been speaking of. Alexie reconciles the void by breaking the rules, by refusing to believe or obey the dictum of contradiction, of dichotomy, of *either/or*. His is a world of *both/and*.

The single-most dominant theme in Alexie's work revolves around the issues of essentialism versus constructionism. As he explains in his poem "13/16," collected in *The Business of Fancydancing*, the essential facts of identity of an American Indian have much to do with certain constructions instigated and instituted by outside forces:

> It is done by blood, reservation mathematics, fractions:
> father (full-blood) + mother (5/8) = son (13/16).

> It is done by enrollment number, last name first, first name last:
> Spokane Tribal Enrollment Number 1569; Victor, Chief.

> It is done by identification card, photograph, lamination:
> IF FOUND, PLEASE RETURN TO SPOKANE TRIBE OF INDIANS,
> WELLPINIT, WA. (16)

While we would not suggest that the idea of purity was initiated solely by European influence—certainly the idea of tribal solidarity and the question of appropriateness of marriage across tribal lines existed to varying degrees before colonial forays into the Americas—the intricate and pseudo-scientific manner in which colonial (mis)rule functioned did (and *does*) increase dramatically not only the awareness but also the degree of importance placed upon difference in racial and tribal settings. Although Native Americans were not the subject of mass slavery in the way Africans were, similar forces surrounding the idea of race were at play in the United States. In each case, political and economic factors pushed the "objectivity" of science toward ridiculous claims that have done irretrievable harm to so many. Needless to say, in hindsight, it seems absurd that segments of the intellectual community would support notions of race that would cause a man or a woman to be "categorized" or "constructed" as an African, a Chinese or an Indian simply because 1/16th or more of that person's bloodline could be traced to an ancestor in the given category.[2] In the case of "13/16," Alexie plays out the range of negative consequences inherent in this system as well as the ways in which his tribe is complicit in this governmental practice.

The idea of racial purity must operate in a closed system. Within closed systems, there is the possibility for living in a world without a "void," for living in such a way that the void cannot be seen or recognized by members within the system. A closed system, for example, in which all the people claim the same racial ancestry, practice the same religious beliefs, follow the same patterns of daily life, *does* offer the potential for solidarity and a way of life that *appears* and *feels* rooted in some absolute, essential, permanent bedrock of truth, of *authentic* existence. (And, of course, such closed systems continue to provide comfort for many, artificial as such systems may be.) Living in a culture like our own, though, in which many different kinds of subcultures exist, makes such insulating behaviors far more difficult to achieve successfully. As we mature, coming into contact with people from other cultures, other communities, we learn, for example, about the differing religious, economic, agricultural, and governmental practices held by those outside of our own culture, and the essential "correctness" of our own position, its rootedness in some foundational, core reality, often is thrown into question by the discovery of these other worlds that are very much unlike our own. "I didn't learn until I was in college about all the other cultures," confesses novelist Kurt Vonnegut, who as a postmodern satirist critiques culture in similar ways as Alexie does, "and I should have learned that in the first grade. A first-grader should understand that his culture isn't a rational invention; that there are thousands of other cultures and they all work pretty well; that all cultures function on faith rather than truth; that there are lots of alternatives to our own society" (Allen, *Conversations* 104). Like Vonnegut, Alexie also recognizes the plurality of not only his own existence but also that of the contemporary Indian, and it is this space that plurality helps to establish and proffers—sometimes to negative consequence, sometimes to positive—that Alexie writes. Alexie's is the world of the devout Spokane Indian Catholic, the world of the Lakota Sioux soldier who fights in the United States Army, the very army that helped to decimate the faith and culture of his ancestors. Alexie creates many characters who expose the difficulty of straddling multiple worlds. He also imagines in other stories the benefits of such straddling and the manner by which one need not live an exclusionary life. What might be described as the art of learning to span diverse cultures, to compensate and to encompass worlds that diverge and converge is depicted in Alexie's stories, often in a cataclysmic fashion.

In the poem "Evolution," collected in *The Business of Fancydancing,* Alexie offers a satiric appraisal of this new time and place where worlds cross and recross, and, sadly, how Indians often continue to find themselves at the short end of the proverbial stick. Alexie uses the iconic figure of Buffalo Bill, transporting him to the present moment in which he opens a pawnshop on the reservation, right across the road from the liquor store. Buffalo Bill keeps his pawnshop open every day of the week, every hour of the day, and we are told that "Indians come running" to sell their possessions, both the mainstream and the traditional: television sets, jewelry, a VCR, a full-length beaded buckskin outfit, and so on. They sell and sell, even their skeletons, until "the last Indian has pawned everything / but his heart." And then Buffalo Bill closes the pawnshop, paints a new sign with the words "The Museum of Native American Cultures," and "charges the Indians five bucks a head to enter" (48).[3] In this surreal vision of a resurrected Buffalo Bill, Alexie showcases the manner in which native culture is stolen and then put on display—the convoluted machinations that coerce Indians to take part in their own undoing. He also calls into question what an *authentic* Indian experience might look like and what it might consist of. Perhaps that is Alexie's true importance as not only a Native American author, but also as a writer in the broader contemporary setting: His ability to demonstrate the constructed nature of our identities without dismissing what we may wish to place our faith in, what we may devote our lives to. In other words, although Alexie combats a form of tribal fundamentalism—as we shall see in several other poems and short stories—he is not willing to dismiss the sacred or the cultural, to lose his faith in his indigenous heritage completely.

According to Terry Eagleton in *After Theory* (2003), fundamentalism "is a neurotic hunt for solid foundations to our existence, an inability to accept that human life is a matter not of treading on thin air, but of *roughness*. Roughness from a fundamentalist viewpoint can only look like a disastrous lack of clarity and exactitude, rather as someone might feel that not to measure Everest down to the last millimeter is to leave us completely stumped about how high it is" (204). Certain kinds of postmodern theory have been critiqued fairly and effectively by those who point out its devotion to relativism, to the equality of all truth claims. In that form of critique, however, too often those who oppose postmodern habits of thought slide comfortably back into the dichotomous model of either/or, and, in doing so, make claims that they possess knowledge grounded in absolute truth. Eagleton perceptively demonstrates that there is a middle ground, that to engage life in its *roughness* is not to dismiss the importance of Everest or to say one does not *know* Everest at all, but rather to say that one understands Everest in part, not to the exact millimeter but in certain ways that are equally significant.

Eagleton explains that "fundamentalists want a strong foundation to the world, which in their case is usually a sacred text. We have seen already that a text is the worst possible stuff for this purpose. The idea of an inflexible text is as odd as the idea of an inflexible piece of string"

(206). The oral storytelling tradition in Native American cultures has the potential to help defend against this kind of inflexibility. Certainly, this tradition does not embrace the rigidness of Enlightenment thought, and time and again in its practice of indigenous rituals, it recognizes the organic nature of a story, the ways in which a story is a living, breathing act that will develop and grow in accordance with the tribe and with the tribal member whose calling it is to carry the story forward. In *The Lone Ranger and Tonto Fistfight in Heaven* (1993), Alexie creates the character of Thomas Builds-the-Fire to demonstrate the power of storytelling and its transformative effect. In "The Trial of Thomas Builds-the-Fire," we are told that "Builds-the-Fire has a history of this kind of behavior. . . . A storytelling fetish accompanied by an extreme need to tell the truth" (93). We are also informed that as "Thomas closed his eyes. . . a new story was raised from the ash of older stories" (98). In many ways, Thomas is Alexie's alter ego, and like Thomas, Alexie does indeed raise his stories from the ash, creating new ways of making meaning from the former traditions and ceremonies.

"Fundamentalism is a kind of necrophilia," Eagleton goes on to explain, "in love with the dead letter of a text. It treats words as though they were things, as weighty and undentable as a brass candlestick. Yet it does this because it wants to freeze certain meaning for all eternity— and meaning itself is not material" (207). One would think that there would be little chance for such textual necrophilia within the Indian community. In such communities, texts are forever changing—perhaps in the smallest, most nuanced fashion, but malleable and flexible nonetheless. The story, in other words, becomes flesh, part of the lived experience of an individual and of his or her community. Alexie appears to have straddled these two approaches to knowledge—the oral and the print—by playing the role of the trickster. At moments, he appears to embrace a kind of essentialism (or literalism) in his explorations of the spiritual, the emotional, the tribal, or the traditional; yet in the very same story—at times, in the very same scene—he undercuts any sense of tribal fundamentalism, understanding that his own traditions will not stand for the textual necrophilia practiced by certain segments of the Western world. Still, surprisingly, some Native American storytellers and scholars have adopted the more rigid and dogmatic rules of a print culture—replete with the strong desire for an essentialist, bedrock truth in the written narrative, a desire for the text to ossify and stand forever as some beacon of unchanging traditional culture.[4] Alexie attempts to counteract such fundamentalist desires, and he is renowned for his performances at readings that undercut many expectations for who a

Native American author is and what he should be. Whether it is a story about Indian heritage and identity or one about sexuality and gender, Alexie pushes against any hard-edged boundaries, continually proffering a position that calls for a porousness of borders, for the rounded and elastic qualities of an ever-changing and ever-expanding narrative string, as Eagleton refers to it.

In "Assimilation," the initial story in *The Toughest Indian in the World*, Alexie demonstrates the manner in which traditional and contemporary storytelling and their attendant artifacts join together—neither canceling the other; neither offering the possibility for the dogma of fundamentalism. From the opening line, "Regarding love, marriage, and sex, both Shakespeare and Sitting Bull knew the only truth: treaties get broken" (1), Alexie assures the reader that culture will be important but not sacred, that more than one culture will be at stake. Mary Lynn, a Coeur d'Alene Indian married to a white man, is troubled in her sexual relationship with her husband. We are told that she is unsure what handsome or ugly "meant anymore and how much relevance they truly had when it came to choosing sexual partners" (1). She has become a "bored angel" in the bedroom with her husband and has to concentrate far too much when making love to him. When she feels the most lonely, she plays powwow CDs by the Big Mom Singers while reading from Emily Dickinson's poetry. (Again, Alexie emphasizes the complicity of more than one culture in shaping the person of Mary Lynn.) Mary Lynn struggles with the essential nature of her marriage and with her husband's whiteness. "Yes, she was a Coeur d'Alene woman," Alexie tells us, "passionately and dispassionately, who wanted to cheat on her white husband because he was white" (3).

Mary Lynn wants to find an anonymous Indian to be her lover. She does not care if he reads Zane Grey or knows the punch lines to dirty jokes. (Again, the cross-cultural nature of character in contemporary America is highlighted in such a description of her potential lover.) She simply wants "to find the darkest Indian in Seattle—the man with the greatest amount of melanin—and get naked with him in a cheap motel room" (3). Alexie stresses Mary Lynn's desire for something essentially different from her husband, something essentially *Indian*. In his usual satiric voice, Alexie emphasizes the absurdity of "Indian-ness" by reducing it to skin pigmentation, to the level of melanin in the skin. In doing so, he accentuates the biological determination of difference, of factual determination, calling it into question. Yet he does not dismiss such difference entirely. As Mary Lynn considers why she wishes to enter into this adulterous act, we discover that she carries with her two possible reasons. "She told herself it was because of pessimism, existentialism, even nihilism," Alexie writes, "but those reasons—those words—were a function of her vocabulary and not of her motivations" (3–4). Language tenders forth the possibility of justification, but Alexie does not allow his character to believe in the unwavering foundation of language. This is not a justification, Alexie intimates, this is the consequence of a good vocabulary. "If forced to admit the truth, or some version of the truth," Alexie tells us, "she'd testify she was about to go to bed with an Indian stranger because she wanted to know how it would feel" (4).

Here is the movement back and forth between language and "lived" experience, between the representation of experience through a sophisticated system of symbols and sounds and the biology that makes our hearts beat and our lungs expand. And even in this struggle, Alexie emphasizes the inability to fully, to completely, to *essentially* grasp "reality" when he says that it would be "some version of the truth"—not *truth* itself. As the story unfolds, Mary Lynn does indeed have sex with an Indian stranger, and it is the outcome of this encounter that is most telling. Before we look at this outcome, however, we should examine her husband Jeremiah's response to race. Jeremiah's understanding of racial difference mirrors much of what Alexie has written on this topic:

> Before he'd married Mary Lynn, Jeremiah had always believed there was too much talk of race, that white people were all too willing to be racist and that brown people were just as willing and just as racist. As a rational scientist, he'd known that race was primarily a social construct, illusionary, but as the husband of an Indian woman and the father of Indian children, he'd since learned that race, whatever its construction, was real. Now, there were plenty of white people who wanted to eliminate the idea of race, to cast it aside as an unwanted invention, but it was far too late for that. If white people are the mad scientists who created race, thought Jeremiah, then we created race so we could enslave black people and kill Indians, and now race has become the Frankenstein monster that has grown beyond our control. Though he'd once been willfully blind, Jeremiah had learned how to recognize that monster in the faces of whites and Indians and in their eyes. (14)

This passage emphasizes the manner in which Alexie straddles essentialist and constructionist ideas, dismissing neither, embracing both. The very title of the story—"Assimilation"—highlights Alexie's struggle to find a middle ground. But who or what is being absorbed or incorporated in this story? Jeremiah has learned to recognize the "monster" in the faces of both whites and Indians, to see it in their eyes. In this particular story—and we would be wise to note that Alexie comes to different conclusions in different stories—Alexie ultimately focuses on the individual and the individual's potential loss. For this reason, "Assimilation" concludes with a unique and telling moment that is fervently necessary to the story of Jeremiah and Mary Lynn.

As they drive home from a dinner date, they come to the scene of a traffic jam caused by a suicidal white woman who is about to leap from a bridge. Jeremiah gets out of the car, leaving Mary Lynn, to investigate what is happening up ahead. The longer Mary Lynn sits in the car the more convinced she becomes that Jeremiah has met some bad end, and she laments her decision to have the tryst with a man of darker pigmentation, with a stranger of certifiable "Indian-ness." "Oh, God, she loved him," Alexie writes, "sometimes because he was white and often despite his whiteness. In her fear, she found the one truth Sitting Bull never knew: there was at least one white man who could be trusted" (19). It is in the individual story of their lives—a story that is not ultimately divorced from the societal and tribal norms that have helped to shape them, but one that is also not ultimately controlled by such norms—that Alexie leaves us. "She and he loved each other across the distance" (20), Alexie concludes hopefully. Race as construct and race as biological difference *do* have the means to generate distance, but our negotiations with race in both areas ultimately determines how it will impact our lives together.

This "monster" of race, which Jeremiah speaks of in "Assimilation," befuddles Alexie, because he knows in some ways it is real and in other ways merely constructed. Race—which consists, for Alexie, of both biological factors (pigmentation, facial structures) and cultural factors (tradition, ceremony)—affects all people within the framework of his stories. In "The Search Engine," collected in *Ten Little Indians*, a young Spokane college student knows that "Indians were obsessed with authenticity. Colonized, genocided, exiled, Indians formed their identities by questioning the identities of other Indians. Self-hating, self-doubting, Indians turned their tribes into nationalistic sects" (40). Although Alexie acknowledges the monster of race and the method by which it controls Native Americans and whites alike, he is not satisfied merely to name it. Using satire as his form of metacritical assessment, in his story "Flight Patterns," Alexie depicts a character in the act of acknowledging the constructed nature of tribalism: "Sure, he was an enrolled member of the Spokane Indian tribe, but he was also a fully recognized member of the notebook-computer tribe and the security-checkpoint tribe and the rental-car tribe and the hotel-shuttle-bus tribe and the cell-phone-roaming-charge tribe" (*Ten Little Indians* 109). The same character later in this story offers the realization that "we're all trapped by other people's ideas, aren't we?" (117). We would add that we often are not only trapped by other people's ideas, but by our own as well.

In many ways, the struggle to name what is "Indian" relates back to dominant Western thinking established by such authorities as the dualistic fourth-century theologian, Saint Augustine of Hippo. As Matthew Fox has argued, Augustine "was a neo-Platonist who believed you have to escape the body to find spirit" (White 183). Certain segments of our culture appear to call for contemporary Indians to escape the trappings of the Western world for them to find the spirit of their indigenous origins. Where does such desire come from? It likely surfaces from a combination of forces, including a belief in, or desire for, the idea of purity, a nostalgic tug toward something we do not understand fully but wish to claim as innocent, as well as varying degrees of guilt over what has been destroyed or transformed by the very existence of whites, the initial expansion of European culture, and now the totalizing effect of American consumerist culture. But Alexie's work seems to suggest that ideas of purity are simply that—*ideas*. Similar to our contention about Mary Oliver and her position as a contemporary Transcendentalist, no tribal person living at the start of the twenty-first century in the United States can claim an unfettered experience, one devoid of the knowledge of nuclear threat or terrorist attack, of alcoholism and drug abuse, of the decimation of the natural world by an industrial complex so monolithic that it appears unstoppable. In other words, Wal-Mart and its kind have become so ubiquitous that aspects of this plastic and processed world have fully infiltrated Indian life. If a Native American wishes to connect back to his or her ancestry, to his or her tribal traditions, he or she must do so from a position of knowledge—and, thus, difference—from his or her forebears.

In this way, today's tribal member is the site of multiple cultural forces coming into being at once. But, unlike some, we would not argue that this makes their way of life any less "Indian." In fact, we would argue that all human culture and behavior—since our earliest forays as homo sapiens—have been a combination of forces in that given moment, not some pure, single, essential force. Because of this Alexie says in his story "Do You Know Where I Am?" that "we all make up our ceremonies as we go along" (*Ten Little Indians* 151). It is Alexie's revelation that the idea of purity may be flawed that pushes his writing into uncharted territories and allows him to tell the stories that populate his life and have resonance with tribal and nontribal readers alike. As Alexie explains in an interview, "I don't know about you, but growing up all I got exposed to was Mother Earth Father Sky stuff, or direction stuff. That's how I thought Indians wrote. I didn't know I actually could write about my *life*. Yeah, I could write about fried bread and fried bologna. And the great thing is I didn't know you could combine the traditional imagery and fried bread and fried bologna. The way I lived my life, and the way inside me, and the way I thought, which is a mix of tradition-alism and contemporary culture" ("Crossroads" 13).

Storytellers must make decisions about the representation of their human experience, and we should not damn or condemn individual storytellers for the difference in these decisions. For example, Oliver sel-dom allows humans to enter into the world of her poetry, let alone the burgeoning world of consumerism that accompanies suburban sprawl. Yet she lives in Provincetown, Massachusetts, a tourist mecca during the summer months. And, although this part of Cape Cod includes a section of national seashore, if we demanded that each writer's perspective—their writerly canvas—include everything that surrounds them, then we would have to say to Oliver that her poems tell lies, not truths.[5] Rather than argue that a writer like Momaday, for instance, does not reflect the factual experience of the contemporary Indian in his writings, we would suggest instead that Momaday gets at one kind of "truth" about the Native American experience, while Alexie gets at another. "Listen: truth is a strange animal haunting my dreams, my waking," Alexie writes in "Sonnet: Tattoo Tears." "In the reservation Kmart, forty televisions erupt in a twentieth-century vision: 500 years of bad situation come-dies" (*The Summer of Black Widows* 59). Perhaps the quintessential exam-ple of Sherman Alexie's operational essentialism—his joining of constructed and biological notions of race represented within a post-modern landscape—is embedded in his stories that depict the tribal use of basketball as a means to get at the "truth."

Over the course of the twentieth century, basketball has grown in importance on reservations across the country, in tribes as diverse as the Lakota Sioux, the Navajo, and the Coeur d'Alene.[6] As Alexie writes in his poem "Father and Farther," "Basketball is / a series of prayers" (*The Summer of Black Widows* 42). For many Indians, basketball has become a sacred rite of passage, a means of restoration, and this game and its "prayers" are symbolic constructions as well as physical actions. They encompass both nonessentialist and essentialist characteristics, merging them in a way that makes it difficult, if not impossible, to tell where biologically determined behavior ends and socially constructed behavior begins. For Alexie, basketball is a metaphor. For Alexie, basketball is also a literal, physical act, and as such it carries something essential, something "real," like the body in motion. It is a sport whose rules are arbitrary: a basket ten-feet high; a hoop large enough that two regulation balls may fit in it at the same time; certain shots made from certain distances are worth two points, while others are worth as much as three or as little as one; each player is allotted five fouls; each player may take one and a half steps before a traveling violation is whistled. It is a sport where despite the arbitrariness of its rules, real flesh and blood collides. It is a game where muscles expand and contract, lungs ache, and desire is made evident by the physical efforts of ten players moving in patterns of meaning around the court, intersecting with one another. These players work toward a common goal, and their work is done both physically and intellectually. Yet the outcome of these games often moves beyond the intellectual, beyond the physical, to encompass the spiritual and the emotional as well.

In "The Lone Ranger and Tonto Fistfight in Heaven," Alexie's narrator tells us that "the most intense competition on any reservation is Indians versus Indians" (188), and the way they play out this competition is through the game of basketball. In the poem "Why We Play Basketball," Alexie demonstrates the conflicted nature of this game and its place among Indians. For them, basketball is not just a game, as the white culture tells them it ought to be. "For us, it is war," Alexie explains, "often desperate / and without reason. / We throw our body / against another / body" (*The Summer of Black Widows* 24). In many of his poems and stories, the basketball court becomes a proving ground, a place where legend begins to take hold, where the story about the game is just as important as the game itself. "We wanted to know / who was best, who could / change the game into / something new," Alexie contends (23). And in this transformation the possibility for renewal and for the means to have faith in something beyond despair emerges: "In basketball, we / find enough reasons / to believe in God, / or something smaller than God" (23). In "Why We Play Basketball," certain Indians come to believe in Seymour, who is blind and deaf. They marvel at the way he plays by the sense of smell, by how he can identify his teammates: "Spokanes smelled like bread; / Flatheads smelled like pine; / Colville smelled like snow; / Lester smelled like wine" (23). For Alexie, in the small acts of playing the game of basketball—feet moving from side to side to defend; ball cradled gently, wrist cocked, until the arm lifts toward the basket and the ball sails through the air—space and time are transcended; the reservation and its limitations settle, at least for the moment, into the background. Each player finds a meaning, a possible myth, for his or her life, for his or her tribe. "We play / because we believe / in our skins and hands," Alexie concludes. "These hands hold the ball. / These hands hold the tribe" (25). Through synecdoche basketball stands for both love and hate, for skins and hands, for each tribe, and the stories that warm them, that sustain them, and that help them to reconcile the void.

In *Crossing Open Ground* (1988), Barry Lopez suggests that we should "cultivate within ourselves a sense of mystery—to see that the possibilities for an expression of life in any environment, or in any single animal, are larger than we can predict or understand, and that this is all right" (202). Interestingly enough, in our desire to honor the ways of North America's indigenous peoples (whose ways were dishonored and desecrated by some of our ancestors and whose lives continue in much hardship due to the living conditions established and perpetuated by current systems of rule), many scholars and creative artists have tried to define or limit what is the "truest" expression of what it means to be an Indian. "Quantum physics," Lopez proposes, "with its ambiguous particles and ten-dimensional universes, is a branch of science that has in fact returned us to a state of awe with nature, without threatening our intellectual capacity to analyze complex events" (202). Perhaps we should borrow this analogy from Lopez and apply it to the work of writers like Alexie—writers who recognize the mystery inherent in all human life, the particles that swirl in the multidimensional universes that we participate in but cannot ultimately control. He understands that biological essence may be shaped by cultural constructions and that cultural constructions in turn are shaped by biological essence. He acknowledges that the very idea of purity is flawed, yet he does not wish to entirely dismiss or give up on the traditional ways of his tribe, the awe with which he holds them. Instead, he embraces the old ceremony and the new, working to change all of the curses into blessings.

6

"Our long national nightmare is over": Moral Repair and Jeffrey Eugenides's *The Virgin Suicides*

My fellow Americans, our long national nightmare is over.

Our Constitution works; our great Republic is a government of laws and not of men. Here the people rule. But there is a higher Power, by whatever name we honor Him, who ordains not only righteousness but love, not only justice but mercy.

As we bind up the internal wounds of Watergate, more painful and more poisonous than those of foreign wars, let us restore the golden rule to our political process, and let brotherly love purge our hearts of suspicion and of hate.

President Gerald R. Ford's remarks on taking the oath of office as President of the United States on August 9, 1974

Life isn't meant to be easy. It's hard to take being on the top—or on the bottom. I guess I'm something of a fatalist. You have to have a sense of history, I think, to survive some of these things. . . . Life is one crisis after another.

President Richard M. Nixon, marking the tenth anniversary of his resignation

For the storytellers under review in this volume, negotiating the void often involves an attempt to effect a solution for the devastating changes that postmodernity has wrought, while continuing to evolve under conditions of fragmentation, alienation, and uncertainty.

As human beings, we inevitably struggle amongst the historical and sociocultural factors that mark our existence, with hope—that peculiarly human sense of optimism—illuminating our way. Yet how can we enjoy hope's comforting manna and appreciate our own selfhood, and the selfhood of others, while living under the disquieting shadow of our fractured historical pasts? How can we establish moral repair—indeed, how can we reclaim our collective particularity— when confronted with both the ethical failures of the institutions in which we place our trust and the vexing, bewildering nature of our contemporary present, with its moral ambiguity and its ethical fissures?

In *The Virgin Suicides* (1993), Jeffrey Eugenides ponders these very questions with the power and beauty of storytelling as a metaphor for understanding the desolation—and potential redemption—inherent in the Watergate crisis that shattered the American political landscape during the early 1970s and beyond. Yet in so doing, Eugenides also proffers a new sense of hope for establishing moral repair in contrast with the insecurity, bitterness, and confusion that the Watergate affair produced in the American political theater. As Jeffrey C. Alexander remarks, Watergate "had initiated the most serious peacetime political crisis in American history. It had become a riveting moral symbol, one that initiated a long passage through sacred time and space and wrenching conflict between pure and impure sacred forms" (155). *The Virgin Suicides* reaches its climax in August 1974, which, in many ways, has emerged as a signal moment in twentieth-century American life—a world founded by waves upon waves of immigration, manifold attempts at sociocultural unification, and the irrevocable sweep of modernity. In itself, post-industrial Americana entails a nationalistic rage for idealism, a frenetic desire for cultural perfection and dominion that produces such phenomena as Prohibition, isolationism, and McCarthyism. This nationalistic zeal for homogenization transmogrifies, in the 1960s and 1970s, into racial disharmony, the political convolutions of the Vietnam conflict, and the sexual revolution. With the disintegration of the nuclear family and widespread cultural malaise in the offing, American notions of idealism and perfection are simply no longer possible. This reality is made resoundingly clear on the evening of August 8th, 1974, when President Richard M. Nixon announces his resignation at the climax of the Watergate crisis. In *The Virgin Suicides*, this very moment symbolizes the collapse of American idealism and a resounding blow to the American Dream. But for Eugenides, it also represents an opportunity, through the auspices of fiction, for creating a genuine sense of moral repair in the wake of national political disaster.

Many thinkers perceive our quests for moral repair—when we bother to undertake them at all—as forms of moral reckoning or, as Miroslav Volf puts it, concerted efforts at achieving reconciliation both with the past and with ourselves. In her valuable work on the intersections between moral philosophy and literary study, Margaret Urban Walker discusses literary texts as important instruments of moral repair.[1] Because such texts create spaces in which the silenced may once again speak, the power of the written word begins to make inroads into the "recovery" of both the oppressed and the oppressor; cultures and histories once hidden or lost because of the tyrannical practices of those in power are reclaimed. For Walker, moral repair refers to a "familiar and unavoidable task human beings face. We need, over and over, to decide how to respond to wrongdoing, whether to ourselves or to others, and whether by ourselves or by others" ("Moral Repair" 112). Walker argues that our desires for achieving moral repair can only be made manifest through a recognition of the temporal contingencies that will inevitably frame our recuperative endeavors:

> Moral philosophers in the twentieth century have often liked to characterize ethics as answering the question, "What ought I to do?" which implies a set of choices on a fresh page. Yet one of our recurrent ethical tasks is better suggested by the question, "What ought I (or we) to do *now*?" after the page is blotted or torn by our own or others' wrongdoing. I am interested here in understanding how responses to moral wrongs can be ways to repair and sustain morality itself. ("Moral Repair" 112–3)

Indeed, our efforts at effecting moral repair are merely short-run solutions unless we attempt to account for the ways in which our actions might continue to produce much-needed senses of ethics and resolution for our communities—not only during our lives in the contemporary moment, but potentially for our lives and the lives of others in an unforeseeable future as well.[2] "Whether morality has its ultimate source and authority in a divine rule, a transcendent order, a natural law, or in the human mind or heart," Walker writes, "the reality of morality in our lives—its importance and its grip, its mattering to us rather than seeming like just somebody else's rules—is something that we human beings must produce and sustain in the real times and spaces of human societies" ("Moral Repair" 113).

With its traumatic effect upon American political life and the visible uncertainty that it brought upon American society, the Watergate crisis presents a vital need for establishing moral repair on a variety of levels. In the scandal's wake, numerous legal and legislative reforms were sponsored in terms of appointing special prosecutors, providing oversight for campaign-financing issues, and affording more clarity to the separation of powers that the Nixon Administration had threatened during the post-Watergate cover-up. Yet such reforms are largely political and legalistic in nature. They represent a concerted effort to restore confidence in the American government, yet they hardly begin to address the interpersonal confusion and uncertainty that Watergate has wrought, nor do they assist us in understanding—and finally coping with—the mystery surrounding the compromise and "pollution," in Alexander's words, of the federal government of the United States.[3] In the ensuing years after the Watergate crisis, the cultural intelligentsia has done surprisingly little in the way of effecting moral reconciliation. As Alexander observes in *The Meanings of Social Life: A Cultural Sociology* (2003), in the post-Watergate world, "many intellectuals, and certainly broad sections of Western publics, experienced a strange combination of optimism and self-satisfaction without an energetic commitment to any particular moral repair" (219). There are literally hundreds of published works of nonfiction that attempt to explain the nuances of the scandal and its principal players, yet there are scant few works of literary art that try to assist readers in transcending the crisis and repairing morality on an explicitly sociocultural level.

One of the first efforts at textualizing the Watergate crisis and achieving some semblance of moral repair is Alan J. Pakula's 1976 film *All the President's Men*, which offers an artful rendering of Carl Bernstein and Bob Woodward's bestselling book about the Watergate scandal. The movie unabashedly depicts Woodward (Robert Redford) and Bernstein (Dustin Hoffman) as heroic reporters—which, indeed, they were, given the public's widespread disbelief that the Nixon Administration would engage in illegal activities, particularly in advance of a lopsided election campaign that the President, for all intents and purposes, had seemingly already won. Worse yet, many of the reporters' peers at the *Washington Post* also doubted the validity of the story, which, as it evolved over the ensuing months, began to implicate key leaders within the world's most powerful governmental body. In one scene, legendary *Washington Post* Executive Editor Ben Bradlee (Jason Robards) interrogates the newspaper's Foreign Editor (John McMartin) about the veracity of the story, as well as about the shadowy nature of the *Post's* coverage of the Watergate issue:

> *Foreign Editor*: It's a dangerous story for this paper.
> *Bradlee*: How dangerous?
> *Foreign Editor*: Well, it's not that we're using nameless sources that bothers me. Or that everything we print, the White House denies. Or that no other papers are reprinting our stuff. . . . Look, there are two thousand reporters in this town, are there five on Watergate? When did the *Washington Post* suddenly get the monopoly on wisdom? Why would the Republicans do it? McGovern's self-destructed just like Humphrey, Muskie, the bunch of them. I don't believe this story. It doesn't make sense.

As the story develops, *All the President's Men* establishes the reporters as a pair of mismatched detectives who, along with the moviegoing audience, follow their journalistic noses in and amongst Washington, DC's corridors of power. For all of the gravity inherent in the film's weighty political material, much of the screenplay is decidedly anti-dramatic— depicting, as it does, Woodward and Bernstein putting long hours into the act of interviewing witnesses, researching various threads of the story in the study carrels of the Library of Congress, and cold-calling nearly anyone who might provide them with clues to unraveling the mystery behind the Watergate break-in and cover-up.

In one of the film's few moments of conventional dramatic intensity, the elusive Deep Throat (Hal Holbrook) emerges from the shadows of a dimly lit parking garage and warns Woodward that the scandal "leads everywhere" and that the reporters' lives "are in danger."[4] The scene culminates, several minutes' worth of screen time later, at the home of Bradlee, who challenges his reporters to raise their level of journalistic intensity, to bring clarity to the country's understanding of the Watergate scandal:

> You know the results of the latest Gallup Poll? Half the country never even heard of the word Watergate. Nobody gives a shit. You guys are probably pretty tired, right? Well, you should be. Go on home, get a nice hot bath. Rest up—15 minutes. Then get your asses back in gear. We're under a lot of pressure, you know, and you put us there. Nothing's riding on this except the First Amendment to the Constitution, freedom of the press, and maybe the future of the country.

It is an instance of piercing drama that is quickly undone by a comparatively lifeless montage that depicts the two reporters hard at work in the newsroom and concludes with a teletype announcing the resignations of various members of the President's staff, and, finally, the President himself. The only explicit effort at asserting any form of moral reckoning occurs in the last frame, which reports that Gerald R. Ford has been sworn in as the nation's 38th president. It is ultimately a half-hearted gesture that fails to do justice to the balance of Pakula's highly provocative film. As Roger Ebert points out, *"All the President's Men* is truer to the craft of journalism than to the art of storytelling, and that's its problem. The movie is as accurate about the processes used by investigative reporters as we have any right to expect, and yet process finally overwhelms narrative—we're adrift in a sea of names, dates, telephone numbers, coincidences, lucky breaks, false leads, dogged footwork, denials, evasions, and sometimes even the truth. Just such thousands of details led up to Watergate and the Nixon resignation," he adds, "but the movie's more about the details than about their results." And in many ways, moral repair is all about reckoning with the wrongs of the past and attempting to generate results.

While it makes for a powerful filmic experience, *All the President's Men* barely begins to accomplish any lasting sense of moral repair, and neither, for the most part, does Oliver Stone's *Nixon* (1995), a biographical study that rather ineffectively mixes great quantities of fact with liberal doses of fiction. For all of Stone's efforts at creating authenticity, he cannot help but loiter in the backwaters of hearsay and conjecture. In one of the movie's most incredible and far-fetched scenes, Stone depicts Nixon (Anthony Hopkins) in Dallas on the very day of the Kennedy assassination—implying, in the same highly speculative and arcane fashion that he employed in the controversial *JFK* (1991)—that Nixon may have been somehow complicit in the terrible events of November 22nd, 1963. Indeed, the movie explicitly suggests that Nixon, with the assistance of a group of wealthy businessmen, had earlier organized an assassination team to murder Cuban President Fidel Castro; after this mission fails, the team allegedly assassinates President Kennedy as an act of political revenge for his neglect of the anti-Castro movement. In the movie, the experience leaves Nixon overwhelmed with guilt for having recruited the team in the first place. In a similar vein, Stone's film depicts First Lady Pat Nixon (Joan Allen) as a tragic footnote to Nixon's political career, as a loyal bystander who suffered for her husband's unchecked ambitions: "How many millions of miles have I traveled?" she asks him. "How many millions of peoples' hands have I shaken that I just don't like? How many thank-you notes have I written? It's as if I—I don't know—just went to sleep a long time ago and missed the years between."

In addition to dramatizing scenes of Nixon's difficult childhood in Whittier, California, under his mother's strict Quaker tutelage, Stone creates a staggering image of Nixon as a bitter amalgamation of arrogance, hubris, and disgust. This characterization is underscored by a scene that takes place later on the day of the Kennedy assassination. As Nixon watches televised reports of President Lyndon Baines Johnson being sworn in, he remarks that "If I'd been President, they never would have killed me." As the Watergate scandal enters its final stages in *Nixon*, Stone conjures up a surreal scene of President Nixon alone in the White House's Lincoln Bedroom, plying himself with alcohol and pills as he fumbles amongst the infamous Watergate tapes in search of the exculpatory evidence that might still save his political life. Yet Stone's portrait of Nixon pointedly softens as the film nears its close. In this manner, *Nixon* achieves a sense of moral reckoning, if only for a moment, during the end credits, which depict President Nixon as he delivers his farewell speech to the White House staff. In many ways, he was authoring his own epitaph: "Always remember, others may hate you, but those who hate you don't win unless you hate them, and then you destroy yourself." By finally highlighting Nixon's self-destructive tendencies, Stone affords us with powerful insight into the death of the Nixon presidency—and in spite of the director's various exercises in unbridled speculation throughout the rest of the film.

In a far more explicit fashion than *The Virgin Suicides*, Michael Cahill's *A Nixon Man* (1998) employs the Watergate crisis as the backdrop for the coming-of-age story of 11-year-old Jack Costello. The title finds its origins in the political leanings of his father, the "Nixon man" who had met the President years before. "My father was a Nixon man," Jack tells us. "Before that he'd been a Goldwater man. On most nights he could be found roaming the house like a ghost, wearing a tattered robe, reading about Ike. But on November 7, 1972, he wore his suit and tie well past midnight" in order to celebrate Nixon's landslide re-election (1). The novel takes place in San Francisco in the early 1970s, a period and setting that is associated, in particular, with rampant sociocultural unrest and political agitation. The novel traces a variety of key events in Jack's pre-teenaged life, including his first brush with romantic love and a comical scene in which he streaks through Haight-Ashbury with his friends. The Watergate affair figures prominently in Jack's world, especially when he orders a Record-a-Jac from the back of a comic book in order to secretly tape his parents during their telephone conversations.

While Jack's juvenile act of surveillance seems clever and funny in its execution, the results of his eavesdropping activities are devastating indeed, as Jack finds himself adrift in the anxiety- and tension-riddled world of his parents' protracted marital struggles. By merging the Watergate crisis with Jack's tender story of growing up, Cahill succeeds in affording Nixon's fall from grace with deeper, more nuanced meanings in Jack's rapidly changing prepubescent world.

And then there's Andrew Fleming's *Dick* (1999), a whimsical film that traces the experiences of a pair of teenaged girls, Betsy Jobs (Kirsten Dunst) and Arlene Lorenzo (Michelle Williams), on a field trip to the Nixon White House during the bleakest days of the Watergate affair. After they get separated from the other students, Betsy and Arlene stroll about the complex, eventually finding themselves outside of the Oval Office. When President Nixon (Dan Hedaya) begins to suspect that the girls may have witnessed the Administration's money-laundering and document-shredding activities, he offers them jobs as the White House's official dog walkers in order to keep them quiet. As the movie continues, the audience is treated to ridiculous explanations for key aspects of the Watergate crisis. In one instance, we learn that Betsy and Arlene accidentally assume the role of Deep Throat and that the infamous 18 and a half missing minutes from the Watergate tapes were inadvertently recorded over as the girls performed their own version of Olivia Newton-John's "I Honestly Love You." Although the film obviously makes little effort at accommodating historical accuracy, it takes great pains to humanize Nixon as a genuinely empathetic character in contrast with the more sinister portraiture that he has received for decades in the popular press. As Stephanie Zacharek writes, *Dick* offers a perceptive vision of President Nixon that reminds us that he was originally motivated to embark upon a career in politics "by an actual desire to serve the people."

In many ways, Eugenides succeeds far more effectively than his precursors at achieving moral repair in *The Virgin Suicides* by shrewdly associating the death knell of the Lisbon family with the degradation of the American Dream during the final days of the Nixon Administration. In the novel, Eugenides illustrates the experiences of the doomed Lisbon family, a flag-waving American success story, as evinced by their privileged suburban livelihood, steady income, and mortgage that promises to grant them literal ownership of a piece of the nation and its destiny. For Eugenides, the Lisbon family represents the hope and possibility that resides in the American Dream, which, since the onslaught of mass immigration to the United States in the early twentieth century, has held out the promise of prosperity for generation upon generation of

Americans—both immigrants and nonimmigrants alike.[5] As Jennifer L. Hochschild notes in *Facing up to the American Dream: Race, Class, and the Soul of the Nation* (1995), "The idea of the American Dream has been attached to everything from religious freedom to a home in the suburbs, and it has inspired emotions ranging from deep satisfaction to disillusioned fury" (15). In its purest sense, the American Dream involves the notion of upward mobility that has been earned through hard work and fortitude. It is, in short, the aspiration for enjoying the fruits of a better life. For many, the American Dream is made manifest through the acquisition of highly visible goods, both material and otherwise. The accomplishment of the American Dream might be represented in a variety of intrinsic and extrinsic ways—from automobiles and real estate through wealth and fame. "American culture is about self-reliance and the individual fighting a way through," BBC reporter Humphrey Hawksley writes. For millions of immigrants, its central tenet was "that the United States is a place where anything is possible."

Yet there are considerably darker sides to the American Dream as well. As Hawksley observes, "American society is starkly divided into winners and losers," and the inability to achieve success and wealth—or, worse yet, the loss of these esteemed attainments—can lead to social and financial ruin. The pursuit of the American Dream, Stella Chess and Jane Whitbread add, can also result in psychological despair and an overarching discontent with a life that produces nothing but anxiety and toil in the service of the great American success myth: "Today's fathers and mothers—with only the American dream for guidance—extend and overextend themselves, physically, emotionally, and financially, during the best years of their lives to ensure that their children will grow up prepared to do better and go further than they did." While a version of the American Dream continues to endure in the present day, the Watergate crisis effectively ended the American *governmental* dream, along with its largely unblemished notions of faith, trust, and democracy. As one of the defining moments in twentieth-century American history, the Watergate affair occurs, rather tellingly, at the apex of unprecedented social change: after more than a decade of racial turmoil, rapidly shifting sexual values, and the cultural cynicism produced during the waning years of the Vietnam War, the nation finds itself beset by a political crisis that questions the legitimacy of the American government, the last bastion of its citizenry's faith and idealism.

In *The Virgin Suicides*, Eugenides depicts the Lisbon family teetering on the cusp of the American Dream, and his recounting of the slow destruction of that dream exists as a parallel text to the Watergate crisis—from its earliest manifestations as a "third-rate burglary" (to borrow a phrase coined by Nixon's Republican apologists) to the political death of the Nixon Administration. The novel is narrated by a group of neighborhood boys who grew up with the Lisbon sisters. Now middle-aged, yet still determined to comprehend the reasons behind the girls' suicides in the early 1970s, the neighborhood boys engage in a quest for redemption—not only for themselves, but for the Lisbon daughters who have disappeared, tragically and unexplainably, into the mysterious ether of the past. But they are not the only unsettled souls who long for a sense of understanding and resolution about the Lisbon sisters' untimely deaths. At the dénouement of *The Virgin Suicides*, the Lisbon family's psychologist Dr. Hornicker adopts the metaphor of a loaded gun in an effort to isolate the causes behind the siblings' suicides: "It was a combination of many factors," he writes in his report regarding the demise of the Lisbon girls. "With most people, suicide is like Russian roulette. Only one chamber has a bullet. With the Lisbon girls, the gun was loaded. A bullet for family abuse. A bullet for genetic predisposition. A bullet for historical malaise. A bullet for inevitable momentum. The other two bullets are impossible to name, but that doesn't mean the chambers were empty" (247–8). In many ways, the loaded gun represents the enigmatic nature of human existence, and Dr. Hornicker's gun metaphor refers explicitly to the untold elements and pressures that determine the course of our lives. Yet, rather pointedly, the metaphor also allows for the unknown—the mysterious and uncontrollable factors that arise unexpectedly only to thwart our trajectories for living and to upset our destinies.

How, then, do we achieve a sense of moral repair in the face of such loss—in particular, the dissolution of the Lisbon family and the concomitant sociopolitical fallout engendered by the Watergate crisis? In order for moral repair to be attained, we must experience "effective processes of interpretation," Alexander writes, and "in contemporary fragmented societies [such as in the United States], political reintegration and cultural renewal depend on the contingent outcomes of specific historical circumstances." But "the successful alignment of these forces is very rare indeed," Alexander cautions (157). Eugenides accomplishes a strong sense of cultural renewal via the memories of the neighborhood boys, as well as the novel's interior detective story, which leads them to discover certain truths about the nature of human existence and, ultimately, about the tragic days that heralded the end of the summer of 1974.

The Virgin Suicides takes place, rather appropriately, in an upwardly mobile suburb outside of Detroit. As the literal engine of progress for the twentieth century, Detroit represents the heart of socioeconomic American culture, the hub of industry for which the suburbs act as a fortifying mechanism and idyllic shelter for the achievers of the American Dream. In Eugenides's fictive world, the residents of suburban America function as the ultimate believers in the figurehead of American values and security, and the traumas of Watergate act as a crushing blow to the idealism at the heart of middle-class values. While the last gasps of the Nixon Administration are being exhaled in Washington, DC, ground zero for the political crisis turns out to be the glossy and pristine suburban outskirts of American industrial progress. It is here that the Lisbons' conservative ways come into conflict with the relaxed value systems in the wake of 1960s counterculture and the sexual revolution. In response to such ethical shifts, Mr. and Mrs. Lisbon exert a totalitarian sense of parental control as their five daughters plunge into the enervating throes of adolescence. The Lisbon parents, jostled by fears of the rampant promiscuity sometimes desired by pubescent girls en route to sexual maturity, inhibit excessive amounts of social interaction between their daughters and others in their age bracket of the opposite sex.

In short, Mr. and Mrs. Lisbon react to changing mores by engaging in a convoluted process of constricting and liberating their daughters at the same time. It is a mechanism that is destined for failure, but it is the only way they know how to respond to a world that seems, from their perspective, to be spiraling out of control. Roused into a brief era of parental openness after the suicide attempt of their youngest daughter Cecilia, Mr. and Mrs. Lisbon host a small party in their basement, allowing the girls to invite several boys from their suburban neighborhood. Reminiscing about the event years later as they try to unweave the untidy threads of memory, the now middle-aged men remember that they

> had never been to a chaperoned party. We were used to parties our older brothers threw with our parents out of town, to dark rooms vibrating with heaps of bodies, musical vomiting, beer kegs beached on ice in the bathtub, riots in the hallways, and the destruction of living room sculpture. This was all different. Mrs. Lisbon ladled out more glasses of punch while we watched Therese and Mary play dominoes, and across the room Mr. Lisbon opened his tool kit. He showed us his ratchets, spinning them in his hand so that they whirred, and a long sharp tube he called his router, and another covered with putty he called his scraper, and one more with a prolonged end he said was his gouger. His voice was hushed as he spoke about these implements, but he never looked at us, only at the tools

themselves, running his fingers over their lengths or testing their sharpness with the tender bulb of his thumb. (27–8)

In a far more substantial instance of parental deference, the Lisbons allow their four surviving daughters to attend the Homecoming dance with Trip Fontaine, a star offensive tackle on the high school football team, and three other grateful members of his squad. Elated by their newly granted freedom, the four daughters, with Mrs. Lisbon in tow and ever-watchful of their exploits, begin to make preparations for their imminent date. "The week before Homecoming, in fact, she had taken the girls to a fabric store," Eugenides writes. "The girls wandered amid the racks of patterns, each containing the tissue paper outline of a dream dress, but in the end it made no difference which pattern they chose. Mrs. Lisbon added an inch to the bust lines and two inches to the waists and hems, and the dresses came out as four identical shapeless sacks" (118).

The Homecoming dance proves to be the catalyst for the Lisbons' final, totalizing retreat from society. The girls' Homecoming experience finds its origins in Trip's raging desires for fourteen-year-old Lux, the youngest surviving Lisbon daughter. Despite her misgivings, Lux makes love to Trip on the soggy high school football field after the dance. In the middle of the act, Lux sobs aloud, "I always screw things up. I always do," but she persists anyway (138). Lux's lethal dance with the hormone-addled frenzy of adolescence gives way to harsh consequences for all four of the girls, prompting Mrs. Lisbon to exercise the most abrasive form of parental authority at her disposal: a total lockdown encompassing the removal of Lux and her sisters from school and an insistence on complete withdrawal from the outside world:

> Given Lux's failure to make curfew, everyone expected a crackdown, but few anticipated it would be so drastic. When we spoke to her years later, however, Mrs. Lisbon maintained her decision was never intended to be punitive. "At that point being in school was just making things worse," she said. "None of the other children were speaking to the girls." Except boys, and you knew what they were after. The girls needed time to themselves. A mother knows. I thought if they stayed home, they'd heal better. (142)

Mrs. Lisbon sees herself acting heroically on behalf of her daughters—caught up, as they are, in the euphoria of pubescence and sexual maturation. In both cases, the parents proceed knowingly against the restless vicissitudes of human nature. They are able to countenance the extremity of their actions by imagining themselves to be engaging in the act of protecting their family from a dangerous and beguiling external world. Yet Mr. and Mrs. Lisbon's quest is utterly doomed to failure. Their desired reality exists at variance with 1970s American culture. The Lisbons expected to live and work within an homogenized American culture in which the promise of the American Dream was sacrosanct, in which gender binaries were rigidly defined, and in which Judeo-Christian values systems went unchallenged. In short, they were completely unprepared for the unprecedented changes inherent in late-twentieth-century life. Eugenides illustrates the family's downfall by pointedly aligning the crucial life experiences of his characters with key instances in the Watergate scandal. In so doing, Eugenides mirrors the events leading up to President Nixon's political ruin with similar moments of disjunction and devolution in the Lisbon household. Cecilia, the youngest Lisbon daughter, begins her suicidal journey on Tuesday, June 13, 1972, when she first attempts to take her own life. The notorious break-in at the Watergate Complex occurs during the following weekend, in the midst of Cecilia's lengthy hospital stay. She returns home on June 23rd, the day in which reports of President Nixon's first blanket denials were flooding the national news wires. In a press conference held the day before, President Nixon remarked that "the White House has had no involvement whatever in this particular incident" (Bernstein and Woodward 29). Even more significantly, June 23rd is the date of the infamous "smoking-gun tape" of a conversation recorded in the Oval Office between President Nixon and H. R. Haldeman, White House Chief of Staff. On the recording, President Nixon can be heard initiating the cover-up that will result in his political ruin. It is hardly surprising, then, that the Lisbon household begins its own doomed transformation roughly coincident with the moment in which the cover-up began to take form. "From that time on," Eugenides writes, "the Lisbon house began to change" (22). On the advice of Dr. Hornicker, the Lisbon parents decide to throw the a chaperoned party in their basement in a desperate attempt to provide a social outlet for their daughters. Within minutes, Cecilia excuses herself from the party and hurls her body from a second floor window, impaling herself on the spiked fence below. On that same July day, *Washington Post* reporters Bob Woodward and Carl Bernstein link enigmatic spy E. Howard Hunt to the White House, beginning the domino effect that would direct them to covert operative G. Gordon Liddy, senior advisor John D. Ehrlichman, Haldeman, and, eventually, to President Nixon himself.

The dissolution of the Lisbons' own house of cards would climax with the aforementioned Homecoming dance, when Mr. and Mrs. Lisbon's experiment in being more lenient, if not more accepting of the rapidly changing world around them, implodes after Lux fails to meet her mother's curfew. Conducting her own Saturday Night Massacre[6] of sorts, Mrs. Lisbon quarantines her daughters, and soon thereafter, Mr. Lisbon quits his job at the local high school and the Lisbon family ceases all contact with the outside world. As with Edgar Allan Poe's "The Fall of the House of Usher," the Lisbon home plunges into a state of utter disrepair with their formerly pristine landscaping devolving into a sea of mud, unread newspapers piling up on the front porch, and shingles falling off of the roof. Eventually, the house itself begins to decay, producing a putrid smell that floats throughout the neighborhood, alerting the other suburbanites to the family's impending doom:

> For even as the house began to fall apart, casting out whiffs of rotten wood and soggy carpet , this other smell began wafting from the Lisbons', invading our dreams and making us wash our hands over and over again. The smell was so thick it seemed like liquid, and stepping into its current felt like being sprayed. We tried to locate the source, looking for dead squirrels in the yard or a bag of fertilizer, but the smell contained too much syrup to be death itself. (165)

It most certainly wasn't death—at least not yet. The girls' suicides would come much later, of course, after Lux took to having sex with random delivery boys and repairmen on the family's tattered roof. Their deaths would be forestalled until after the girls' final, desperate effort to make contact with the outside world. Engaging the neighborhood boys in a series of late-night musical exchanges, they played popular love songs from the early 1970s to each other over the telephone, culminating with the painful, unerring distance of Carole King's "So Far Away." Their meticulously orchestrated suicides occur during the following summer, concurrent with the death throes of the Nixon Administration.[7]

For the neighborhood boys, the idea of moral repair is inextricably bound up with their effort to make sense of why the girls chose to kill themselves in the bloom of youth. Given the evidence presented in *The Virgin Suicides*, it would be reasonable to blame Mrs. Lisbon for her daughters' self-destruction. Mrs. Lisbon's "maximum-security isolation" of the girls represents her last desperate attempt to stave off the sociocultural pressures wrought by sexual liberation and various other paradigm shifts away from traditional American morality (141). Mrs. Lisbon unknowingly creates the confining setting—"one big coffin," Eugenides writes (163)—that allows the girls to make their deadly decision, severing her daughters from the outside world by extinguishing the girls' social ties—even going so far as to force the girls to destroy several of their rock albums. In a confused state shaped by a genuine yearning for love and comfort, Lux begins escorting random suitors to the roof of the Lisbon home for a series of sporadic trysts. A feigned pregnancy and a dire need to escape from the increasingly dreary Lisbon household affords Lux with a visit to the hospital, where Dr. Hornicker diagnoses her as suffering from a form of manic-depression. "She was in deep denial," Dr. Hornicker later told the neighborhood boys, "She was obviously not sleeping—a textbook symptom of depression—and was pretending that her problem, and by association, her sister Cecilia's problem, was of no real consequence. But even her delight had a manic quality to it," he added. "She bounced off the walls." Dr. Hornicker's diagnosis—which he neither shared with Lux nor her parents—proved to be remarkably accurate, even down to his conclusion that "there is a high incidence of repetitive suicides in single families" (156–7). Could Dr. Hornicker have saved the girls from doom by acting on their behalf, by functioning as a conduit between medical science and their parents' staunch resistance to allowing their daughters to merge with the external world?

Mrs. Lisbon's own fatal error in judgment finds its origins in her belief that the problem was social rather than medical. Even more problematically, she failed to comprehend, as with nearly everyone else in the novel, the perilous nature of her daughters' predicament. Eugenides makes this point resoundingly clear when he depicts the girls staging a protest against the Parks Department's decision to remove a diseased tree from the Lisbon lawn: "Three rings formed around the tree: the blond ring of the Lisbon girls, the forest green of the Parks Department's men, and, farther up, the ring of onlookers." In a frantic plea to save the tree from demolition, Therese crafts the very argument that might have saved the Lisbon daughters' lives. "There's no scientific evidence that removal limits infestation," she said. "These trees are ancient. They have evolutionary strategies to deal with beetles. Why don't you just leave it up to nature?" (181). By stifling her daughters' own evolutionary potentialities, Mrs. Lisbon opts to countermand the girls' opportunities for living well and flourishing beyond their parents' control. Although her motives were clearly not punitive, Mrs. Lisbon forced her daughters, nevertheless, into making life-or-death decisions while they were lingering in a collective state of psychological trauma.

As *The Virgin Suicides* comes to a close, Eugenides offers a rather open-ended conclusion in which the neighborhood boys posit no easy answers to the pain and suffering evoked by the girls' untimely loss:

> It didn't matter in the end how old they had been, or that they were girls, but only that we had loved them, and that they hadn't heard us calling, still do not hear us, up here in the tree house, with our thinning hair and soft bellies, calling them out of those rooms where they went to be alone for all time, alone in suicide, which is deeper than death, and where we will never find the pieces to put them back together. (248–9)

They will achieve moral repair, but not through any clear, unmitigated understanding of the reasons behind the girls' suicides. Instead, they accomplish new senses of renewal and reconciliation by giving voice to the lost Lisbon sisters, by reincarnating them once again through the artifice of narrative. In *Ethics and the Limits of Philosophy* (1985), Bernard Williams observes that "critical reflection should seek for as much shared understanding as it can find on any issue, and use any ethical material that, in the context of the reflective discussion, makes some sense and commands some loyalty. The only serious enterprise is living," Williams adds, "and we have to live after the reflection" (117). For the neighborhood boys, their act of moral repair in *The Virgin Suicides* exists as a critical moment in their own efforts to "live after the reflection." While they recognize that they will never fully comprehend the nature of the girls' demise, they are better for having simply attempted the reflection in the first place. In *The Sovereignty of Good* (1970), Iris Murdoch argues that such forms of recognition lie in the mysterious and communal fabric of the self. "The self, the place where we live, is a place of illusion," Murdoch observes, and "goodness is connected with the attempt to see the unself, to see and to respond to the real world in the light of a virtuous consciousness" (93). For the neighborhood boys, now wizened and ensconced in middle-age, the world has become a more expansive place filled with mysteries that will never be unraveled, yet it is also a world in which a quest for selfhood and goodness genuinely makes a difference—no matter what they may find there. They may never truly reclaim the Lisbon girls, but they may very well reclaim their own misplaced senses of selfhood in their stead.

But how, then, does Eugenides's careful alignment of the girls' fate with that of the Nixon Administration function as an act of moral repair? It is the American Dream, of course, that fails to materialize for the Lisbons—or at least it fails to materialize according to their socio-cultural expectations. But then again, the American Dream exists in an incredible state of flux during the Lisbon family's final, catastrophic years among the other Detroit suburbanites. They simply cannot cope with such rampant postmodernity, and they cannot, for the life of them, reconcile the impending void. But neither could the Nixon Administration, which, through its own massive ethical breaches, contributes part and parcel to the acceleration of that selfsame void. By establishing a confluence between the Lisbon family's ruination and the Watergate crisis, Eugenides asks us not only to reconsider the place of the lost sisters in our readerly imaginations, but also to reassess the role of the Nixon Administration in our historical memories. He does not invite us to forget the Watergate affair, nor does he entreat us to minimize President Nixon's responsibility for changing the ways in which we think about the government, for breeding the cynicism that characterizes the American political void of the present. Instead, Eugenides asks us in *The Virgin Suicides* if we might yet be willing to transcend the failures of the past, to reclaim our idealism, and to restore, in Walker's prescient words, "the reality of morality in our lives."

7

"What's Filipino? What's authentic? What's in the blood?": Alterity and Ethics in the Novels of Jessica Hagedorn

> What is literature for? You don't go to literature and say, "I need to feel good about my race, so let me read a novel."
>
> Jessica Hagedorn

Migration—the desire to explore, to reposition, to overcome—is a fundamental human impulse. It is an urge characterized by movement, adaptation, and progression, yet it is also fraught with dislocation and uncertainty. In such visionary novels as *Dogeaters* (1990) and *The Gangster of Love* (1996), Jessica Hagedorn explores the impact of Americanization and cultural bifurcation upon the Filipino pre- and post-immigrant experience. In *Dogeaters*, Hagedorn examines the turbulent world of Manila during the Marcos era, a morally convoluted environment in which the importation of American movies seems to provide her high and low characters with a means of escape from their politically corrosive world. Yet at the same time, their vast consumption of American popular culture continues to obliterate their sense of national identity. In *The Gangster of Love*, Hagedorn traces the story of the Rivera family after they make their immigrant journey from the Philippines to the United States. Haunted by the lingering memory of their homeland, the Riveras find themselves confronted with ubiquitous sexual promiscuity, the artificiality of the American success myth, and the moral vacuousness of Western materialism. Interpreting Hagedorn's narratives in terms of their ethical positions regarding alterity and otherness affords us with a powerful mechanism for understanding the larger cultural and literary significance of *Dogeaters* and *The Gangster of Love*, novels in which Hagedorn addresses the realities of identity loss and interpersonal reaffirmation in a world increasingly complicated by globalization and the seemingly relentless exportation of Americana. Hagedorn's narratives about the pre- and post-diasporic lives of a wide array of Filipino characters allow her to construct a literary model of the immigrant experience particularized to refugees during the Marcos era. More significantly, Hagedorn's novels function as a binary representation of the important interpersonal associations between self and others inherent in the process of immigrant transformation.

The uneasy relationship that marks our philosophical understanding of self and otherness is perhaps most usefully considered via Emmanuel Levinas's conceptions of alterity, contemporary moral philosophy's sine qua non for considering the nature of our innate responsibilities to our human others. The notion of alterity itself—which Paul-Laurent Assoun characterizes as "the primal scene of ethics" (96)—refers to our responsibilities and obligations to the irreducible face of the other. These aspects of our human condition find their origins in the recognition of sameness that we find in the realization of otherness. This similarity of identity and human empathy establishes the foundation for our alterity—in short, the possibility of being "altered"—and for the responsibilities and obligations that we can afford to other beings via our own ethical conversions. For Hagedorn—already a renowned poet and performance artist prior to the success of *Dogeaters*—the novel clearly provides an expansive forum for exploring larger and more wide-ranging ideas about the heterogeneity of contemporary media and the manner in which its various manifestations succeed in exporting globalization, with its attendant economic aspirations, to virtually every nook and cranny of the planet.

In *Dogeaters* and *The Gangster of Love,* Hagedorn challenges us to rethink our understanding of these virtual and nonvirtual global spaces through a form of Levinasian alterity in which otherness becomes defined in terms of its capitalistic currency. As Saskia Sassen contends in *Losing Control?: Sovereignty in an Age of Globalization* (1996), the phenomenon of globalization "has contributed to a denationalizing of national territory" (30) in which a given country's dominion becomes displaced by a host of competing forces marked by an ongoing struggle among international marketplaces, governmental interests, human-rights groups, ethnic factions, and supranational organizations. "Today," Sassen writes, "the old hierarchies of power and influence within the state are being reconfigured by increasing economic globalization" (99). In such an inherently unbalanced system, proponents of globalization seek to manage alterity, as it were, by intentionally complicating existing notions of identity formation in terms of race, gender, and nationalistic desires. In a world in which wealthy nations expand third-world markets by devaluing their own domestic unemployment positions—and, in turn, by increasing their trade and budget deficits in the bargain—former President George Herbert Walker Bush's formulation of a "new world order," as related to Congress and a worldwide television audience in March 1991, seems like mere pretext for exporting capitalism on a truly international scale.[1]

By ultimately reconfiguring the ways in which we think about ourselves in relation to the larger worlds in which we live, globalization clearly offers a host of social and economic implications that threaten to alter our existing notions of identity. As David Harvey observes in *Spaces of Capital: Towards a Critical Geography* (2001), "Through changing our world we change ourselves" (200). Indeed, what becomes of identity in such a conflicted and rapidly shifting set of global spaces in which our senses of geopolitical selfhood become altered by media and market forces at nearly every turn? For Hagedorn's readership—an audience that presumably includes Filipinos, Americans, and that Westernized amalgam of "Filipino Americans"—the act of conceptualizing alterity demands an understanding of the ways in which identity operates in such a constant state of flux and uncertainty. In short, the notion of Filipino identity remains both an unknown quantity and an overly inscribed space of cultural confusion. As E. San Juan Jr., astutely observes

> By grace of over 400 years of colonial and neocolonial domination, the inhabitants of the islands called the "Philippines" have acquired an identity, a society and a culture, not totally of their own making. We share this fate with millions of other "third-world" peoples. We Filipinos have been constructed by Others (Spaniards, Japanese, the *Amerikanos*); recognition of "our" utterances and deeds remains scant. We are still misrecognized. What is ours and what has been imposed is still a burning issue, reflecting divisions across class, gender, ethnicity, religion, and so on. (6)

These already convoluted Filipino conceptions of self and identity become further confounded, of course, by the momentous events of 1946, when the United States granted independence to the Philippines as well as by the later emergence of the Marcos regime. After nearly five decades as a colonial territory, the Philippines found itself confronted by the challenge of imposing democracy and self-rule in the shadow of its American benefactor. Yet, as history tells us, the inception of President Ferdinand Marcos's dictatorship (1965–1986) forced Filipinos once again to question their larger sense of cultural identity in a post-colonial world characterized by the competing value systems of quasi-American democracy, the insurgency of Soviet communism, and Marcos's own strikingly *un*original brand of wholesale corruption.

In *Shadows of Ethics: Criticism and the Just Society* (1999), Geoffrey Galt Harpham contends that "ethics does not solve problems, it structures them" (37). In *Dogeaters*, Hagedorn structures her novel's ethical dimensions by imagining a vast textual landscape that illustrates the highly complexified layers of Filipino cross-colonization. Hagedorn's multi-voiced narrative features an array of characters across various nonlinear historical dimensions, beginning with the 1950s-era Rio Gonzaga, a young *mestiza* whose wealthy Filipino family includes a half-Spanish father and a half-American mother. Their union exemplifies the colonization of the Philippines by Spain and the United States. Fittingly, the novel proper begins in 1956 with images of Rock Hudson and Jane Wyman—the *faux* signifiers of healthy American glamour and sexuality—wafting through the "air-conditioned darkness" of a Manila cinema (30). Rio idolizes Hollywood's whimsical and overtly stylized productions as sterling examples of the incredible possibilities, spurious as they may be, of American life. The novel pointedly shifts to the 1970s, the heyday of Marcos-era corruption and graft. Hagedorn depicts this period via a series of micro-narratives that orbit around the two "dogeaters"—Joey Sands, a drug-addled prostitute and Lolita Luna, a heroin junkie and B-movie star. The phrase "dogeaters" finds its etymological roots as a Filipino epithet, yet in Hagedorn's more deliberate usage it refers to society's most sordid creatures, the people who exploit and manipulate others in their zeal for self-sufficiency and survival.[2] Like Rio, Joey's parentage underscores his symbolic representation of the postcolonial world. As the son of an unknown African American serviceman and a Filipino prostitute, Joey exists as the bastard spawn of the protracted American military presence in the Philippines.

Dogeaters depicts Rio vicariously—and, in colonial terms, rather submissively—living her life through the artificiality of Filipino radio serials such as *Love Letters* and the alluring fantasy of American movies like *All That Heaven Allows*. While Joey takes on a more active role in his process of self-emergence, his principal means of identity creation, as with Rio's, involves the establishment and maintenance of a new reality grounded in American popular culture. Joey resolves the dilemma of his mysterious paternity by adopting his surname after receiving a postcard from Las Vegas's Sands Motel. By "naming himself after a monument of American entertainment," Rachel C. Lee asserts, "Joey locates his origin and destiny in U.S. celluloid space" (76). As a genuine child of the Marcos era, Joey shapes the boundaries of his reality via his experiences as a prostitute with his predominantly Western clientele. A bisexual dilettante, Joey views sex strictly as a means of securing upward mobility in an impersonal food chain that elevates corruption and assertiveness over equality and fairness. "Most sex is charity, on my part," Joey exclaims. "I'd rather dance alone" (132). In one instance, Joey scuttles his job as a DJ at the CocoRico, a Manila sex club, after he anticipates that an affair with Rainer, a visiting German film director, might prove to be more lucrative: "The German director will cast me in his next movie," Joey tells himself. "All my problems will be over, ha-ha" (131). Later, at an airport hotel, Joey happens upon the assassination of Senator Domingo Avila, a staunch critic of the country's dictatorship.[3] Fearing the consequences of being an eyewitness to Avila's murder, Joey goes into hiding and finds his destiny with a faction of armed rebels in the steep and isolated mountains of the provinces, rather than in the cultural mythology of the increasingly distant United States: "Joey is overwhelmed by a sense of fear and wonder," Hagedorn writes. "His life in Manila is only a memory now" (232). For Joey, the possibility of alterity suddenly exists in his capacity for remaking himself as a revolutionary and, perhaps even more importantly, as a potential participant in the future ethical makeover of the Philippines.[4]

Like Joey, Lolita engages in aggressively ambitious behaviors designed explicitly to achieve her materialistic goals of self-sufficiency and survival in a world characterized by the realities of political corruption and martial law. Lolita initially enjoys renown as a result of her work as a *bomba* star in B-movies and soft pornography. Literally meaning "bomb," the Marcos-era phenomenon of the *bomba* star refers to ambitious—indeed, *explosive*—women like Lolita who covet the kind of power associated with a vaunted place, no matter how transitory, in the national spotlight. *Bomba* stars like Lolita were the deliberate creations of the government to provide a tonic—or, more appropriately, a diversion—for the national viewing audience.[5] Lolita's sexual affair with the powerful General Nicasio Ledesma, the highest-ranking member of the government's morally bankrupt military establishment, affords her with the social cachet necessary for living a posh and extravagant lifestyle replete with a stylish Manila apartment and a ceaseless supply of heroin. Eventually recognizing the constructed nature of her fame, as well as the diminishing economic and social returns of her relationship with the General, Lolita opts, like so many before her, to make her way to America, where she dreams of reinventing herself in a new world. Yet

Lolita realizes "that she is not going to get what she wants," Hagedorn writes. "She will rot in Manila for the rest of her life, or else he will have her killed; it's that simple. It is a revelation for the movie star, and almost invigorating" (176).

Restricted by her extremely colonized and highly stratified existence, Lolita finds herself confronted with two choices: secure an immigrant visa from General Ledesma or raise the necessary funds by starring in an "experimental art film" that "would involve lengthy close-ups of Lolita Luna's vagina, shot by professional cameramen in living color and in a variety of simulated settings." The film's producer reassures Lolita that "we will only allude to violence"—her vagina would be "teased by the gleaming blade of a knife, for example, or perhaps a stubby black pistol. Or by the edge of a samurai sword" (177). When Lolita subsequently chooses the predictability of General Ledesma's sexual desires over the indelicacy of the smut film, she "dismisses her fears" by telling herself that "the General is just another old man" (178). Hagedorn's tone clearly suggests the inevitability of the actress' doom. As Lolita's colonizer, the General can only perceive his *bomba* star in terms of her sexuality; hence, he remains ethically unequipped to enjoy an altered relationship with her. In regard to her personal salvation, Lolita has realized the abject nature of her relationship to her neocolonial others far too late, and her fascination with the illusory qualities of fame and fortune will undoubtedly seal her fate.

Like some postcolonial *Heart of Darkness*, *Dogeaters* eventually finds its way up the river to Malacañang Palace, where First Lady Imelda Marcos—perhaps the most visible dogeater of them all—lies in wait at the novel's core. Re-imagined by the novelist as the loquacious "Madame," Hagedorn's metaphorical "Mistah Kurtz" wallows in power and privilege. Reclining in an "exquisite armchair inlaid with intricate mother-of-pearl designs," Madame conducts an interview with a fawning Western journalist in which she defends her unquenchable cravings for footwear and conveys her enduring respect for astrology, psychic healing, and Oscar de la Renta (221). Unlike Joey and Lolita—mere peasants, in comparison to the "Steel Butterfly," who recognize their inequitable positions in her national tapestry—Madame refuses to register her relationship between the self and the multitudinous others who make her extravagant life possible. Simply put, she eschews alterity in favor of a grossly pejorative status quo.[6] Madame denies otherness by claiming victimhood and ignoring her husband's crimes against humanity: "Because I happen to look great—they assume—they put two and two together—they accuse me of stealing food from children's mouths.

Absurd, *di ba?*" (221). In addition to refuting her husband's role in Senator Avila's assassination, Madame attributes her social malaise and political failings to an irrepressible penchant for "being a great dreamer." Momentarily suspending the interview before the stunned journalist, Madame fills a yellow legal pad with childlike drawings of "dozens of cartoonish, twinkling stars" and "moons of all shapes and sizes" (223). When her reverie concludes, Madame waxes rhapsodically about her dreams of becoming a movie star:

> "I could have been an actress in one of those romantic musicals, back in the days when movies were movies and everyone loved romance! *Ay*—where is romance, these days? . . . What would life be without movies? Unendurable, *di ba?* We Filipinos, we know how to endure, and we embrace the movies. With movies, everything is okay *lang*. It is one of our few earthly rewards, and I longed to be part of it!. . . Obviously, God had greater things in mind. I met my husband, and our destinies entwined. Together, we served our country, and together we sacrificed everything. We were chosen by God to guide and to serve—" Her braceleted arm sweeps over the room, over her blue women, the imposing furniture, and her scattered blue, mother-of-pearl peau-de-soie pumps. "What greater destiny could there be?" (224)

Attributing her bounty of good fortune to a larger, divine purpose, Madame remains unable to see beyond the rigid boundaries of her self. As Myra Mendible perceptively remarks, the First Lady "indulges in a postmodern logic that denies the existence of any real social or political problems" (299). Indeed, Madame's self-sustaining ethical system operates in a moral void where concepts such as obligation and accountability have become devoid of meaning. For the life of hers, Madame simply cannot (or, perhaps more accurately, *will* not) see the Levinasian faces of the larger Filipino populace that suffers under her husband's dominion.[7]

By self-consciously declining to engage in an altered relationship with her people and refusing to recognize the extent of their plight, Madame suspends the possibility of genuine alterity and ethical renewal in the Philippines. The novel's melancholy musical coda, entitled *"Kundiman,"* underscores Hagedorn's powerful rejoinder to the First Lady's self-serving pontifications.[8] A reconfiguration of the Lord's Prayer, the novel's bittersweet coda laments the "spilled blood of innocents" rendered "dead by the bullet, the dagger, the arrow; dead by the slingshot of polished stones; dead by grenades, hunger, and thirst; dead by profound longing and profound despair." In addition to cataloguing the human tragedy of colonialism, the coda's quasi-spiritual language transmogrifies from a sorrowful dirge into a searing indictment of the Marcos regime's manifold transgressions against the motherland: "Dammit, mother dear. There are serpents in your garden. Licking your ears with forked tongues, poisoning your already damaged heart. I am suffocated by my impotent rage, my eyes are blinded by cataracts blue as your miraculous robes, I listen intently for snatches of melody, the piercing high-pitched wail of your song of terror" (250–1). As *Dogeaters* comes to its embittered close—as "we flap and beat our wings in our futile attempts to reach what surely must be heaven" (251)—Hagedorn offers scant hope for the beleaguered children of the postcolonial era.

In addition to illustrating the manner in which many of these same Filipinos will ultimately reject life in the Marcos-era Philippines and find their way to America, Hagedorn's next novel, *The Gangster of Love*, offers a powerful study of the complicated nature of that three-headed cultural monster—immigration, assimilation, and Americanization. More than 20,000 Filipinos have immigrated to the United States on an annual basis since the advent of the Immigration Nationality Act of 1965. If *Dogeaters* exposes the inability of its authority figures to embrace alterity and reshape the lives of millions of socially and economically disenfranchised Filipinos, *The Gangster of Love* seeks to demonstrate what transpires when an immigrant family transplants itself in America, where the family members hope to enjoy the fruits of personal freedom and the possibility of material success. Confronted by the harshness and impersonality of American life, the Riveras must contend with identity loss, the erosion of extended familial relationships, and the all-encompassing power and elusiveness of the American dream. For the Rivera family, alterity entails the realization of the particularity of their Western others as well as their own acceptance as Filipino Americans. Can the Riveras flourish in a new world that asks them to consent to wholesale assimilation yet maintain their sense of cultural identity, their "Filipinoness"?

As *The Gangster of Love* begins, the Rivera family arrives by ship in San Francisco in 1970, the final year in the truncated life of Jimi Hendrix, the legendary guitarist whose metaphysical presence pervades the novel. The refugee from a broken marriage as much as from the villainy of the Marcos regime, Milagros Rivera escapes to America with her son Voltaire and her daughter Raquel, who is affectionately known as "Rocky" among her friends and relations. Their story of acculturation inevitably collides with two principal aspects specific to the Filipino immigrant experience: the concept of the "yo-yo" and the linguistic distinction between being "Pilipino" or "Filipino." In addition to being a crude weapon and, much later, a toy first exported to the United States by Filipino Pedro Flores and popularized in the 1920s, the yo-yo refers, in terms of its ethnic implications, to people who go back and forth between their allegiance to Filipino and American sensibilities.[9] Such intercultural vacillation makes it difficult, quite obviously, for genuine assimilation—for the notion of becoming altered—to occur. The second concept addresses the pronunciational differences between "Pilipino" and "Filipino." For some Filipino Americans, the former pronunciation signifies the phrase's indigenous Tagalog origins; the latter articulation—with its European connotations of Spain's Crown Prince Philip II—implies a colonial antecedent.[10] Americanized Filipinos, particularly second-generation immigrants and beyond, often display the latter pronunciation as their accents soften and they begin to conform to the sound and idioms of American English. Both issues—the yo-yo phenomenon and the significance of Pilipino v. Filipino—intersect notions of ethnic authenticity and confront immigrants with a vexing double-bind: on the one hand, comprehensive cultural assimilation (Americanizing one's accent and not succumbing to the yo-yo effect) indicates a progressive degree of successful integration in terms of the immigrant experience; on the other, the ostensible subjugation of the immigrants' authenticity via language and cultural demeanor might suggest a betrayal of the motherland and of their attendant devotion to their ethnicity. In their bleakest manifestations, such phenomena can force immigrants into feeling a sense of nonbelonging—as though they are the citizens, in effect, of nowhere.

As first-generation immigrants who become naturalized American citizens, the Riveras face particular challenges as they attempt to assimilate with the dominant culture of their adopted homeland.[11] The Korean immigrant Haewon Han explains that the intergenerational hierarchy inherent in immigrant families functions as a determining factor in the degree of success or failure in the assimilation process: "When we look at immigration history," he writes, "all the first-generation immigrants brought their own culture, customs, and language and continued associating mostly with their own people." Hence, genuine "assimilation was usually achieved only during the second generation." First-generation immigrant parents like Milagros typically consider themselves strictly in terms of the identity that they created during their lives as members of their pre-diasporic culture. As the children of a first-generation immigrant parent, Voltaire and Rocky face a host of altogether different assimilation challenges. For school-aged immigrant children, "Learning a new language, adjusting to a different educational system, and experiencing native prejudice and hostility toward those with a foreign accent and culture are major obstacles," Kathleen Mullan Harris observes (287). In this manner, Milagros, Voltaire, and Raquel share—and each thrives and suffers under—a paradoxical system of social and cultural stimuli that compels them to grasp for their increasingly distanced ethnic origins, while also permitting them to give in to their acculturated desires for benefiting from the commercial manna of American life. As San Juan notes, the Riveras' "situation can be read as an allegorical rendering of the post-1965 cohort of Filipino immigrants whose neocolonial roots can only prompt a clinging to fragments of indigenous, damaged culture while aping the suburban lifestyle of conspicuous consumerism" (11). Given these constraints, how can each family member attain an altered state of being in relation to their larger sense of self, the other members of their immediate family, and the immigrant and nonimmigrant others who populate their environment?

Understood in this context, the yo-yo phenomenon's capacity for producing a schizophrenic mindset among first-generation immigrants becomes strikingly clear. For Voltaire, life in the United States seems especially unbearable. Sporting his self-styled "Filipino Afro" and wearing a crushed velvet tunic accented with royal purple bell-bottom jeans, Voltaire fashions himself after Hendrix and dabbles as an electric guitarist, although not a particularly gifted one: "It's okay for me to dream, isn't it?" (5). Unable to establish a sense of ethnic identity for himself amidst his mother's yearnings for her cultural past and the seductive, omnipresent trappings of Western materialism, Voltaire suffers, tellingly, from manic-depressive tendencies and falls victim to the yo-yo phenomenon. For much of the novel, he travels back and forth to Manila, where he attempts to recapture his fragmented Filipino soul and reconnect with Luz, the older Rivera sister who stayed behind as well as Francisco Rivera, his estranged father. In *The Gangster of Love*, Voltaire points out that "in Spanish, *yo-yo* means 'I, I'" (225), which denotes the very form of dual subjectivity that underscores the cultural bifurcation of his immigrant self. Determined to halt the fluctuating rhythms of his yo-yo-inscribed persona, Voltaire permanently resettles in the Philippines and pledges to renounce his US citizenship: "Voltaire, you're really backward," one of his relatives exclaims. "Everyone else in this godforsaken country is trying to leave, and you're trying to stay!" (295).

As with her son, Milagros also suffers from the boomerang effect of the yo-yo phenomenon. Milagros's Tagalog name translates as "miracle" in English, and her experiences with Americanization are miraculously successful in comparison to her son's uneasy relationship with the West. Having made her escape from a tyrannical husband—her de facto colonizer who marries another woman illegally on September 21, 1972, the day, ironically enough, when President Marcos declares martial law in the Philippines—Milagros longs for a new world in which to enjoy the advantages of personal freedom as well as from which to prod her alienated husband into altering his totalitarian perspective about their marriage and her individuality: "Our deluded, beautiful mother thought that by running away and spending money my father didn't really have," Rocky remembers, "she could force him to mend his ways. She was a romantic, defiant, and proud woman" (12). Francisco Rivera never chooses to modify his behavior, of course, and the disavowal of his immigrant family begets their inability to move forward in their new lives without the psychological comfort of closure. Milagros spends the rest of her days in America pining for her lost husband and dreaming of the Philippines. While Milagros's yearnings for a love affair with her landlord Zeke Akamine never resulted in the consummation of their intensely romantic relationship—she simply cannot betray Francisco, despite his many ethical failures and his sham marriage to another woman—she succeeds nevertheless in establishing the Lumpia X-Press, a thriving Bay-area business that sells lumpias, the indigenous Filipino variety of egg rolls characterized by their hearty portions of pork, shrimp, or ground beef. Thrilled with her business' success and delighted by her acceptance among her American others, Milagros concocts several lumpia innovations to please her Western customers, including "Mexi-Lumpia (stuffed with avocado and jalapeño chili, salsa on the side) and New Wave Lumpia (bite-sized, vegetarian)" (19).

Yet even as her life comes to a close, Milagros cannot elude the colonizing specter of her Filipino past. In the summer of 1990, Milagros visits Rocky in New York City, the location of Imelda Marcos's sensationalized trial on charges of fraud and racketeering. Simultaneously fascinated and repelled by the sight of the former First Lady, Milagros becomes entranced by Imelda's commanding presence. At one point, "Imelda glances in her direction. Perhaps she notices the genuine pearls around Milagros's neck," Hagedorn writes. "Milagros is sure that Imelda, at the very least, retains a good eye for authentic jewelry" (218). After more than 20 years, the Marcos regime still possesses the power, it seems, to transport Milagros into her colonial past, where her husband and her distant homeland taunt her from afar. Later, as Milagros lies alone on her deathbed in her San Francisco apartment, she reflects upon her life as a reluctant immigrant bent on finding salvation in a foreign land: *"I sailed on a ship for an eternity of seventeen days to California and shut my eyes to save myself and dream"* (252; Hagedorn's italics). While life in America results in many hardships and heartachesfor her, Milagros ultimately experiences an altered post-diasporic perspective distinguished by her ability to transcend the yo-yo phenomenon and shape the course of her own destiny.

In addition to narrating her family's immigrant experiences in the United States, *The Gangster of Love* traces Rocky's cultural journey from Manila to San Francisco, New York City, and then back again to the world of her colonized youth. Rocky's initially effective assimilation owes a particular debt to the realization of her childhood dream of becoming a recording artist in a hard-driving rock-and-roll band. Known as Gangster of Love, the band includes Rocky, the group's vocalist and songwriter as well as Elvis Chang, the flashy guitarist with whom she enjoys a lengthy, torrid affair. As with Milagros and Voltaire, Rocky frequently finds herself at odds with the yo-yo effect and vacillates between her zeal for American life and a stultifying sense of homesickness that culminates in bouts of protracted depression. Rocky intuitively recognizes the semantic distinctions that exist at the heart of her cultural dejection: "The English language confuses me," she confesses. "What is at the core of that subtle difference between *homesick* and *nostalgic*, for example? Why is one preferable over the other? I don't get it." Rocky's analysis of her emotional ties to the Philippines prompts her to address larger questions about the authenticity (or lack thereof) of her postcolonial sense of selfhood: "What's Filipino? What's authentic? What's in the blood?" (57). In such moments, Rocky seeks solace among her relatives and the trappings of her Filipino childhood: "It was back to Uncle Marlon's orchid-filled house to heat up a batch of my mother's party-mix lumpia and my uncle's famous *adobo* and rice," Rocky tells us. "We gossiped, laughed, pigged out, until the sun came up. Filipino soul food, Filipino therapy, the best cure for hangovers and general spiritual malaise" (150).

Rocky's post-diasporic crisis of the self reaches its emotional nadir after the disbandment of Gangster of Love, the demise of her stormy relationship with Elvis, and the birth of her baby, Venus. In many ways, her various attempts at assimilation came to naught. Although the birth of her daughter brings her great joy, her dysfunctional relationship with Jake Montano, Venus's father, only serves to sour her expectations for the future. Rocky's pursuit of the quintessentially

American dream—the cultural touchstone that includes, in some fashion or another, the inalienable right to seek commercial success, romantic love, and a family—leaves her unfulfilled. Desperate for avenues of reconnection with her Filipino soul, Rocky imagines an encounter with the "Carabao Kid," a street poet whom she knew during her childhood in Manila, as well as a fantasy sequence in which she interviews Hendrix, her musical idol. During her imaginary conversation with the Carabao Kid, she chides herself for being too "ambitious" and "trapped in my media-saturated, wayward American skin" (203). Responding to Rocky's cultural impasse, the Carabao Kid tells her to "stop beating yourself up. Your mother's not Imelda Marcos, your father's not that greedy tyrant [Ferdinand Marcos]. What went wrong isn't your fault" (212). Rocky's fantasy interview with Hendrix finally forces her to reconsider her place in the world, to look outward for new spheres of interpersonal connection. With Hendrix's "Voodoo Chile" playing in the background, Rocky lashes out at the dead guitarist for his inability to assist her in healing her cultural bifurcation: "Damn, aren't you listening? Haven't you heard a thing I've said? Everybody I love is dead or dying. I have outlived most of my friends. I have a baby" (236).

In a symbolic effort to repair her sense of cultural vacancy, Rocky inaugurates a self-conscious quest for pathways of reconnection with her late mother and her estranged father. Sifting through the remnants of her mother's San Francisco apartment, Rocky dons Milagros's favorite dress, an "amazing mermaid gown" of "emerald green and completely beaded with shimmering sequins." To Rocky, the form-fitting, shimmering outfit with a matching sequined purse is "very Imelda." Yet when the gown envelops her body, it feels like a "second skin." Suddenly transported back to the islands of her tropical memory, Rocky imagines that "I am a torch singer at the Bayside Club in Manila. I am my mother giddily dancing on a tabletop in Hong Kong twenty-five years ago" (271–2). Rocky completes her voyage of self-rediscovery when she visits the Philippines for the first time in more than two decades. Gazing at a crowded Manila streetscape, she revels in the sight of the "*sampaguita* leis, painfully sweet peanut brittle. Rice cakes wrapped in banana leaves, still steaming. White squares of carabao cheese. Whimsical pot holders stitched from colorful rags" (293). Dazzled once again by her homeland's rich culinary tapestry, Rocky ends her journey at the home of her elderly father. Hagedorn shrewdly leaves the effects of Rocky's visit to the readerly imagination, opting instead to narrate the reunion in silence. By merely depicting Francisco as he anxiously prepares for his daughter's arrival, Hagedorn offers a pointedly neutral conclusion regarding Rocky's future as well as about whether or not she successfully eclipses the lingering wounds of her colonial past.

For Hagedorn, the postcolonial future for culturally bifurcated, first-generation immigrants like Rocky remains inexorably undecided. In *The Gangster of Love*, Hagedorn refuses to provide any facile solutions for an increasingly dispersed community that still reels from the ethical convolutions of the Marcos regime. While individuals may achieve altered states of being through generation after generation of Western immigration, the larger Filipino populace exists in a kind of postcolonial stasis, where identity remains indeterminate and where the future subsists as an empty cultural space. Yet for readers in the post-Marcos period, novels such as *Dogeaters* and *The Gangster of Love* perform important ethical functions by acting as vital correctives for the dominant master-texts of the colonial era. "In the act of narrating the homeland," Nerissa S. Balce writes, "the Filipino American writer inevitably narrates more than memories. Memory and/or the imagination is no longer mere fantasy, simple escape, or contemplation for the writer whose roots lie in the colonial past of a colonized people. By narrating the colonial past," Balce adds, writers like Hagedorn create "counter-narratives" in an express effort to "challenge the colonizer's lies and distortions," as well as to subvert the colonizer's hegemony over their victims' cultural memory. As vivid counter-narratives about the lives of pre- and post-diasporic Filipinos, *Dogeaters* and *The Gangster of Love* afford us with powerful ethical rejoinders to the Philippines' colonial past, while gesturing toward a more hopeful—and potentially altered—postcolonial future.

Part III Music, Image, and Activism: A Means to an Open Ending

8

"Everybody had a hard year": *The White Album* and the Beatles' Poetics of Apocalypse

> We tell ourselves stories in order to live. . . . We look for the sermon in the suicide, for the social or moral lesson in the murder of five. We interpret what we see, select the most workable of the multiple choices. We live entirely, especially if we are writers, by the imposition of a narrative line upon disparate images, by the "ideas" with which we have learned to freeze the phantasmagoria which is our actual universe.
>
> Joan Didion, *The White Album*

> It's hard to describe, even with the clarity of memory, the moment the apple falls. The thing will start moving along at a speed of its own, then you wake up at the end of it and have this whole thing on paper, you know?
>
> John Lennon

Music possesses an innate power to move us in myriad emotional, spiritual, and sensual ways, and the Beatles understood this concept implicitly. They pulsed our adrenaline with "I Want to Hold Your Hand"; they broke our hearts with "Yesterday"; they thrilled our minds with *Sgt. Pepper's Lonely Hearts Club Band* (1967); and they touched our souls with "Let It Be." But with *The White Album* (*The Beatles* 1968), the Beatles literally took us everywhere that music can go. In a self-consciously constructed song cycle that guides the listener from the Cold War-inspired "Back in the USSR" through the psychosexual "Happiness Is a Warm Gun," the somber realities of "Blackbird," and the sheer terror of "Helter Skelter," *The White Album* pits our yearnings for love, hope, and peace in sharp contrast with an increasingly fragmented postmodern void.[1]

Through parody, hyperbole, and bitter irony, *The White Album* tells the story, in highly metaphorical fashion, of the sociocultural calamity that the world experienced in 1968. From assassination and racial unrest to political disjunction and the growing shadows of the Vietnam War, 1968 displaced the optimism of 1967's Summer of Love with equal doses of alienation and uncertainty. And *The White Album*—with the blank, empty space of its glossy pearl cover—dares us to re-inscribe the Beatles' art with our own passion, our own reality, our own terror.

Recorded in January 1969, the coda from "I've Got a Feeling" finds Lennon lamenting that "everybody had a hard year." And it was a hard year indeed. In April 1968, Dr. Martin Luther King Jr. was gunned down in Memphis, Tennessee, by sniper James L. Ray. The assassination of the American civil rights leader spawned riots in more than 60 American cities, resulting in the deaths of 39 people. In contrast with the previous year's Summer of Love, the summer of 1968 replaced the decade's growing senses of hope and optimism with bloody despair. Less than two months later, surging Democratic presidential candidate Robert F. Kennedy was felled by Sirhan Sirhan, a Palestinian who opposed the senator's support for Israel. Kennedy's murder led to a power vacuum that effectively destabilized the antiwar faction of the Democratic party. The summer's awful events reached their nadir in August at Chicago's Democratic National Convention, where thousands of people, including members of Students for a Democratic Society and the Youth International Party (the "Yippies"), gathered to protest against the Vietnam War and the policies of President Lyndon B. Johnson. After violent confrontations erupted between the demonstrators and the Chicago police, Mayor Richard J. Daley ordered some 12,000 officers to attack the protesters with clubs, dogs, and tear gas for nearly three days. Broadcast to a horrified American television viewing audience, the convention's tragic turn of events weakened the support for Democratic candidate Hubert Humphrey, who lost the November 1968 election to Richard Nixon. If you are the Beatles—for whom *Sgt. Pepper* served as the soundtrack for the Summer of Love—how do you go about textualizing the Summer of Hate and Despair?

There is little argument among musicologists and cultural critics alike about the Beatles' inherent literary qualities. After all, their songs—like our greatest works of literature—almost exclusively concern themselves with the human condition and the dilemmas that confront us regarding the interpersonal relationships that mark our lives. The Beatles' albums offer a range of decidedly literary characters, from Mean Mr. Mustard, Eleanor Rigby, and Polythene Pam to Nowhere Man, Lady

Madonna, and Billy Shears. These personages, in addition to the psychological dimensions of the band members' personalities themselves, imbue their works with a particularly literary texture. "The Beatles treated the album as a journey from one place to another," Tim Riley observes. "They built cornerstones into their records by positioning their songs in relation to one another: beginnings and endings of sides can sum up, contradict, qualify, or cast a shadow over the songs they introduce or follow" (29–30). For this reason, one can hardly imagine hearing the final *a cappella* chords of "Because" without anticipating "You Never Give Me Your Money" and the bittersweet nostalgia of the symphonic suite that punctuates the end of the band's career in *Abbey Road* (1969). Similarly, the manner in which "Drive My Car" and "Taxman" introduce *Rubber Soul* (1965) and *Revolver* (1966), respectively, not only signals us about the musical direction of various stages of the band's development, but also becomes inextricably bound up in our successive "listenings" of those recordings. Hence, the positioning of the Beatles' songs on their albums underscores the ways in which the band intended for us to receive—indeed, to interpret—their artistic output. Who could conceive, for example, of listening to the beginning of *The White Album* and not hearing the soaring jet engines that announce the familiar opening strains of "Back in the USSR"?

Perhaps it is the band's abiding self-consciousness about the overall production, design, and presentation of their art that invites us to *read* (and re-read) the Beatles in the first place. From their heyday as recording artists from 1962 through 1969, the Beatles enjoyed a staggering musical and lyrical leap that takes them from their first album *Please Please Me* (1963), which they recorded in a mere 16 hours, to *Sgt. Pepper, The White Album*, and *Abbey Road*, which took literally thousands of hours to complete. Paul McCartney astutely recognized the artistic integrity of their musical *oeuvre* when he referred to their albums as a singular and sacrosanct "body of work." When considered in this fashion, the Beatles' corpus reveals itself to be a collection of musical and lyrical impressions evolving toward an aesthetic unity that appears to reach its artistic heights during the late 1960s and the band's studio years. A number of music critics echo McCartney's sentiments, including Ian MacDonald, who notes that "so obviously dazzling was the Beatles' achievement that few have questioned it." Their recordings, he adds, comprise "not only an outstanding repository of popular art but a cultural document of permanent significance" (1, 33). Riley similarly describes their canon as a "very intricate art. . . .The Beatles are our first recording *artists*," he writes, "and they remain our best" (9, 26; italics added).

In many ways, *Sgt. Pepper* and *Magical Mystery Tour* (1967) exist as mere warm-ups—psychedelic diversions, if you will—in advance of *The White Album*'s more considerable achievement as a compelling act of extended storytelling.[2] Released in November 1968 and the product (in contrast, most notably, with *Please Please Me*) of thousands of hours of studio time, *The White Album* affords its listeners with a host of literary figures, from Dear Prudence, Bungalow Bill, and Rocky Raccoon to Sexy Sadie, a sty of political Piggies, the ghostlike Julia, and a pensive Blackbird "singing in the dead of night." Conceived when albums existed as the self-consciously imagined "sides" of long-playing records, *The White Album*'s first side is a mind-bending suite characterized by moments of arch parody, simple romantic pleasures, and bitter drama. There is "Back in the USSR," complete with its tongue-in-check mergence of Chuck Berry's "Back in the USA" and the Beach Boys' fun-in-the-sun, bikini-clad "California Girls." The result is a brilliant send-up of life behind the Iron Curtain, a world of ostensible mystery and danger—particularly from a Western ideological perspective nursed on *Sputnik* and James Bond—where "Moscow girls make me sing and shout," while the singer entreats his listeners to "come and keep your comrade warm." With the jet engines disappearing beyond the horizon, "Dear Prudence" draws a warm bath of guitar balladry. "Won't you come out to play?" the speaker beckons. The song makes for one of the album's most pleasing interludes, with its daisy chains and carefree romantic disposition. It reveals itself to be transitory, though—like the album's other oases of comfort and solitude—as Ringo Starr's staccato drumbeats usher in "Glass Onion," the Beatles' most self-referential and self-conscious track.

While "Glass Onion" encounters a wide range of Beatles' characters and songs—from "Lady Madonna" and "The Fool on the Hill" to "Fixing a Hole" and "Strawberry Fields Forever"—it takes place, John Lennon reports, on Liverpool's "cast-iron" shore, a paradoxical universe in which the notion of comely beach terrain is undercut by the rust and decay of a dying shipbuilding town.[3] As with the embedded layers of meaning in a composition, peeling back the transparent layers of the Glass Onion reveals a narrative that constantly turns inward upon itself until meaning becomes diffuse, even meaningless. The song's impetus becomes resoundingly clear in its waning moments, as Lennon barks, "Trying to make a dove-tail joint." A work of metapoetry, "Glass Onion" acts as a parable about the act of storytelling, about the difficulty of plying a writerly trade—like Wallace Stevens's "motive for metaphor," where "everything is half dead" with "an obscure moon lighting an obscure world," where the "wind moves like a cripple among the leaves / And repeats word without meaning" (288). The parody thickens in "Ob-La-Di, Ob-La-Da," with its white reggae, south-of-the-border connotations, the hippie nonchalance of "Wild Honey Pie," and "The Continuing Story of Bungalow Bill," which transforms the cold-blooded, thrill-killing of a tiger with the lighthearted air of a children's song. By contrast, George Harrison's "While My Guitar Gently Weeps" is a bitter pill to swallow. The song's maudlin lyrics and pessimistic orchestration reek of unrequited love and wasted life. It is a fitting introduction to what is, quite arguably, the album's philosophical centerpiece, "Happiness Is a Warm Gun," with its cynical lechers, its junkies, and its madmen. The female lead, Lennon sings, is "not a girl who misses much. . . . She's well-acquainted with the touch of the velvet hand / Like a lizard on a window pane." Her sleazy male counterpoint is "the man in the crowd with the multicolored mirrors / On his hobnail boots." He masturbates publicly—"Lying with his eyes while his hands are busy / Working over-time"—before Lennon's psychosexual nether world dissolves into a denunciation of 1950s-era notions of faux innocence and veiled sexuality. "Happiness Is a Warm Gun" is a revolution unto itself: on the one hand, it basks in the seamy residue of unfettered lust, while on the other, it whitewashes our sins with a doo-wop chorus lost amidst its own restless insincerity. In the end, it is a hall of mirrors, and the only way out, it seems, is through an Id-cleansing time warp.

The White Album's rollicking second side reveals—and perhaps more so than any other Beatles album—the ways in which the band's musicality contributes to the lyricism of their narratives. With their dizzying array of musical styles, the nine tracks from "Martha My Dear" through "Julia" loom as masterworks of artistic virtuosity. They also illustrate *The White Album's* stunning eclecticism—the true measure of the album's resilience. McCartney's baroque-sounding "Martha My Dear," with its crisp brass accompaniment, introduces the sequence, which meanders, rather lazily, into Lennon's bluesy "I'm So Tired." Lennon later recalled the song as "one of my favorite tracks. I just like the sound of it, and I sing it well" (quoted in Dowlding 232). Written during the Beatles' visit to the Maharishi Mahesh Yogi's retreat at Rishikesh during the early spring of 1968, McCartney's folksy "Blackbird" imagines a contemplative metaphor for the United States' civil rights struggles during the 1960s. The sound of a chirping blackbird eventually segues into Harrison's edgy political satire, "Piggies." Interestingly, the songwriter's mother, Louise Harrison, composed the tune's signature lyric—a punishment suitable for misanthropic politicians everywhere: "What they need's a damned good whacking!"

The White Album's song cycle continues with McCartney's countrified "Rocky Raccoon," a track that shifts, rather astonishingly, from the disquieting universe of cowboys, gunplay, and saloons into a gentle paean about nostalgia and loss. Having ventured into the "black mountain hills of Dakota," Rocky is dead, quite literally, before the song even starts. Future commutates into present when Rocky, with only Gideon's Bible to nurture his aching heart, pledges to avenge the loss of his beloved—in a masterstroke of ambiguous identity, "Her name was Magil, and she called herself Lil / But everyone knew her as Nancy"—who has left him, it seems, for another man. The expected showdown is intentionally anticlimactic, resulting, as it does, in Rocky's fatal shooting. As he teeters toward death on the drunken physician's table, Rocky optimistically plots his revival: "Doc, it's only a scratch / And I'll be better, I'll be better, Doc, as soon as I am able." With precious little time remaining, Rocky returns to his hotel room, where Gideon has already "checked out," leaving the gunslinger to die alone. In contrast with the Biblical Gideon's theophanic mission to inspire the Israelites, Rocky's spiritual savior sees scant value in rescuing yet another relic from the Old West. With no place in the future and a desolate present spread out before him, Rocky fades away into a quickly receding past. As with the lover's waning romantic aspirations in *Revolver's* "For No One," Rocky can only contemplate the inevitable measure of his loss in an alien world in which nostalgia engenders nothing but sadness and death, spiritual or otherwise.

Starr's "Don't Pass Me By," with its barrelhouse piano chorus, steers the sequence abruptly into the sudsy world of the beer hall. Originally entitled as "Some Kind of Friendly," the song became a number-one hit, rather fittingly, in Scandinavia. One of McCartney's finest blues effusions, "Why Don't We Do It on the Road?" explodes from the embers of "Don't Pass Me By" and brilliantly sets the stage for the side's final two numbers, "I Will" and "Julia." A soothing melody about the tenuous interplay between romance and commitment, "I Will" remains one of McCartney's most memorable experiments in brash sentimentality. Arguably his most powerful ballad, Lennon's "Julia" memorializes the songwriter's late mother while simultaneously addressing his spiritual deliverance at the hands of his new-found soul mate, the "ocean child" Yoko Ono. The somber quietude of "Julia" acts as an ironic counterpoint to side two's rampant animalia, its mock seriousness, and its whimsy. As with the rest of the album, it finds the Beatles seeking to undermine the act of meaning-making at every turn. Just as we are about to bring our interpretations to fruition, the group draws the curtain on the scene before raising it above an entirely different setting. And the resonances shift yet again.

Side three begins with "Birthday"—a spontaneous guitar-bash that the Beatles conjured up on the spot in the studio. It makes for yet another moment of parody, as the band reconceives the act of birthday celebration in their own image. The album shifts gears rather precipitously into "Yer Blues," a razor-edged musing about all-out desolation and suicide. "Yes, I'm lonely / Wanna die," Lennon sings, before invoking Bob Dylan's Mister Jones, the aloof, freakish everyman from "Ballad of a Thin Man": "something is happening here / But you don't know what it is / Do you, Mister Jones?" Ever-mindful of the dislocating power of contrast, the Beatles take yet another musical right turn—in this instance, into the folkways of McCartney's "Mother Nature's Son," which pursues a starkly different line of inquiry. With "Mother Nature's Son," McCartney imagines a pastoral environment in which his speaker lives in an interminably idyllic present: "Born a poor young country boy, Mother Nature's son / All day long I'm sitting singing songs for everyone." Rather than blithely memorializing the past in the vein of *Magical Mystery Tour*'s "Your Mother Should Know," "Mother Nature's Son" establishes an artificial present in which the speaker's yearnings for transcendence have seemingly already been satisfied. Yet as surely as the sun goes down, McCartney's "swaying daisies [that] sing a lazy song beneath the sun" will die. The song rather pointedly avoids the discussion of life's cyclical maneuvers between birth and death, even though the recording's very fleeting subject matter necessarily prefigures a nostalgic experience in some distant (or perhaps not so distant) future.[4] As with "In My Life," "Penny Lane," and "Strawberry Fields Forever," "Mother Nature's Son" depicts life as a generally benevolent experience with scant regard for its corporeal limits.

With a fire bell highlighting its raucous introduction, "Everybody's Got Something to Hide Except for Me and My Monkey" explodes its precursor's sweetness with all of the subtlety of an atomic bomb. Once again connoting the album's larger themes of chaos and uncertainty— "Your inside is out and your outside is in"—the song offers a manic interpretation of love's capacity for effecting disruption and dis-ease. A moment of pure excitement and adrenaline, the guitar riff at the conclusion of "Everybody's Got Something to Hide Except for Me and My Monkey" accentuates an otherwise peculiar song about social politics with the bruising panache of rock-and-roll. It is a rhythmic burst of high-octane modulation that is undermined, rather intentionally, by the clanging, mid-bar introduction of McCartney's piano preamble to

"Sexy Sadie." As Lennon's acidic footnote to the Beatles' experiences under the Maharishi's dubious tutelage, "Sexy Sadie" displaces the previous song's hyper-realized sincerity with pure salaciousness: "We gave you everything we owned just to sit at your table / Just a smile would lighten everything." As McCartney's tinkling piano phrases spar with Harrison's bristling guitar, "Sexy Sadie" maneuvers effortlessly through chord changes and one harmonic shift after another. When the song finally ascends to its closing musical interchange, the Beatles' instrumentation and Lennon's spellbinding vocal coalesce in a breathtaking instance of blissful resolution. For the first time since the plaintive brass accompaniment to "Mother Nature's Son," the album seems to achieve a sense of wholeness. It is a fleeting sensation, of course, that is spoiled by the electric terror inherent in "Helter Skelter." With its shouts and its screams and its scorching guitar work, "Helter Skelter" heightens our sense of trauma through a series of false endings, punctuated by Starr's most notorious moment on record: "I've got blisters on my fingers!" It's a breathless effusion that puts our nightmares to bed, if only temporarily, with Harrison's overtly somber "Long Long Long."

With side four, *The White Album*'s brilliant psychosocial palette reveals a number of instances in which the band presents intentionally contradictory canvases for our inspection, particularly in terms of the so-called "Revolution" series that helps bring the album to a close. In "Revolution 1," Lennon sings about the tempting qualities of revolution and revenge: "When you talk about destruction / Don't you know that you can count me out—in." As with "Happiness Is a Warm Gun," Lennon delivers his polemic against the dislocating backdrop of a 1950s-era "bam shoo-be-doo-wop" refrain. Interestingly, with "Revolution 1," the composition's first iteration, Lennon teeters between revolutionary and antirevolutionary stances: "I put in both because I wasn't sure," he later remarked (quoted in *Anthology* 298). In the more up-tempo, raucous version of the song (entitled simply as "Revolution" and released as the B-side of "Hey Jude"), Lennon abandons his militant extremism, thus embracing the peace movement's pacifist outlook. What renders the song even more compelling, of course, is its author's own uncertainty about violence as a viable interpersonal solution. As Walter Everett observes, the song's "slow tempo, laid-back brass, restful lead vocal, and smooth backing vocals have the calming effect counseled in the lyrics, an effective counterpoise to the revolution sizzling in the distance with metric stabs and distorted electric guitars" (174). And then there is "Honey Pie," a McCartney non sequitur that defuses the inner tension wrought by its predecessor with the white noise of a phonograph needle alighting a 78-RPM record. The guitar rock of "Revolution 1" is exploded by the big-band sounds of yesteryear. "Honey pie," McCartney sings, "You are making me crazy / I'm in love but I'm lazy / So won't you please come home?"[5] The Beatles intend to take us home alright, but not before traversing the dessert fare of Harrison's "Savoy Truffle," with its sax-driven melodies and, as with Lennon's "Glass Onion," its intertextual reference— "We all know Obla-Di-Bla-Da"—that affords the Beatles' larger musical narrative with a sense of coherence and continuity. "Cry Baby Cry" distorts the album's momentum yet again with a series of nonsensical children's nursery rhymes about being "old enough to know better," an implicit reminder that human beings so rarely take their lessons from the past—in spite of the wisdom that it contains. In many ways, it is precisely these sorts of backhanded motifs that set the Beatles apart from the other practitioners of their genre—songwriters who, more often than not, substitute bombast for subtlety.[6]

The Beatles conclude the album with what amounts to their most purposefully disconcerting trio of recordings: the unlisted "Can You Take Me Back?"; the fiercely chaotic "Revolution 9," a jarring montage of indiscriminate noise, tape loops, and sound effects; and "Good Night," the lushly over-sentimentalized lullaby that brings *The White Album* to a close. As the coda for Lennon's "Cry Baby Cry," McCartney's haunting fragment literally pleads for a transcendent return to a simpler past: "Can you take me back where I came from? / Can you take me back?"—a question that will be revisited with dramatically different results in *Abbey Road*'s "Golden Slumbers." The speaker's answer arrives in the menacing form of the Stockhausen-inspired "Revolution 9," some eight minutes of nightmarish surreality. Lennon describes the track as "just abstract, *musique concrète*, [tape] loops, people screaming. . . . I thought I was painting in sound a picture of revolution—but I made a mistake, you know. The mistake was that it was anti-revolution" (*Anthology* 307). Alan W. Pollack rightly describes the recording as a "random anti-narrative effect," which indeed it is. Yet by accruing disruptive layer upon layer throughout that same anti-narrative's stultifying vision, the track succeeds in establishing one of popular music's most disturbing listening experiences. The answer to McCartney's desperate appeal for a return to innocence is nothing short of a resounding negative. "As one of the more infamous achievements of the mid-twentieth-century *avant-garde*," Pollack writes, "Revolution 9"

challenges the listener on both psychological and philosophical grounds. The extent to which the pervasive ambiguity of content teases the listener into projecting a personalized vision of continuity onto the music opens up a radical new dimension to the experience we call "listening." Similarly, the extent to which the background "noise" of real life provides the same kind of narrative ambiguity [is telling;] if we bother to attend to it as thoughtfully as we do to so-called music, then the line between what we call a "composition" and what is merely "random noise" is significantly blurred if not eradicated.

As the haunting landscape of "Revolution 9" recedes from view, a distant harp ushers in the seeming comfort and solace of "Good Night," complete with Starr's warm farewell to the band's understandably disoriented listeners: "Good night, everybody / Everybody everywhere." In this way, *The White Album* pointedly concludes with the intentionally syrupy mawkishness of "Good Night," the band's explicit attempt to console their audience, to provide palpable reassurance in the cataclysmic wake of "Revolution 9." In this way, the Beatles' poetics of apocalypse finds them tempering their larger sense of cultural despair with the lingering images of peace and resilience afforded by "Good Night." In so doing, they opt to mute the chaos and horror with an overtly hopeful gesture.

By reconciling the void on their own terms—by dramatizing it with all of its narrative detachment and terror before euthanizing it with a lullaby of their own making—the Beatles succeed in trumping the fragmentation of their age and achieve something larger and more lasting. With such works as *The White Album* and *Abbey Road*, the Beatles fashioned an abiding legacy based upon our innately human needs for hopefulness and reconciliation. As McCartney remarks, "I'm really glad that most of the songs dealt with love, peace, and understanding. There's hardly any one of them that says: 'Go on, kids, tell them all to sod off. Leave your parents.' It's all very 'All You Need Is Love' or John's 'Give Peace a Chance.' There was a good spirit behind it all, which I'm very proud of" (*Anthology* 357). By seeking wholeness in the midst of life's manifold contradictions, conflicts, and absurdities, *The White Album* suggests that self-awareness and pure human resilience continue to matter in a world beset by violence and turmoil. *The White Album* pointedly reminds us that we can take our broken wings and fly, that we can still say "good night" after the revolution, that we will always find a way to endure. Is there any grander narrative than that?

9

Finding Forgiveness, or Something Like It, in David Mamet's *House of Games, The Spanish Prisoner,* and *State and Main*

> I think that Movies, with few exceptions, have always been trash. I would like to aver that this trash has, historically, been better spirited but, on reflection, I cannot.
>
> David Mamet, *Make-Believe Town*

When we speak about confidence games, we consider them almost entirely in terms of their artfulness, the cleverness with which their perpetrators succeed in the act of deception. We speak about con artistry as being "choreographed," as something to be admired, as being the product of deft timing and intellectual skill. In his screenplays, David Mamet functions as the *auteur* behind many of contemporary cinema's most intricately staged confidence games. Mamet asks his audience to revel in the well-timed sleight of hand, to set aside their ethical preconceptions to enjoy the mastery of his textual masquerade. In short, Mamet's dramaturgy tempts us to lose ourselves in his films, to become conned along with his characters. As viewers of Mamet's films ponder the implications of his con games—pulling back the veil, examining how the cloth was hung so deftly—the gravity of where these lies and deception take both his characters and audiences becomes clarified in terms of Mamet's ethical intentions. Rather than being reduced to a simplistic moral code, Mamet's ethical imperatives find their embodiment in his enduring interest in the mysterious nature of human relationships.[1] As Mamet astutely observes, a dramatic work that functions as pure didacticism or as a morality play whose sole purpose is to impart one-dimensional moral lessons about virtuous behavior, simply cannot account for the rough edges of real life: "It might make a good tract," he remarks, "it might make a good political platform, it might make a good speech. But it can't be art" (quoted in Weber 136).

For a work of literary art to transcend didacticism, it must necessarily challenge its audience by asking them to engage in an experiential narrative event instead of rehearsing an existing canon of laws.[2] For this reason, Mamet self-consciously strives for asymmetry and misdirection in his plays. While reminiscing in his memoir *South of the Northeast Kingdom* (2002) about constructing stone walls at his home in rural Vermont, Mamet compares the act of building walls to his work as a writer: "My wall is falling, here and there, after twenty [years]. I did love building it. Here is an odd-shaped stone. Turn it this way or that, it will not square, set it aside, and now and then, by magic, its asymmetry completes an otherwise unbridgeable gap," Mamet writes. "Perhaps all of us artists like to think of ourselves that way" (60). For Mamet, art's complexity exists in its asymmetry, in its movement away from straight lines and toward the circuitous shapes that human existence inevitably takes. In his screenplays, Mamet illustrates his characters in the act of making complicated choices that will affect the direction of their lives. "Everyone from petty thieves to movie producers in Mamet's canon," Leslie Kane writes, "is judged by his or her behavior and viewed through the lens of ethical choice" (4). The complexity of these decisions ensures that such choices lack the clarity for which didactic or morality plays strive. In a Miltonic understanding of characterological free will, Mamet points out that "any of us has the capacity for atrocity—just as each of us has the capacity for heroism" (*Make-Believe Town* 142). Hence, Mamet's world—founded, as it is, upon a necessarily complicated textual ethics—exists somewhere in the untidy median between absolute good and evil, the place where real human beings pursue their workaday lives.

For Mamet, ethical conceptions of forgiveness and empathy comprise the very soul of his dramaturgy. As Levinas suggests, forgiveness and empathy—an act or leap of faith—can only take place if a person is willing to imagine him- or herself in the life of another, taking on, imaginatively, the other's joy and suffering, the other's confinement and freedom. When this imaginative act of empathy occurs, the distance between the players is closed, and the violence that each might perpetrate upon the other is collapsed. In short, alterity occurs. The perpetrator becomes the victim of his own violence; the victim becomes part of her perpetrator. In this ethical and emotional shift, the possibility for renewal and redemption emerges. A reading of *House of Games* (1987), *The Spanish Prisoner* (1997), and *State and Main* (2000) affords us with a powerful forum for discussing alterity and forgiveness' evolving place in Mamet's textual ethics. As with Hagedorn's novels, the concept of alterity in Mamet's fictive universe does not necessarily connote goodness per se. For Mamet's characters, the recognition of otherness can occur in moments in which they make either positive or negative ethical choices. "There are a number of different kinds of Other," David Corker writes. "There is the Other who is an integral part of oneself because it [involves] the as yet unacknowledged and un-integrated aspects of one's own being; this is the Dialectical Other. There is the Other who is the negative reference group for one's own identity—that is everything which one believes one is not [but may well be]. And there is the Other who is Alien in a more dramatic way because their difference is not able to be utilized as part of oneself." Corker's schema usefully correlates with Mamet's depictions of otherness in *House of Games*, *The Spanish Prisoner*, and *State and Main*, respectively. In each instance, Mamet portrays his characters in the act of achieving various states of otherness as well as different levels of forgiveness with divergent purposes and outcomes. His characters frequently become altered in a Levinasian sense, although they apprehend alterity in radically different ways—and often in relation to the ethical particularities, or lack thereof, of their attendant professions.

In *House of Games*, Mamet devises perhaps the most enigmatic character among his vast dramatic canon. In the film, psychiatrist and self-help author Margaret Ford (Lindsay Crouse) engages in a desperate search for selfhood. By definition, her profession requires her to interpret otherness from a variety of vantage points; in this manner, she creates alternate story lines for her clients as a form of treatment. Played by Crouse with extreme detachment and stoicism, Margaret compulsively takes notes—as psychiatrists are wont to do—to capture the essence of another's sense of self, an aspect that she struggles with in her own life. While her workaholic demeanor has resulted in a thriving practice and a best-selling self-help guide entitled *Driven: Obsessions and Compulsions in Everyday Life*, this same quality finds her grasping for an increasingly fragile sense of selfhood, a blank slate, of sorts, waiting to be inscribed. A visit to the aptly titled House of Games brings her into the orbit of Mike (Joe Mantegna), the flim-flam man who orchestrates a series of confidence games that will transform Margaret's life. While on a mission to settle a gambling debt for a wayward client, Margaret agrees to help Mike fleece a cardsharp during a high-stakes poker game. In so doing, Margaret becomes unknowingly enmeshed in a larger scheme designed to cheat her out of her life savings.

In the process, Margaret develops what she believes to be a friendship with Mike and his gang. She ultimately enjoys a romantic interlude with

Mike, although it is difficult to tell where her love for the confidence game begins and her affection for the con artist ends. As Margaret ventures into the interior layers of Mike's convoluted ruse, she begins to perceive psychiatry as a con game in its own right, a conclusion that finds her shifting allegiances and energies from her profession to the more seductive world—from her socially conflicted perspective—of the confidence game. She is particularly attracted by Mike's capacity for reading the other. As a con artist, he gives her lessons about how to recognize a "tell," the physical gesture that reveals a person's intentions despite his or her best efforts to conceal them. In contrast with psychiatry—a profession whose validity she increasingly doubts—the con game explicitly works to change a person's behavior with gratifying results. For Mike, the con exists as a depersonalized activity, as a business transaction devoid of pleasure or emotional connection. Unlike Mike, Margaret cannot differentiate between these two realms of meaning. As a psychiatrist, Margaret suffers from similar boundary issues—the very phenomenon that brought her to the House of Games in the first place.

The otherness that Margaret seeks initially through her profession and subsequently via her relationship with Mike proves to be as illusory as any two-bit con game. Using Corker's terminology, Mike functions as Margaret's Dialectical Other because she remains unable to establish a unified sense of self that acknowledges or integrates fundamental aspects of her personality into its being. Margaret denounces her profession as a "sham" and a "con game" to a fellow psychiatrist because of her overarching compulsion to help her patients—*all* of her patients—to overcome their maladies. This unacknowledged aspect of her persona drives her even deeper into the arms of the con men, who, from Margaret's troubled perspective, never seem to fail at hoodwinking their clientele. Seemingly recognizing Margaret's desire to change her life, Mike observes that she needs "somebody to come along, somebody to possess you, to take you into a new thing. Would you like that? Do you want that?" Later, he entreats her to "call yourself what you are." Margaret's telling response—"What am I?"—prompts Mike to provide the film's most prescient advice—a lesson, incidentally, that Margaret is psychologically ill-equipped to absorb in any healthy fashion: "There are many sides to each of us," Mike tells her. "Good blood. Bad blood. Somehow all those parts have got to speak." When Margaret realizes the extent of her victimization within Mike's highly structured con game, she self-consciously opts to eschew alterity—and its potential for bringing her sense of selfhood into bold relief—rather than follow Mike's advice about learning to separate business from pleasure. In short, she refuses to see the other, thereby denying herself of the possibility of experiencing empathy.

By personalizing Mike's duplicitous behavior, Margaret can no longer recognize the spheres of otherness that he purports to possess. Unable to reconcile the complexity of Mike's various façades, Margaret fashions a con game of her own to exact revenge upon the Dialectical Other whom she intends to destroy. Simply put, she self-consciously chooses to kill Mike—to erase the face of his otherness—when he refuses to apologize for his profession: "You say I acted atrociously. Yes, I did," he readily admits. "I do it for a living." Mike seals his fate when he exposes Margaret's own complicity in her descent into the shadowy world of the confidence game. "You learned some things about yourself that you'd rather not know," he tells her. When Margaret kills Mike, she does so in an attempt to expunge the self-knowledge that Mike has revealed. Without the ethical counterpoint that Mike represents, alterity becomes impossible for Margaret because of the absence of sameness and her capacity for self-recognition. "All alterity is negated by murder," Levinas reminds us. "Being myself," he continues, "I already ask myself whether my being is justified, whether the *Da* of my *Dasein* is not already the usurpation of someone's place" (*Alterity* 28). When Margaret usurps Mike's existence, she enters into the film's most elaborate con game, a self-fulfilling ruse in which she succeeds in conning herself into believing that self-forgiveness mitigates any ethical responsibility or consequences. "When you've done something unforgivable, you must forgive yourself," she avows. By forgiving herself without impunity, Margaret silences her good conscience—the "good blood" of which Mike speaks— and, in so doing, damns and diverts any possibility for genuine absolution, the kind of self-reflexive critique that allows for an authentic sense of emotional reparation.

With *The Spanish Prisoner*, Mamet shifts his attention from the Dialectal Other to an Other, in Corker's parlance, who functions as the negative reference group for shaping a character's identity. The film depicts the priggish, albeit kindhearted Joe Ross (Campbell Scott) in an identity crisis of sorts that finds its origins in conflicting aspects of his personality. On the one hand, he comports himself as an earnest, hardworking businessman—"a real Boy Scout," as one of the characters observes; yet on the other, he longs for the material rewards that he believes his ethical mindset and industriousness should merit. In short, he is a perfect mark for the long con orchestrated by Jimmy Dell (Steve Martin), a smooth-talking grifter who poses as a well-heeled entrepreneur replete with all of the extravagances and trappings of a prosperous lifestyle. In its cinematic representations, the long con requires the existence of a reference group with which the mark has little experience. Existing on the fringes of this group, the mark desires entrée into its ranks, often becoming so enticed by its wealth and privilege that his ethical perceptions seem murky, rendering him even more vulnerable to the con's seductive façade.

In the latter stages of developing the "Process," a deliberately vague business scheme for establishing market supremacy, Joe finds himself rectangulated—for lack of a better word[3]—by his boss, Mr. Klein (Ben Gazzara), who seems intentionally noncommittal about Joe's compensation for the Process' imminent success; by Jimmy, who suddenly materializes in Joe's life as the manifestation of the affluent otherness that he desires with ever-increasing desperation; and by Susan Ricci (Rebecca Pidgeon), Joe's congenial secretary who seemingly offers the possibility of romance, thus creating yet another diversion in his increasingly complicated life. Figuratively boxed in by his ostensibly conflicting relationships with Mr. Klein, Jimmy, and Susan, Joe is afforded with a litany of unsolicited advice from his triumvirate of new friends. "If we all do our jobs, we will each be rewarded according to our just desserts," Mr. Klein tells him. Meanwhile, Jimmy counsels Joe to "always do business as if the person you're doing business with is trying to screw you, because he probably is. And if he's not, you can be pleasantly surprised." Finally, Susan renders Joe's outlook even more muddled, pointing out that "it just shows to go you, you never know who anybody is." With growing paranoia about his fate as the inventor of the Process, Joe begins to doubt both the ethics of his profession and his apparently inconsequential role in its machinations. Only Jimmy and Susan, it seems, can offer Joe the possibility of being rewarded for his toil as well as for transforming his life into something more substantial, more lucrative. Joe's trusty colleague, attorney George Lang (Ricky Jay), unwittingly provides him with the catalyst for his naïve progress into the waiting arms of the flim-flam men: "Do you know what your problem is, Joe? You're too nice. You do everything for everybody else, and nothing for yourself." By highlighting his friend's earnest devotion to principles of fairness and responsibility, George succeeds in making Joe's negative reference group appear even more alluring.

Determined to do something for himself for a change, Joe accepts Jimmy's professed friendship and Susan's increasingly flirtatious overtures.[4] Waxing sincere in an effort to appeal to Joe's Boy-Scout persona, Susan remarks that "I'm a helluva person. I'm loyal, and I'm true, and I'm not too hard to look at." As with Jimmy's wealth and largesse, Susan presents Joe with yet another possibility for changing his life. Joe is seduced by his encounters with one false other after another, each of whom belongs to a negative reference group in contrast with their mark's most glaring weakness—his intensely ethical demeanor, particularly his steadfast desire for fairness and justice in his own life. In many ways, these aspects of Joe's identity signal a lack of maturity on his part in terms of his personal ethical philosophy; indeed, a value system based upon recompense and retaliation only succeeds in creating a hollow, self-serving sense of equality. His devotion to justice renders him ill-equipped, then, to recognize the artificial boundaries inherent in the philosophical complexities of pursuing an ethical life under real-world conditions. Hence, we witness Joe in the act of discovering the painful truth about the duplicity of each member of his negative reference group.

After Jimmy's friendship is revealed to be mere sham and pretense to steal the Process—a feat that he accomplishes with the assistance of a group of con artists masquerading as undercover FBI agents—Joe's world continues to unravel with the murder of George, an innocent bystander in Jimmy's long con as well as with Mr. Klein's mounting pressure for Joe to retrieve the Process. Ultimately, Joe's belief system—and the long con itself—collapses when he realizes Susan's considerable role in his undoing. Only Mamet's *deus-ex-machina* conclusion in the form of a pair of undercover federal marshals prevents Jimmy from killing Joe— and with Susan's rather spirited approval, no less. Susan's betrayal of him and his near-death experience force Joe into an ethical retreat from the corrupt value systems of his negative reference group and back toward the safer parameters of his self-contained, albeit unsophisticated philosophy of individuation and justice. Levinas contends that individuation involves a self-conscious effort to disconnect or disengage oneself from the other. As Levinas observes

> Subjective existence derives its features from separation. Individuation—an inner *identification* of a being whose essence is exhausted in identity, an identification of the same—does not come to strike the terms of some relation called separation. Separation is the very act of individuation, the possibility for an entity which is posited in being to be posited not by being defined by its references to a whole, by its place within a system, but starting from itself. The fact of starting from oneself is equivalent to separation. But the act of starting from oneself and separation itself can be produced in being only by opening the dimension of interiority. (*Totality* 299–300)

By re-asserting his sense of interiority—and thus completing his separation from the other—Joe fulfills his return to the more dependable confines of his emergent selfhood. As *The Spanish Prisoner* comes to a close, Susan begs Joe to rescue her from the fate that she and Jimmy, as his victimizers, have authored for themselves. "Can you help me?" she pleads. "You're the Boy Scout. Can I be your good deed for the day?" Recognizing that Susan desires a form of forgiveness that he simply cannot provide, given the rigidity of his ethical system, Joe reverts to the flirtatious banter that characterized their relationship throughout the con. "I'm afraid you're going to have to spend some time in your room," he tells her. With the possibility of genuine alterity looming before him, Joe greets the face of the other with playful insincerity. He has seen the other alright—but he has also seen far more than his ethical system can stomach.

As with *House of Games* and *The Spanish Prisoner*, *State and Main* finds Mamet in the act of skewering the ethical failings of yet another profession—his own. In *State and Main*, Mamet dissects Hollywood's questionable value systems within the relatively bucolic environs of small-town America. Much of the film is focalized through the character of Joe White (Philip Seymour Hoffman), a neurotic playwright making his screenwriting debut as the author of *The Old Mill*, the Hollywood production that steamrolls its way into Waterford, Vermont, where it infiltrates nearly every facet of the townspeople's lives. In many ways, the film's director Walt Price (William H. Macy) functions as Joe's ethical foil, contrasting movieland's self-serving nihilism with Joe's naïve belief in the limitless power of the pen. For Walt, language exists as an express tool for disguising the falsehood and insincerity that he peddles with veritable ease: "It's not a lie," he proclaims. "It's a gift for fiction." While Walt registers little, if any, remorse or self-consciousness for the repercussions of his serial duplicity, Joe obsesses at nearly every turn about the awesome responsibility that being an artist entails, especially a Pulitzer Prize-winning playwright like himself.[5] As with his screenplay's nineteenth-century-era protagonist, Joe is absorbed in a "quest for purity" of his own.

At the beginning of *State and Main*, Joe consistently asserts the authority and autonomy of the self through his insistence that his screenplay cannot be distorted by the commercially driven desires of Hollywood's short-sighted value systems. Hollywood functions as Joe's Alien Other, in Corker's postulation—the ethical counterpoint to his personal rage for purity. Simply put, Hollywood exists as the long con writ large. In short order, Joe discovers that the production of a Hollywood movie is a confidence game in itself, an enterprise that employs ethical compromise as the modus operandi of its business and creative practices. Joe's ethical conversion involves an ironic shift from an inflexible belief in the power of art to allowing himself to be corrupted by Hollywood, a movement away from a self-contained philosophy of individuality toward a more balanced perspective of his place in the world. Joe's ethical transformation begins, rather appropriately, when his typewriter—the symbol of his search for purity as an artist—is lost during the production's relocation to Vermont. His search for a replacement brings him into the orbit of Ann Black (Rebecca Pidgeon), the owner of an independent bookstore who dreams of transforming Waterford into a viable arts community by revitalizing the *Waterford Sentinel*, the town's defunct newspaper, and creating a thriving amateur-theater scene.[6] As with Joe, Ann is no stranger herself to the notion of compromise, given her engagement to local politician Doug MacKenzie (Clark Gregg), a shameless, self-promoting grandstander.

Joe's alterity emerges via the finite sense of Levinasian freedom that his budding relationship with Ann provides. Through her society, he comes to realize that his conception of absolute freedom and his misconstrued notions of purity originate from his fallacious idea of a limitless self. "Does the finitude of freedom signify the necessity by which a will to will finds itself in a given situation which limits the arbitrariness of the will?" Levinas asks. "In finite freedom, there can then be disengaged an element of pure freedom, which limitation does not affect, in one's will" (*Otherwise* 123–4). For Joe, the writerly autonomy that he enjoys as a playwright allows him to dissociate himself from the Alien Other. Joe is altered via Ann's artful ruse in the film's final reel, a short con that allows him to commit an ethical transgression without any ultimate consequence. The film's central crisis concerns the fallout from an accident at the corner of State and Main, where Joe witnesses a car wreck involving *The Old Mill*'s leading man, Bob Barrenger (Alec Baldwin), a lecherous B-movie actor with a penchant for seducing underage girls. After Bob and his latest conquest, local high school student Carla Taylor (Julia Stiles), emerge from the accident with minor injuries, Bob convinces her to leave the scene in a hasty effort to conceal their illegal liaison. Still reeling from his broken romance with Ann, Doug appropriates the incident to exact his revenge by destroying the movie production that brought Joe to Waterford in the first place.

As the car accident's only witness, Joe could tell the truth by testifying to Bob's unlawful relationship with Carla. Conversely, he could lie about Carla's role in the accident, thus preventing Bob's imprisonment and saving the movie from ruin. Using the courtroom set of a community theater production aptly entitled *Trials of the Heart*, Ann arranges for Joe to testify before a local actor portraying a judge.[7] Motivated by self-interest and under considerable pressure from Walt and Marty Rossen (David Paymer), the movie's merciless producer, Joe perjures himself. Almost immediately, Joe recognizes the extent of his falsehood, believing that his behavior has defeated his cherished quest for purity. Later, when Joe discovers Ann's ruse, he realizes that her act of deception has given him a second chance to redeem himself no matter the consequences. "I thought that you needed to get it out of your system," she tells him. In this manner, Ann's miniature con game allows Joe to forgive himself for his perjury as well as to move beyond his unyielding personal philosophy of freedom and individuality.

As with *The Spanish Prisoner*, Mamet effects yet another *deus-ex-machina* conclusion in *State and Main* through the 11th-hour arrival of the studio executive Howie Gold (Jonathan Katz) who brings $800,000 from Hollywood, which Walt and Marty use to buy Doug's—and ultimately, Waterford's—complicity. The film's *deus ex machina* acts as an engine of universalizing forgiveness via which the town can coexist with Hollywood's Alien Other. Perhaps even more significantly, this same engine affords Joe with the opportunity to negotiate a new philosophical system for himself in which he can work for Hollywood without being cannibalized by his association with its ethically vacuous dream factory. In contrast with the more cynical marks in *House of Games* and *The Spanish Prisoner*, Joe enjoys a genuinely altered relationship with the ethically conflicted others who pock his personal universe. Yet, despite Joe's ultimate complicity in *The Old Mill*'s production, Mamet clearly refuses to demonize his protagonist.[8] As the film comes to a close, Mamet pointedly depicts Joe as an enthusiastic participant on the set who implicitly approves of *The Old Mill*'s greatest ethical *faux pas*—a ridiculous product-placement scheme cooked up by Marty involving an anachronistic advertisement for a computer company. Within nearly the same instant in which it foments a sense of communal forgiveness, Hollywood cannot help but betray the moment by reverting to the very same bankrupt value systems that drove it to the brink of ruin in the first place.

In addition to exposing the long con that Hollywood perpetuates across the globe, *State and Main* reveals Mamet in the act of questioning the ways in which producers, directors, and screenwriters deliberately involve us—and often with the blessing that we evince by paying the price of admission—in a con game that inevitably reveals something about ourselves. Even more intriguingly, *State and Main* demonstrates

Mamet, in a moment of metatextual exuberance, in the act of forgiving himself for participating in Hollywood's ethically problematic system. Obviously, Mamet could not produce a film like *State and Main* without recognizing that he is complicit within the very system that he seeks to critique. How else could he succeed in getting his films made in Hollywood? Mamet's depiction of Ann's selfless generosity of spirit underscores his own struggle with the complexities of forgiving others and effecting self-absolution within—or perhaps in spite of—a system that is at once profoundly perverse and at the same time filled with so much possibility for interpersonal redemption. In this way, Mamet encounters the "paradox of the pardon of fault" that Levinas addresses in *Totality and Infinity*. "Why is the beyond separated from the below?" Levinas asks. "Why, to go unto the good, are evil, evolution, drama, separation necessary?" For Levinas, forgiveness entails "a rupture of continuity" followed by "a continuation across this rupture" (284). If nothing else, Mamet's films demonstrate the other in the process of creating or facilitating this rupture. Only alterity, it seems, can afford us with a map for moving beyond the wreckage of our lives.

10
Performing Empowerment: Revisiting Liberation Pedagogy in Eve Ensler's *The Vagina Monologues*

> Art is not merely contemplation, it is also action, and
> all action changes the world, at least a little.
>
> Tony Kushner

As we learned in our discussion of the poetry of Mary Swander, the body is a highly performative text that is capable—in its own, uncanny way—of extracting particular truths about the nature of our humanity and our capacity for endurance. This is especially true of the work of playwright Eve Ensler, who challenged an entire civilization's perspectives about the female body.

Our story begins on the evening of June 9, 2001, as an eclectic group of women and men, largely consisting of tourists, pensioners, and young professionals, waited nervously for the house lights to extinguish before a performance of Ensler's controversial one-woman show, *The Vagina Monologues*. Staged at London's New Ambassadors Theatre in the heart of the city's West End theater district, *The Vagina Monologues* seemed like an unlikely offering among the more commercially driven productions such as *The Lion King*, *The Phantom of the Opera*, and *Mamma Mia!* As Ensler uttered her famous opening line—"I bet you're worried. *I* was worried"—the set's lighting system began to fail. Frustrated about being thrust into darkness on one too many occasions, Ensler eventually interrupted the show and challenged her audience to subject themselves to something unique among her play's storied history. Simply put, she proposed performing the balance of *The Vagina Monologues* under the house lights. Audience members would no longer be able to experience the play's frank talk about female genitalia and sexuality under the cover of darkness. When the lights went up on the tiny New Ambassadors Theatre, Ensler invited her audience to render themselves even more emotionally defenseless than usual, to become self-conscious about the mutual vulnerability that each member shared with the other theatergoers in attendance. In short, she asked her audience to liberate themselves by becoming *part* of the text, as opposed to being the mere consumers of its sensational contents who may or may not opt to ponder the play's significance in the future. For the West End audience at *The Vagina Monologues* on that June night, the time for reflection had suddenly arrived.

In *The Vagina Monologues*, Ensler liberates our conceptions of the female body via the theater of empowerment that she fashions out of a series of intimate anecdotes and performative villanelles.[1] Drawing upon the revelatory critical lens inherent in Paulo Freire's *The Pedagogy of the Oppressed* (1970), we can understand the rhetorical machinery of Ensler's play in terms of its capacity for raising consciousness and engendering social change. In particular, Freire's notion of a liberation pedagogy affords us with a mechanism for addressing the nature of political education, the synergy that exists between teachers and learners, and the transformative power of establishing a critical consciousness through dialogue and the construction and solution of problems. Freire's model of a liberation pedagogy advocates education and knowledge making as the means for counteracting the frequently overwhelming "discursive gestures" of a patriarchal culture. Reading Ensler's monologues through Freire's eight principles of a liberation pedagogy reveals the manner in which her play attempts to create a global dialogue about the veil that envelops female sexuality and violence against women. In *The Vagina Monologues*, Ensler's theatrical representation of female sexuality allows her to pierce the "culture of silence"[2] that problematizes women's experiences with their bodies in Western society. As Jeanie Forte astutely observes, "At this point in history it is politically imperative that feminists construct the language, the theoretical models, that will enable analysis of feminine praxis and the oppressions of the female body" (259). By speaking about the unspeakable, Ensler's play implores her audience members—male as well as female—to enter into the kind of dialogue that may yet liberate them from contemporary society's convoluted sexual tyranny. She does not merely ask her audience to reconcile the void—she dares them to usurp it.

A previously obscure playwright and actress, Ensler first conceived of the idea for *The Vagina Monologues* after having a conversation with an older woman about her vagina. The woman was "saying contemptuous things about her genitals that shocked me and got me thinking about what other women thought about their vaginas," Ensler recalls in her introduction to the play. "I remember asking friends, who surprised me with their openness and willingness to talk" (xxiv). Since its debut in 1996 at an off-Broadway theater, *The Vagina Monologues* has been performed in some 31 countries in 26 different languages. The recipient of a 1997 Obie Award, the play has been performed by such luminaries as Erica Jong and Linda Ellerbee during its three-year run at New York City's Westside Theatre. More than 500 college theatrical troupes performed the play in 2002 on behalf of V-Day, a nonprofit organization that raises millions of dollars per year for various women's organizations. "The miracle of V-Day, like *The Vagina Monologues*, is that it happened because it had to happen," Ensler writes. "*In order for the human race to continue, women must be safe and empowered.* It's an obvious idea, but like a vagina, it needs great attention and love in order to be revealed" (xxxvi; Ensler's italics). In this way, *The Vagina Monologues* performs an explicitly activist function in the world of contemporary theater, an increasingly global marketplace that often sacrifices any semblance of a social agenda in favor of the demands of commercialism and the bottom line.

According to the organization's website, V-Day embraces a vision of human life "where girls and women live free, safe, equal and with dignity." Founded in 1998, V-Day champions "a spirit affirming that life should be lived, creating and thriving, rather than surviving victimization and recovering from atrocities." Finally, V-Day supports "a determination to end violence against women."[3] In itself, the organization's program for women's empowerment offers a prescription for a liberation pedagogy based upon principles of human dignity and equality. Similarly, Freire's conception of a liberation pedagogy functions as a process for learning and knowing about ourselves and our relation with the larger communities in which we live within the context of power, agency, and history. As a kind of "discourse of experience," in Freire's words, a liberation pedagogy attempts to create a dialogue that inspires an innate human curiosity about the acquisition of knowledge and its capacity for effecting change. In *The Pedagogy of the Oppressed*, Freire describes this process as a "pedagogy which must be forged *with*, not *for*, the oppressed (whether individuals or peoples) in the incessant struggle to regain their humanity." Freire contends that this "pedagogy makes oppression and its causes objects of reflection by the oppressed, and from that reflection will come their necessary engagement in the struggle for their liberation. And in the struggle this pedagogy will be made and remade" (48). In short, Freire advocates a process through which the oppressed achieve a greater sense of their own humanity by ensuring that their oppressors participate directly in their liberation.

Originally conceived as a program for addressing the plight of Brazil's massive population of illiterate urban poor people, Freire's liberation pedagogy provides us with a powerful critical language for exploring the gender issues in *The Vagina Monologues*. As with Brazil's crisis of the dispossessed, women's sexuality continues to be marginalized by a patriarchal culture that colonizes our notions of the female body—whether we be male *or* female—by a variety of means that includes religion, psychology, the media, and the entertainment industry, among a host of other power bases. For Freire, the notion of a liberation pedagogy operates as a "pedagogy of humankind." His pedagogy of the oppressed involves two stages as well as the eight principles that will be discussed in detail below. In the first stage, "the oppressed unveil the world of oppression and through the praxis commit themselves to its transformation." In the second stage, "the reality of the oppression has already been transformed" and a pedagogy emerges that accounts for "all people in the process of permanent liberation" (54). By tracing the evolution of Ensler's narrative in *The Vagina Monologues*, we can demonstrate the ways in which her text underscores the capacity of Freire's pedagogy to establish a self-empowering environment with the potentiality for "permanent liberation."

In the three decades since its publication, Freire's *Pedagogy of the Oppressed* has endured a number of critical attacks regarding its relevance to the experiences of the oppressed in Western society, his perceived usage of sexist or elitist language, and what some of his detractors consider to be his over-arching emphasis upon the class struggle to the detriment of other social issues.[4] While conducting a course on "Media and Anti-Racist Pedagogies," for example, Elizabeth Ellsworth argues that "we produced results that were not only unhelpful, but actually exacerbated the very conditions we were trying to work against, including Eurocentrism, racism, sexism, [and] classism. . . . To the extent that our efforts to put discourses of critical pedagogy into practice led us to reproduce relations of domination in our classroom." Ellsworth adds, "these discourses were 'working through' us in repressive ways, and had themselves become vehicles of repression" (44). In dramatic contrast with Freire's findings in *The Pedagogy of the Oppressed*, Ellsworth's experiences during the course led to the understandable conclusion that her students could only realize actual social progress by disengaging themselves from the subject instead of grappling directly with the spurious ideologies inherent in racism and sexism.

Interestingly, the textual construction and theatrical effect of *The Vagina Monologues* itself answers many of the criticisms regarding the contemporary efficacy of Freire's postulation of a liberation pedagogy, particularly in terms of the issues leveled by Ellsworth. As a highly performative text, Ensler's play compels audiences to engage in a debate with the prevailing social and political structures that have resulted in female inequality and the disenfranchisement of the female body. The act of performance in Ensler's case conforms explicitly to Jeanne Colleran and Jenny S. Spencer's notion of "staging resistance"—their terminology for denoting works of contemporary drama that necessarily seek to disrupt cultural or ideological norms. Any drama that stages resistance, Colleran and Spencer remark, functions as a self-conscious forum "for public debate, a gauge of national aspirations, an enactment of social critique, and a space for imagining alternatives" (10). By drawing her audience into a resistant text of her own making, Ensler urges us into a kind of self-dissociation from our socially encoded value systems that allows audience members to share in the theatrical experience and to enjoy a sense of unity, however illusory it may be, during any given performance. In addition to leading her audience as they chant *Cunt!* in an effort to ease their socially inscribed inhibitions about genital euphemisms, Ensler accomplishes this end through a series of simultaneously moving and disconcerting dialogues about the female body. According to Susan Broadhurst, such gestures produce a liminal form of theatrical excitement as well as intentional feelings of disquiet and discomfort. "Liminal performance," Broadhurst writes, "strives to play to the edge of the possible, continually challenging not only performance practice but also traditional aesthetic concepts."[5] Hence, the liminality of overtly political plays such as *The Vagina Monologues* ultimately establishes "an experimental extension of our social, cultural, and political milieu" (1–2). In this way, Ensler exploits the play's performative components to confront her audience with radically different ways of thinking about the place of women and the female body in contemporary life. Indeed, do we engage in any genuinely open discussion about female genitalia other than as an intentionally conspicuous form of derision?

Freire's eight principles of a liberation pedagogy afford us with an epistemology for examining the ways in which Ensler's various monologues attempt to disrupt the socially constructed systems of repression that characterize our perspectives about the female body.[6] The first of Freire's principles advocates a value-driven and politically activist educational stance. In this precept of Freire's liberation pedagogy, teachers challenge their students to conceive of themselves as participants in the creation of more democratic and liberating value systems. In her introductory monologue, Ensler—via the activist-teacherly persona that she adopts in her performances in *The Vagina Monologues*—sets in motion a process for deconstructing our prevailing cultural ideologies about the vagina. In addition to providing a context for understanding the ways in which women come to devalue their own anatomy, Ensler assists her audience in comprehending the veil of secrecy that cloaks our conceptions of the vagina by desensitizing its multifarious (and often ridiculous) euphemisms. She delivers a lengthy catalogue of slang that ranges from "pussycat," "pooki," and "twat" to "coochie snorcher," "nappy dugout," and "split knish," among others (5–6). Ensler also engages her audience in an educational manner by reciting a series of "vagina facts" throughout the play. In what is clearly her favorite of these factoids, Ensler clarifies the explicit purpose of the clitoris:

> It is the only organ in the body designed purely for pleasure. The clitoris is simply a bundle of nerves: 8,000 nerve fibers, to be precise. That's a higher concentration of nerve fibers than is found anywhere else in the body, including the fingertips, lips, and tongue, and it is twice. . .twice. . .twice the number in the penis. Who needs a handgun when you've got a semiautomatic. (51)

Ensler encourages audience participation by inviting spectators to request impromptu encores of this particular vagina fact throughout each performance. In this way, she draws audience members into a multidirectional forum in which they may interact with her play's central thesis, as well as the motivation for her crusade on behalf of the female body: "I am worried about vaginas" (6).

Freire's second principle for a liberation pedagogy contends that teachers and learners exist in a synergistic relationship in which both parties contribute their experiences and perceptions to create knowledge. Freire's detractors often take issue with this particular aspect of his pedagogy because it seems to suggest that people generally do not reflect critically upon the nature of their own lives and experiences. As George Dei argues, "There is a disturbing failure [in Freire's pedagogy] to recognize that local peoples do theorize in their communities as part of community life, that they not only articulate but also interpret their experiences" (140). Yet in *The Vagina Monologues*, Ensler clearly assumes that her spectators possess prior knowledge and have reflected about various issues regarding their conceptions of female anatomy. She simply draws these perspectives into a discursive space by self-consciously providing her audience with opportunities to identify with women's experiences regarding their vaginas and the role of their genitalia in shaping their selfhood. Ensler deftly illustrates the validity of Freire's second principle through her monologue entitled "The Vagina Workshop." In this narrative, Ensler takes on the persona of a matronly English woman who, on her own volition no less, attends a workshop designed to help women achieve self-awareness about their bodies. As the workshop comes to a close, the woman locates her clitoris, climaxes, and demystifies the source and nature of orgasm: "*My vagina is a shell, a tulip, and a destiny. I am arriving as I am beginning to leave. My vagina, my vagina, me*" (50; Ensler's italics). In this guise, Ensler invites her audience to share in the woman's most cherished moment of self-discovery in an effort to engender new perspectives about ourselves. Perhaps even more importantly, she empowers us via the woman's story to assume responsibility for our own sexuality and reminds us of our own capacity for initiating and celebrating self-transformation in our lives.

Freire's third principle concerns the creation of a mechanism in which people attempt to understand and alter their perspectives through dialogue and a teacher-facilitated process of naming. This dialogical methodology encourages learners to imagine and put into practice new senses of reality. As Freire remarks in *The Pedagogy of the Oppressed*, "To exist humanly is to name the world, to change it. Once named, the world in its turn reappears to the namers as a problem and requires of them a new *naming*" (88). In short, the namers author their own liberation pedagogy through the auspices of language. In *The Vagina Monologues*, Ensler fashions a series of soliloquies that address this very issue by asking women to engage in the process of renaming—indeed, recapturing—the essence of their bodies. The content of these monologues finds its origins in Ensler's interviews with women about the appearance and personalities of their vaginas. When asked "*If your vagina got dressed, what would it wear?*" Ensler's subjects offered a range of responses, which she incorporates into her performance as a series of humorous one-liners. Their answers—which include such apparel as "a beret," "a leather stocking," "a pink boa," "combat boots," and "a pinafore"—reveal women in the act of re-presenting aspects of themselves about which they wish to learn more (15–17; Ensler's italics). A similar question "*If your vagina could talk, what would it say, in two words?*" elicited a variety of frequently hilarious, albeit equally illuminating responses, including "slow down," "feed me," "brave choice," "I'm here," and "let's go" (19–20; Ensler's italics). Simply put, the act of renaming affords Ensler's interviewees—and, hence, her audience—with a process for taking control of their bodies and fashioning new perceptions of themselves.

With his fourth principle, Freire's liberation pedagogy proposes the exploration of relevant interpersonal issues in an effort to stir up a passion for activism among students. In her monologues entitled "My Vagina Was My Village" and "My Angry Vagina," Ensler attempts to stimulate an emotional connection between her audience and the women's experiences in her narratives. Both monologues depict female characters as they recall the emotional effects of bodily invasion. Effecting a lifeless, desolate voice, Ensler embodies the spirit of a Bosnian refugee who fell victim to the unspeakable traumas of a rape camp:

> My vagina [was] a live wet water village.
> They invaded it. Butchered and burned it down.
> I do not touch now.
> Do not visit.
> I live someplace else now.
> I don't know where that is. (63)

In addition to attempting to generate empathy among her audience, Ensler's monologue underscores the debilitating effects inherent in the erasure of her subject's essence. In "My Angry Vagina," Ensler adopts a strident pose as she voices the outrage of her narrator's vagina about the proscriptive practices of workaday life that seek, in one fashion or another, to control women and mitigate their avenues toward self-actualization. Lashing out against the commodification of the female body, Ensler's fuming voice derides thongs, tampons, and gynecological exams as instruments of silence, containment, and limitation: "An army of people out there thinking up ways to torture my poor-ass, gentle, loving vagina. . . . Spending their days constructing psycho products and nasty ideas to undermine my pussy. Vagina motherfuckers" (69).

Having vented her anger and aroused her audience's passions for her cause, Ensler shifts into a problem-posing mode, the basis for Freire's fifth principle for a liberation pedagogy, in which *The Vagina Monologues* emerges as a forum for pondering the sources of female dysfunctionality regarding self-esteem and the body. Ensler's rhetorical stance allows her to submit two monologues, "Hair" and "The Flood," for her audience's deliberation. Each monologue represents socially constructed barriers to women's self-fulfillment. In "Hair," Ensler narrates a woman's futile efforts to satisfy her husband's desires for dominating and infantilizing her by forcing her to shave her vagina:

> My first and only husband hated hair. He said it was cluttered and dirty. He made me shave my vagina. It looked puffy and exposed and like a little girl. This excited him. When he made love to me, my

vagina felt the way a beard must feel. It felt good to rub it, and painful. Like scratching a mosquito bite. It felt like it was on fire. There were screaming red bumps. (9–10)

For Ensler's character in "Hair," the act of shaving her genitalia fails, rather pointedly, to save her marriage. Her husband ultimately leaves her in favor of another woman who presumably acquiesces to his demands. In "The Flood," Ensler takes on the persona of an elderly Jewish woman from Queens who speaks euphemistically of the "cellar down there" (25). Her disconnection with her body occurs in 1953 after a traumatic sexual encounter in which she stains the upholstery of her would-be boyfriend's Chevy BelAir: "I got excited, so excited, and, well, there was a flood down there" (27). His angry rebuff forces her to endure a form of spiritual vacancy and shame for the balance of her life. Ensler's dramatic recreation of the woman's story allows her to challenge her audience into thinking critically about the social formation of our sexual identities. The narrator of "Hair" feels violated and sexually unworthy. For the woman in "The Flood," her genitalia simply ceases to exist: "It's a place. A place you don't go. It's closed up, under the house. It's down there" (30).

For Ensler, the act of problem posing allows her to prepare her audience for building a critical consciousness about the oppression of the female body. "In problem-posing education, people develop their power to perceive critically *the way they exist* in the world *with which* and *in which* they find themselves," Freire writes. "They come to see the world not as a static reality, but as a reality in process, in transformation" (83). Hence, Freire's sixth principle of a liberation pedagogy involves a process of "conscientization." As the sine qua non of liberatory education, conscientization entails the act of breaking through prevailing social mythologies to create new levels of reality for the oppressed. In *The Vagina Monologues*, Ensler shares the moving accounts of two extraordinary men who defy gender expectations. In "Because He Liked to Look at It," Ensler traces the story of Bob, the man who loved vaginas: "He was a connoisseur. He loved the way they felt, the way they tasted, the way they smelled, but most important, he loved the way they looked" (55). Bob's unabashed appreciation for the narrator's body affords her with a new sense of self in dramatic contrast with the negative sexual identity established through her experiences with previous lovers:

I began to see myself the way he saw me. I began to feel beautiful and delicious—like a great painting or a waterfall. Bob wasn't afraid. He wasn't grossed out. I began to swell, began to feel proud. Began to love my vagina. And Bob lost himself there and I was there with him, and we were gone. (57)

In another vignette from *The Vagina Monologues*, Ensler remembers meeting a woman in Oklahoma who had been born without a vagina. Rather than being dismissive and embarrassed about his daughter's plight, her father embraces her dilemma, provides her with unconditional love, and nurtures her through the painful process of reconstructive surgery: "Don't worry darlin'. This is all gonna be just fine," he tells his daughter. "As a matter of fact, it's gonna be great. We're gonna get you the best homemade pussy in America" (99). By virtue of their inclusion in Ensler's play, these monologues demonstrate her keen interest in depicting men in the act of participating in women's liberation. In Ensler's liberatory pedagogy, then, the oppressors ultimately evolve by sharing in the emancipation of the oppressed.

Freire's seventh principle for a liberation pedagogy concerns a process of communal transformation in which educators seek to humanize the world. As Tom Heaney perceptively observes, "The transformation of the world is humankind's entry into history. As people act upon the world effectively, transforming it by work, consciousness is in turn historically and culturally conditioned." Rather than functioning as an individualistic mechanism, Freire's concept of a liberation pedagogy attempts to enact change on a multiplicity of societal levels. In her monologue entitled "Reclaiming Cunt," Ensler attempts to demythologize the usage of the vagina's most notorious euphemism. Through a series of verbal gestures, she deconstructs *cunt*'s status as a four-letter word by renaming each of its phraseological components:

> Listen to it. "Cunt." C C, Ca Ca. Cavern, cackle, clit, cute, come—closed c—closed inside, inside ca—then u—then cu—then curvy, inviting sharkskin u—uniform, under, up, urge, ugh, ugh, u—then n then cun—snug letters fitting perfectly together—n—nest, now, nexus, nice, nice, always depth, always round in uppercase, cun, cun—n a jagged wicked electrical pulse—n [high-pitched noise] then soft n—warm n—cun, cun, then t—then sharp certain tangy t—texture, take, tent, tight, tantalizing, tensing, taste, tendrils, time, tactile, tell me, tell me "Cunt cunt," say it, tell me "Cunt." "Cunt." (101–2)

By literally converting it into a multisyllabic phrase, Ensler desensitizes *cunt* by pronouncing it in a wide range of vocal registers and modulations during her performance, ultimately inviting the audience to chant the word along with her in triumphant unison. In this way, she redefines *cunt* and reclaims its inherent power after 5,000 years in the hands of a pejorative, patriarchal culture.[7]

Freire's eighth and final principle of a liberation pedagogy concludes—as does *The Vagina Monologues*—by acknowledging that genuine education invariably operates as an ongoing praxis involving the interplay between reflection and action. "Praxis comprises a cycle of action-reflection-action which is central to liberatory education," Heaney writes. "Characteristics of praxis include self-determination (as opposed to coercion), intentionality (as opposed to reaction), creativity (as opposed to homogeneity), and rationality (as opposed to chance)." Ensler's closing monologue, "I Was There in the Room," evinces these characteristics by celebrating the vagina as a locus of social reparation.[8] As she describes her experiences while witnessing the birth of her grandchild Colette, Ensler marvels at her daughter-in-law Shiva's vagina and its capacity for producing life through transformation, expansiveness, and sacrifice. "As I stared," Ensler recalls, "her vagina suddenly became a wide red pulsing heart" (124). For Ensler, the vagina functions as a metaphor for forgiveness and social repair. Ensler intuitively recognizes that cultural change inevitably occurs, as with the process of birth, via anguish and disarray. For this reason, she reconceives of the vagina as a restorative, inclusive space that "can change its shape to let us in" and "expand to let us out." Simply put, Ensler's vaginal metaphor addresses the convoluted fashion in which real change comes to fruition as the product of a reciprocal cycle of action-reflection-action. Mindful that we must reflect periodically upon our efforts to change the world, Ensler's liberation pedagogy implicitly understands the vagina's considerable power as a metaphor for our abiding need for spheres of reconnection and renewal: "It can ache for us and stretch for us, die for us, and bleed us into this difficult, wondrous world" (125).

While a reading of *The Vagina Monologues* in terms of Freire's eight principles demonstrates its revolutionary potential for engendering social transformation, how can we realistically assess the play's sociocultural influence? Perhaps the real power of *The Vagina Monologues* as a form of liberation pedagogy can be measured by its impact at the grassroots level of our college campuses, the site of the hearts and minds of the future. As one student-director from Colorado State University recalls, "To sit in the audience watching my once-shy actresses laugh and moan and cry about their vaginas, and feel the power that their words had over the people surrounding me was indescribable." For yet another student—also a former victim of sexual abuse—the V-Day project "has reminded me what I lost in my rush to recover: I lost my body and now I know I will get it back." Finally, a male student from the University of Oklahoma writes that *The Vagina Monologues* "gets people who ordinarily wouldn't even think about women's issues to come to the play and most of them leave with a new understanding and a lot more respect for the experiences of women in our society" (quoted in Obel 141, 143, 145). The poignant words of these students clearly speak to the transformative power of Ensler's play. Yet to suggest that *The Vagina Monologues* operates as a kind of all-inclusive panacea would be utterly naïve. As Peter McLaren astutely remarks, "Freire acknowledges that decolonization is a project that knows no endpoint, no final closure. It is a lifetime struggle," he adds, "that requires counterintuitive insight, honesty, [and] compassion" (170). In this sense, *The Vagina Monologues* is merely the first step on a much longer road to universal awareness.

11

How Do You Solve a Problem Like *Magnolia*?

For the historical ache, the ache passed down
which finds its circumstance and becomes
the present ache. . . .
> Stephen Dunn, "To a Terrorist"

Or suppose you are a teacher and one student after
another comes to ask you how to deal with despair.
What would you tell them?
> Scott Russell Sanders, *Hunting for Hope*

The past isn't dead. It isn't even past.
> William Faulkner

Paul Thomas Anderson's third film, *Magnolia* (1999), is at once a solemn and terrifying cinematic experience, a crushing and a heartening movie encounter. It is the kind of film whose structure and content spin you backward into your seat with the centrifugal force of narrative. It represents the work of a young auteur who not only ignores the pressures of crass commercialism, but also eschews the even stronger and divisive forces of ideology and philosophy. It dispenses with Hollywood's simplistic dichotomies between the more serious aesthetic of the independent film and the crowd-pleasing aesthetic of popular cinema's happy endings. *Magnolia* makes use of postmodernity's metafictional techniques to draw attention to its own textual nature, while still pleading that we see what is "real" within it. In other words, Anderson gathers us around the complex, despairing lives of his characters—literally pushing us closer and closer to the void—and then he offers a possible way out, a means to begin negotiating a postmodern humanism based on the constructed ideas of connection, forgiveness, and love. In the midst of this earnest and heartfelt film is a storyteller seeking to assemble a bridge of inclusion—of both/and, *not* either/or—and the story he tells of a past that does not stay in the past and of a future that must acknowledge the ways the past becomes part of our lived, bodily selves still proffers hope based on the ways we may participate in its construction through language and action.

Anderson utilizes the film's initial scene as a philosophical epigraph of sorts, a means for constituting the manner in which we will take part in the creation of his narrative. Through the common technique of voice-over narration, he tells us about three historical cases of seeming coincidence, all of which end in tragic deaths. The initial incident involves the hanging of three men who, in an attempted robbery, murder Sir Edmund William Godfrey, a pharmacist. The last names of the three killers—Green, Berry, and Hill—comprise the name of Godfrey's hometown, Greenberry Hill. The narrator states that he "would like to think this was only a matter of chance." The second case relates the death of Delmer Darion, a blackjack dealer and recreational scuba diver from Reno, Nevada, and Craig Hansen, a volunteer firefighter who pilots an air tanker while fighting forest fires. In an instance of tragic happenstance, Darion goes scuba diving in the lake where Hansen comes to draw water into his tanker. Accidentally, Hansen scoops Darion into the plane's tank—where, incidentally, Darion has a heart attack—and then dumps his body onto the fire along with the lake water. We are then told that only the evening before, Hansen had physically and verbally abused Darion in the casino for dealing him the "wrong" cards. The intersection of these seemingly unrelated events is too much for Hansen, and, he takes his own life by placing a shotgun to his head and pulling the trigger. The narrator tells us that he is "trying to think this was all only a matter of chance."

The final episode concerns Sydney Barringer, a 17-year-old boy who steps off the roof of a nine-story building in an attempted suicide. As he falls past a window on the sixth floor, a bullet smashes through the glass and into Sydney's stomach. Ironically, he falls into a safety net below that had been installed only three days before. The net would have saved him from the crushing blow that the concrete would have dealt, of course, had he not been the victim of an incidental murder. We are told that his parents often fought and that the mother usually threatened to shoot the father with the family's shotgun. The key to the benign outcomes of these disputes is that the shotgun is never loaded; there is no real threat. On this day, though, unbeknownst to his parents, the shotgun holds live ammo. Sydney himself had loaded the gun six days prior because he hoped that his parents would indeed kill each other. Thus, an unsuccessful suicide becomes a successful homicide, and Sydney's mother is charged with the murder of her son, who is listed as an accomplice in his own homicide. After relating this bizarre sequence of events, the narrator struggles with how such things might come to pass: "And it is in the humble opinion of this narrator that this is not just 'something that happened.' This cannot be 'one of those things.' This, please, cannot be that. And for what I would like to say, I can't. This was not just a matter of chance. These strange things happen all the time." The most remarkable aspect of the film's introduction is that the narrator—who in the world of film ordinarily occupies a space of authority, of nearly omniscient knowledge, privy to the thoughts and actions of the characters—is unsure of himself, of what he is narrating. He stumbles. He pleads with us to grant that this cannot be "one of those things." As he frames the story that is about to unfold before us, he does more than merely suggest that these portentous happenings are not the workings of chance, he proclaims it, albeit beseechingly.

These so-called incidents of haphazard synchronicity, upon closer inspection, reveal deeper, more troubling associations. The effects or outcomes of randomness may appear to have no relation to some broader "plan" until we begin to strip away the thin veneer of "reality" and expose how our most personal actions and motivations ultimately impact others. Anderson takes the theoretical construct of relationality—the idea that the beat of a butterfly's wings in the Pacific Ocean may play a part in generating the strength of a hurricane in the Atlantic Ocean, for example—and applies it to a very specific group of people to demonstrate the ways we are all linked, all related, all responsible to and for one another. In "*Magnolia* and the Signs of the Times: A Theological Reflection," Mario DeGiglio-Bellemare contends that "the film asks us to ponder how labeling something a coincidence can mask more telling undercurrents." It is the telling undercurrents of our lives that Anderson seeks to expose. But to what end? It is the answer to this question that reveals the core elements of postmodern humanism, the manner in which it urges us forward, asks us to acknowledge the seen and unseen relationships between us, and, ultimately, exhorts us to forgive, to do what we can to heal the ways that we betray one another.

Perhaps betrayal and judgment are the "sins" that sit at the center of Anderson's film. As A. G. Harmon explains, judgment is at the root of the kinds of revelations we encounter in *Magnolia*, and "these self-revelations (often, but not exclusively, involving fathers) are striking because the characters stare at a part of themselves they have made manifest, a part they have sculpted out of a lifetime of error, until it springs forth and faces them down" (111–2). Certainly, Jimmy Gator (Philip Baker Hall) has betrayed his daughter Claudia (Melora Walters) by molesting her in years past, and Earl Partridge (Jason Robards) has definitely transgressed against his son Frank T. J. Mackey (Tom Cruise) in his lack of care for him as well as in his infidelity to his wife and his abandonment of her as she suffered and died of cancer. Similarly, Rick Spector (Michael Bowen), in his lustful rush for fame and game show fortune, pushes and prods and ultimately humiliates his son Stanley (Jeremy Blackman). Even Donnie Smith, a former quiz-kid phenomenon, feels the heavy weight of his past and, in the end, may be his own worst adversary. Linda Partridge (Julianne Moore), Earl's trophy wife, consistently deceives her husband out of spite, only to discover as he lies on his deathbed that she actually loves him. For all the characters whose individual stories swirl in a mélange of interconnection and interrelation, unfaithfulness and duplicity come raging forth from the past to stand in judgment of the present. "The idea of judgment, of being called to account for the way we have lived in the world," Kathleen Norris remarks "*is* solemn, and terrifying" (316). Indeed, we see terror, confusion, even resignation in the face of such failures and the accompanying condemnation. "What is more terrifying in life than staring at our selves, as our selves stare back?" Harmon asks (112). In seeing who we are and how we have helped to shape the lives of others, Harmon contends, the weight of self-recognition wears us down. Indeed, as Earl rages to his nurse Phil Parma (Philip Seymour Hoffman) that "this is the regret that you make," that this is the "goddamn regret," we bear witness to the visible signs of the devastating effects of self-recognition in Earl. "I'm so embarrassed, so embarrassed for what I've done," Earl confesses, and at this point in his life there is a certain level of impotence, of a weariness and shame that is stultifying. After all, what can Earl do on his deathbed? He rages and stutters incoherently to Phil that "this is so boring. . .so goddamn. . .and dying wish and all that, old man on a bed. . .fuck. . .wants one thing!" Yet even incapacitated, Earl has not completely given up. These moments waiting for death to claim him may be boring, and the idea of a dying man's wish may seem both cliché and impossible, but it is Earl himself who suggests that we might employ our regret for something better—an idea that will play an integral role in the film's dénouement.

With skill and acumen, Anderson allows his story to unfold at a leisurely pace. We witness Frank in his present element, conducting misogynistic self-help workshops for other men who have been damaged in their search for love and by love's failures. We watch as police officer Jim Kurring (John C. Reilly) attempts to muster enough confidence to simply do his job after his many inept fiascos at work. We also see Claudia Gator thrust herself into abusive self-hatred, having sex with strangers and snorting cocaine. We observe Linda Partridge on the verge of a nervous breakdown as she scurries from one pharmacy to another, collecting anti-depressants to combat her despair. Meanwhile, we are privy to the despondency of Donnie Smith as he mumbles and bumbles his way through a life of disappointment and failure after his 15 minutes of quiz show fame, and we perceive the same possibilities for the future of Stanley Spector as the pressure of winning on the same game show gradually mounts with the taping of each new episode. Finally, we watch as Earl Partridge wastes away in his bed, the demons of his past life seemingly represented by the severity of his painful end.

As the film progresses, however, Anderson increases the speed of the film's cuts from scene to scene, transitioning from the many different character-settings with mounting frequency. He does so to generate the intensity of the narrative, to make the visual storytelling component respond to the grim reality that these characters must collide with the consequences of their combined histories. There is simply no escaping the weight of the past. As we shift from character to character, these moments of gut-wrenching,[1] despairing calamity, suggest that all of their lives—in obvious and not so obvious ways—are linked, that not only is there no way to escape their own individual pasts, but there also is no way for them to escape their collective past. Ultimately, Anderson demonstrates the ways in which past, present, and future can never be characterized as separate or distinct. Ironically, while it is the past that each member seeks to escape, it is this same past that ultimately holds the key to their judgment and potential absolution. What each of them fails to realize is that the past not only cannot be eluded or fooled, but that it resides in the very fabric of their lives, that although they have not recognized its patterns, they have been dressing themselves in the cloth spun from its source with each passing day. And so we see Officer Kurring lose his gun at a potential crime scene—a transgression of great import in his field of work. And we watch as Claudia continues to deceive others and herself, frenetically imbibing drugs and sex and any other substance that might help numb her to the tragic truth of her father's transgression against her. And Frank, having been confronted with his own lies about his past by a reporter, sits wordlessly, stoically, the mask of his professional self no longer of any use against the truth of his father's abandonment of his mother and him. "I'm quietly judging you," he tells the reporter. And Donnie, like Jim Kurring, fails continually in his position as an electronics salesman, ultimately losing his job and retreating to a bar where he hopes to proclaim his love for Brad the bartender (Craig Kvinsland), whose affections he spars for with another patron. Linda Partridge, having acquired her many prescriptions, sits in her car inside the garage, the engine running, the poison slipping into the air, as she tries to decide whether she will turn off the engine and go inside or simply drift away into death's arms. And all the while, Stanley struggles against the callousness of his father, the imposition of his role on the game show that is taking away what little normalcy his childhood might have provided.

While Anderson has been praised for this "edgy, messy, wildly ambitious portrait of American angst" (Kempley C1), some critics find his turn toward love and forgiveness to be less than show stopping. Charles Taylor complains that "by the close of *Magnolia*, you're painfully aware of how everything in the movie is put at the service of Anderson's trite message," and Janet Maslin of *The New York Times* concurs with Taylor, suggesting that the "great uh-oh moment" in *Magnolia*—here she refers to the scene in which all of the characters sing along with Aimee Mann as she bleakly states that "It's not going to stop / Till you wise up"—is one of "directorial desperation," not of storytelling brilliance or insight (E1). As Wesley Morris explains, "Anderson's only cure is 'love.' And that's a terribly corny, grossly uncool, perfectly obvious solution to what is the emotional equivalent of the common cold." Perhaps this is what is at stake in postmodern humanism. Certainly, it is the reason that certain schools of thought lambasted Kurt Vonnegut's idealism and his unabashed commitment to characters like Eliot Rosewater who declares in *God Bless You, Mr. Rosewater*, "God damn it, you've got to be kind" (110). How can we take love and redemption seriously, sincerely, when we look around and see the world mired in war and famine and disease? When we note the manner in which so many of us treat one another—using and abusing another human being to gain some profit, some power—how can we even think of a world in which the ideas of "love" or "redemption" might facilitate something better? Surely, the irony and cynicism of certain artistic or theoretical schools of thought offer more protection and security against the failure of so simplistic a notion. But this safe and sheltered means of combating despair and angst does not satisfy everyone. Roger Ebert refers to the fruits of irony and cynicism as the "timid postmodernism of the 1990s," and he lauds Anderson's new approach, calling *Magnolia* "operatic in its ambition, a great joyous leap into melodrama and coincidence." He goes on to say that it is the kind of movie that does not "apologize for [its] exuberance, or shield [itself] with irony against suspicions of sincerity."

Magnolia is a film that wants us to believe—in some magically real way—that all of these characters can and do sing together in their darkest, most destitute moment, that as they sing they might begin to recognize a way out of their despondency and desolation.[2] Despite the fact that such a musical moment highlights the filmic nature of the text, Anderson allows the scene to carry real emotional weight. In other words, we suspend our disbelief—or perhaps for many there is no disbelief to begin with because of the way Anderson has constructed the film—and enter fully with the characters into the confluence of emotion and language and music. Perhaps the most apt metaphor for such a scene comes from the High Church tradition. In one sense, Earl and Frank and Claudia and Phil and the rest of the characters sing the same words as they partake in the film's "liturgy." Just as in Christian worship, these people allow the same language to order their existence, to give meaning to their actions. Such a scene seems to suggest that after so much degradation, after so much pain, the kindness of strangers may actually make a difference. Of course, there is no way to convince the viewer of this. If facts are necessary, if the scientific method is the only means by which validation can occur, then irony and cynicism will win out. But a postmodern working faith that still imagines a way to construct something different, something better that might alter the ways in which we live with each other, is another matter entirely.

Paradoxically, Anderson makes use of postmodern aesthetic devices to achieve this result. Chief among these methods is the tool of metafiction, a stepping outside of or above the textual experience to draw attention to the text *as* text, a self-referential exercise that taps the reader or viewer on the shoulder and points to the artwork only to say, "See, it's art; it's artifice; it's not real life." By doing so, Anderson is more than aware that he is reminding us of the film's own constructed nature—a move used by many postmodern artists. But unlike John Barth or Thomas Pynchon, Anderson does not use this maneuver to undercut the validity or reality of his text. Instead, he implores us to believe in the text, not to dismiss it just because of its constructed nature. He still wants us to believe that his text is about "real" life. As Phil cares for Earl—dispensing painkillers, listening to his confused and distorted speech—he discovers that Frank is Earl's son, and Phil decides that a dying man might best be served by speaking to his son one last time. After attaining the phone number to Frank's *Seduce and Destroy* self-help program in a porno magazine, Phil finds himself trying to convince a tele-operator that he is the nurse for Frank's father and that Frank's father is in the final stages of cancer. Needless to say, Phil has difficulty explaining all of this because Earl and Frank neither share the same last name nor have they spoken to each other in years. There is a moment in the conversation, however, that suddenly makes what transpires possible. The tele-operator asks what kind of cancer Earl is dying from, and Phil tells him that it is of the brain and lung. The tele-operator confesses that his mother had breast cancer, breaking down the distance between them, making an association that represents a bond—however small—that matters. This apparently minor moment in the film, so easily overlooked, is representative of Anderson's conception of how we might make a difference, how we might actually break out of patterns of destructive behavior that the past wishes to perpetuate in this present moment. It is in human connection, in taking the time to actually listen and extend what little we may have to offer to another, that the possibility of countering habitual patterns occurs. Ultimately, Phil pierces the barriers we all erect when he drops any pretense of professionalism and simply states his needs and his desires, nakedly and unabashedly:

> I know this all seems silly. I know that maybe I sound ridiculous, like maybe this is the scene of the movie where the guy is trying to get a hold of the long-lost son, but this is that scene, you know? I think they have those scenes in movies because they're true, because they really happen. And you gotta believe me: This is really happening. I mean, I can give you my phone number and you can call me back if you wanna check with whoever you can check this with, but don't leave me hanging on this—please—please. See—See—See, this is the scene of the movie where you help me out.

Indeed, this is the very scene in the movie where Phil, in trying to grant Earl's dying wish, is helped out by a complete stranger, and, as Phil has already pointed out, this is not just a movie—this is real; *these things really do happen.*[3]

Such moments represent a shift in postmodernity's approach to the notions of the "textual" and the "real." Instead of amplifying the dichotomous and contentious relationship that exists between these two ideas, Anderson suggests that something can be both "textual" and "real" at the same time. Early practitioners of this mode appeared to draw attention to the textuality or constructedness of the world to distance the reader or viewer from any notion of a "real" shared human experience. Highlighting the artifice of human existence—and, thus, its relative value and shifting morality—preoccupied such writers, and tendered forth easy targets for cultural conservatives. During the 1990s, a shift occurred, however, and we began to see films like Lars Von Trier's *Breaking the Waves* (1996) and David O'Russell's *Three Kings* (1999) as well as books like Michael Martone's *Seeing Eye* (1995) and Dave Eggers's *A Heartbreaking Work of Staggering Genius* (2000), in which the same postmodern techniques that were used to highlight the mere artifice of existence were employed to different effect. It was as if the artist wished to demonstrate that he or she was savvy enough to know that we live in a "constructed" universe, that all around us artifice structures our lives, but having displayed such a knowledge and the artistic skills to represent it, these same artists turned to heartfelt earnestness, to notions of love and trust and forgiveness as something real, something to be sought after.[4]

Perhaps this is the reason why Anderson risks everything by inserting a moment of Biblical proportion toward the end of the film; perhaps this is why he is willing to let Officer Jim Kurring tell us that "as we move through this life we should try to do good and not hurt anyone else." Anderson knows that he has created a target for the cynical, that there will be those critics who believe such statements only demonstrate a degree of naïveté and triteness that we are unaccustomed to in the work of a filmmaker whose first movie focused on gambling (*Sydney* [1996]) and whose second celebrated the "familial" qualities of the pornography industry (*Boogie Nights* [1997]). Yet Anderson takes this risk just the same. After offering myriad clues, including, most notably, the placards held aloft by members of the studio audience at the quiz show,[5] the director introduces a rain of frogs straight out of the book of Exodus. In the midst of the culmination of so many different crises—Stanley has humiliated himself on the game show by peeing in his pants; Donnie has failed in his attempt to rob the electronics store where he worked before being fired; Frank has come to his father's bedside and broken down uncontrollably—the frogs begin to fall from the sky. Early in the film, Anderson foreshadows his rain of frogs in the prophetic rap of Dixon (Emmanuel Johnson), a young African-American boy who promises to help Kurring solve the crime he is investigating: "Check that ego—come off it—I'm the profit—the professor. Ima teach you 'bout The Worm, who eventually turned to catch wreck with the neck of a long time oppressor. And he's runnin' from the devil, but the debt is always gaining. And if he's worth being hurt, he's worth bringin' pain in. When the sunshine don't work, the Good Lord bring the rain in." Dixon's final lines echo the book of Exodus: "Thus says the Lord: Let my people go, so that they may worship me. If you refuse to let them go, I will plague your whole country with frogs" (8:1–2). Obliquely, Anderson has connected his story to the idea of separation—from God and from one another—and as frogs splatter upon the Earth, their dead bodies mounting, we begin to see our characters' stories converge.

Anderson uses this unaccountable phenomenon in much the same way as magical realists do in their fiction. He does not have his characters gasp in amazement or shudder at the extraordinary, the surreal quality of this occurrence. Instead, after their initial shock, they go on about their business. But their business changes. As Kurring—the film's moral compass of sorts—tells us, "You can forgive someone." And Anderson concludes his film with scene after scene of potential forgiveness: Kurring helps Donnie put back the valuables he has stolen; Frank leaves his father's bedside to attend to Linda, who is in the hospital now herself; Stanley returns home after running away and tells his father, "You have to be nicer to me." Anderson wisely avoids offering any pat or definitive conclusions to these stories. He proposes that certain kinds of redemption may be within reach, but that the key will be in figuring out what we can forgive and how we might reach across the distance of our pasts to embrace one another. Hence, as Claudia pointedly breaks the fourth wall and smiles at the end of the film—the final note in this film's song—Anderson offers hope but no confirmed, ultimate happy ending. Kurring certainly decides that any past transgression on the part of Claudia is not only forgivable but redeemable. He does not worry about his position as a police officer or his faith as a Christian. The fact that Claudia is an addict who has slept with numerous men, that her own father has harmed her sexually, does not faze Kurring. "Yes, they're going to get together and form a relationship," Anderson explains in an interview, "but in no way is it going to be easy or entirely possible. But it is a surrender to falling in love, no matter how much shit that's going to entail" (207).

"There can be no truth between people without the will to embrace the other," Miroslav Volf writes (258). If postmodern humanism points toward a healthy and helpful means of negotiating the void, then we must begin with the embrace of the other, and such an embrace, tellingly, must often navigate the waters of forgiveness, the past that bears up our complicity in the wronging of others, as well as the ways in which we have been wronged. "I really do hath love to give, I juth don't know where to put it," Donnie says through a mouthful of broken teeth near the film's conclusion. Yes, we all have the possibility of love, but before we can put it anywhere, we would do well to heed the words of the film's narrator as he reminds us that "the book says, 'We may be through with the past, but the past is not through with us.' " Out of the past, all of our relationships—to ourselves and to others—are made, and the only way we stand a chance at moving beyond our present, at helping to construct a better future—a way of negotiating the possibilities that loom over the void—is to embrace one another in forgiveness and love. It may seem facile, and it may seem naïve, but for Anderson, such a conclusion is precisely *that* simple and exactly *that* clear. It is *Magnolia*.

Conclusion: Postmodern Humanism and the Ethical Future

> If the artist could explain in words what he has made,
> he would not have had to create it.
>
> Alfred Stieglitz

How, then, do we reconcile the void?

For Jim Harrison, there is ecology as a revitalizing force.

For Mary Swander, there is the mystery of the body and the essence of the soul.

For Mary Oliver, there is an Emersonian quest for selfhood and spiritual transcendence.

For John Irving, there is the search for redemption in spite of a world of fragmentation and chaos.

For Sherman Alexie, there is the essentializing power of identity in an uncertain, impure universe.

For Jeffrey Eugenides, there is ethical reconciliation—the notion of living well and flourishing against all odds.

For Jessica Hagedorn, there is the creation of counter-narratives to salve the wounds of a colonized past.

For the Beatles, there is the dream of wholeness in an era beset by absurdity, contradiction, and revolution.

For David Mamet, there are stories of forgiveness amidst a corrosive age of liars, cheaters, and confidence games.

For Eve Ensler, there is an effort to describe the indescribable, to posit awareness in spite of a millennium of silence.

For Paul Thomas Anderson, there is the brash sincerity of absolution and love as antidotes for interpersonal disconnection and loss.

And these stories—every last one of them—are made possible by simple human utterance. But with this recognition of the awesome power of the word comes an understanding, disturbing as it may be, that language also shared in, if not spearheaded, the creation of the postmodern void. That it was language that wrought a spate of world wars, a legacy of holocaust, and the ceaseless perils of colonialism. That it was language that spawned racism, hegemony, and bifurcation. That it was language that bore the identity politics and institutional malaise that renders governments ineffectual. That it was language that engendered crass consumerism and its exportation across an entire planet. That it was language that tore humankind asunder even though we possess so much possibility for interpersonal connection and renewal.

The solution, of course, is decidedly simple, yet nearly impossible, it seems, to effect—especially when life's inertia urges us toward silence, passivity, placation, and complacency. Cultures of community have been displaced by global marketplaces and multinational corporations. The faux dream of a "new world order" has been unmasked as a panacea for the masses, the promise of greener pastures of freedom for everyone, while increasingly we have placed the reins of power in the hands of the few. These are mixed metaphors, to be sure, but their intellectual freight is no less germane when it comes to snake-oil salesmen and realtors peddling swampland.

We have traded in a world of experience and relationship for a world driven by desire and satisfaction. Where once we depended upon each other for community, for sustenance, for joy, we now find gratification in slaking the needs of the self—by ourselves and for ourselves. As Paul McCarthy points out, one of the touchstones of the postmodern world is the establishment of spheres of desire that must be quenched. The bombardment of television advertisements tells us that we need a newer, faster, better automobile, so we buy one to sate our desire. Identity politics tells us that we need a more beautiful, more seductive, more pliant lover, so we covet one, upsetting the relationships—the families that we have created—in the bargain. Commercialism tells us that we need the trappings of a better life—more exotic vacations, a larger television, a luxurious house—so we crave for them. We desire these things as never before in the course of human history. And in the process, we diminish the quality and value of the people and things that already exist in our lives. We no longer yearn for experience and sharing human interrelationships, but rather we long for more and better things for the sheer bragging rights to be able to say to others—to ourselves—that we are living the good life, that we are enjoying the life that we have always

deserved. It is the life that television, that our highly portable and mech-
anized culture, tells us we should have. It is a fearful symmetry indeed.

What we no longer have—in addition to genuine human community
and self-awareness—are authentic opportunities for reflection. If our
commodity culture has taught us nothing else, it has cautioned us against
the real and present danger of free, unfettered time. There is no room for
silence and inactivity in the postmodern world. Commercialism prods us
to always be in motion, *to always be doing something.* Is it possible to cruise
along an American interstate highway and not see a family, in their late-
model minivan, being pleasured by—being placated by—the sweet
sounds from an iPod, the iterative thrills of a Nintendo Gameboy, and the
passive contentment afforded by a flip-down video screen?[1]

And when mass culture fails us—when it falls short of feeding our every
whim for universal fulfillment—we find ourselves inevitably looking
backward, contemplating a simpler time, dreaming of the good-old days.
We find ourselves waxing nostalgic. We yearn (often unconsciously) for
transcendence amidst the malaise and fragmentation of postmodern life.
"When the real is no longer what it used to be," Jean Baudrillard cautions,
"nostalgia assumes its full meaning" (12). Does it ever.

Interestingly, Kimberly K. Smith argues that our contemporary notions
of nostalgia first came into being through various nineteenth- and
twentieth-century conflicts over the political significance of the past.
According to Smith, nostalgia finds its origins in the historical transi-
tion from the relative stability of an agrarian society to the mounting
anxiety of a largely industrial world. In this sense, nostalgia emerges as
a means for recontextualizing the past in terms of the present, as a form
of social constructivism in which the past accrues greater meaning
because of its significance and desirability in contrast with an uncertain
and highly volatile contemporary moment. "To experience a memory
nostalgically is not just to have certain feelings along with that memory,"
Smith suggests, "but to adopt a particular attitude towards it: to understand the memory and its associated feelings as the product of a psychological propensity to romanticize the past, and to value it as a vehicle
for a Proustian sort of heightened sensibility or self-awareness" (509). In
this way, nostalgia exists as an acculturated behavior through which we
develop a perspective toward the past as a place where we might fulfill
our collective longing for an "archetypal paradise" (514).[2]

When we can no longer enjoy the manna of an "archetypal paradise"
in our real lives, we draw upon the language of our nostalgic dreams to
concoct an idealized past. We engage in a sentimentalized longing for a
past that never existed in the first place by reflecting upon memories

that we never had or much less experienced. And when we find ourselves seeking out explicit moments of self-delusion, what have we accomplished? What do we really possess if all we can show for our toil and existence are fakery and wishful thinking? Consider the following poem, in which the poet struggles with the concept of expressing identity through language, of engaging in action among a world that calls for passivity and consumption. How can individuals contemplate their own selfhood—their places in the universe—if mass culture is constantly telling us to look elsewhere for our fulfillment?

The Great Traveling Medicine Show

There are, as I have become dolefully aware,
certain limitations on what we can and cannot say—

Even in the politest of company, amongst the finest friends and
relations
in whose estimation we invest everything that we are, and
everything that we hope to become, on some sunny day.

There are no rousing elixirs, I have since discovered,
that can assist us in living out loud—no miracle cures, no magic
bullets,
no homespun remedies, no herbal concoctions for nudging us
into the fray.

We linger in dank back alleys, nooks and crannies, haunted
garrets—and,
oh my yes, haunted garrets really do exist—secret places where we
gird ourselves from
peering into the maelström that is ourselves.

There is no map, and a compass wouldn't help at all. (Womack)

While commodity culture may be able to provide us with prescriptions for nearly everything that ails us—for our bald spots, for our high cholesterol, for our unruly bladders, for our sexual inadequacies—it falls decidedly short when it comes to giving us the will to flourish within ourselves, to find solace and contentment in the aspects and desires that derive who and what we are. How can a brand new vehicle make us whole when the most that we can really hope for in this world is to peer into the secret garrets of our own hearts and unlock the mysteries of the self?

There is no map, and a compass wouldn't help at all, the poet tells us, by way of the inspired lyrics of Björk. Is this true of the postmodern void? Are we beyond the pale of understanding, when there are no more reliable maps or compasses left to help us find our way? The artists under review in *Reconciling the Void* remind us, often through markedly different approaches and genres, that we can triumph over the chaos of our malaise through the discovery of our own voices. As McCarthy argues, a "re-orientation is called for."[3] It is high time that we seek a new understanding of the place of the individual within the fabric of human relationships.

For Jim Harrison, our desires for sounding out meaning can find affirmation through an immersion with nature in its starkest manifestations. For Mary Swander, the human voice may be ascertained within our struggle to particularize the body. For Mary Oliver, language might be honed through a re-engagement with the spiritual essences of ourselves. For John Irving, words make possible our capacity for recognizing and enjoying the power of redemption. For Sherman Alexie, language emerges through our efforts to find ourselves within a universe of myriad identities, to transform our curses into blessings. For Jeffrey Eugenides, language assists us in achieving a renewed sense of community and finding our own ways to endure. For Jessica Hagedorn, language offers the potentiality for salvation in spite of the memories of a barbaric, colonial past. For the Beatles, words and music serve to stay the chaos when they flower into the phrases of a hopeful lyric or a searing guitar. For David Mamet, the language of the con artist can be reconfigured by words of altruism and forgiveness. For Eve Ensler, language affords us with the power to erase the pain of intercultural silence with the sustenance of glorious, uncompromised meaning. For Paul Thomas Anderson, language illuminates the truth about the families that we have lost and makes it possible for us to imagine structures of wholeness yet again.

In the end—as in the beginning—it is language that matters. And it is ultimately via language that we fashion hope, that we articulate love, that we build community. It is through language that we reconcile the void.

Notes

Introduction: Necessary Negotiations

1. In *Kurt Vonnegut's Crusade, Or, How a Postmodern Harlequin Preached a New Kind of Humanism* (2006), Todd F. Davis contends that "although many postmodern philosophers see the effects of poststructuralism's critique of essence and centrality as an opportunity for negative freedom or endless play, there exists among the masses a reluctance to embrace the postmodern.... Instead, we find large groups of people calling for a return to traditional morality, for a belief in the spiritual or mystical. Sadly, at times these groups find the clarity they seek in the company of fascists, racists, and warmongers. In our own country we have seen the tragic consequences of Charles Manson, Jim Jones, and David Koresh, while witnessing the growth of the religious right promulgated by such leaders as Pat Robertson and Jerry Falwell. Not surprisingly, the New Age movement, including the growing furor surrounding angels and astrology and the practice of witchcraft known as Wicca, has been consistently exploited by tabloid television. The sweeping success of the likes of Bill O'Reilly and Rush Limbaugh—as they confidently tell their listeners in no uncertain terms what is right and what is wrong with the political and social sphere in the United States—certainly indicates the seductive appeal of the demagogue to those who wish to have, as Ihab Hassan puts it, meaning anchored" (23). See also Terry Eagleton's chapter, "Revolution, Foundations, and Fundamentalists," in *After Theory* (2003).

2. As we suggested in *Formalist Criticism and Reader-Response Theory* (2002), "the critic wears scholarly lenses that cause certain elements of a literary work to rise from the page, similar to the shift that occurs when one views an image with 3-D glasses" (37). To be sure, these lenses comprised or are polished from the materials of theory, but when theory begins to limit the vision of the critic, keeping important sections of a text out of sight, then the hybrid nature of humanity is lost. What makes us most interesting (and, we would contend, healthiest) as readers and writers of a story is our mixed nature, the amalgamation of all that we have experienced distilled into the act of telling and interpreting.

3. Related to the idea of subjectivity and objectivity is the role that religion plays in the act of interpretation and meaning-making. In *Telling Stories: Postmodernism and the Invalidation of Traditional Narrative* (1995), Michael Roemer offers a shrewd observation about the "gods" that structure and control our everyday living. "Many of us no longer believe in an all-knowing, just, and loving deity," Roemer remarks. "But we also tend to think that *all* the gods are dead, though their names may have simply changed to biology, history, economics, culture, the unconscious, grammar, and chance. They don't know we exist, but determine our lives as completely as the gods of old" (353).

4. As critics, we do not offer allegiance to any one form of theory, but we have made use of such forms of theoretical practice as family-systems

psychology, ecocriticism, feminism, Marxism, reader-response theory, formalism, tropology, narratology, ethical criticism, myth criticism, and postmodernism.

1 Embracing the Fall: Reconfiguring Redemption in Jim Harrison's *The Woman Lit by Fireflies, Dalva, and The Road Home*

1. In a revealing passage from his long poem, *After Ikkyū*, Harrison reflects on the current spiritual state of his culture and the political and theological leaders whom he loathes. The speaker in the poem faces a crisis of sorts but looks to the Christ he knew in his youth and the Buddha he follows now, both of whom admonish him to "pay attention," a form of sacred attentiveness:

> The World is wrenched on her pivot, shivering.
>   Politicians
> and Preachers are standing on their heads, shitting
> out of their mouths. Lucky for us Stephen Mitchell
> has restored the Gospels, returning the Jesus
> I imagined at fourteen, offering up my clumsy life
> in a damp shroud of hormones. Most of all he said
> "pay attention," Buddha nodding from the wings. (45)

2. We are told in a later passage that for Clare's husband "the world itself was a marketing possibility" (214). As they drive through Iowa, Donald comments that local acreage prices are recovering from the 1985 downturn, and Clare remembers his worry that the black walnut tree in their yard— "worth seven thousand bucks as furniture veneer" (215)—might be cut down by lumber thieves while they are away on vacation. Donald cannot see beyond the seductive realm of the financial world to some other form of worth, a fact that injures Clare's psyche and leads to the dissolution of their marriage.

3. Harrison appears to adhere to Emerson's notion that stasis is nothing more than another kind of death, that spiritual truth may only be experienced by recognizing that it can never be captured in language. Clare's own experience echoes a passage in "Nature" when Emerson asks, "Who looks upon a river in a meditative hour and is not reminded of the flux of all things?" (32).

4. For further discussion of Harrison's conception of landscape as it relates to one's spiritual centeredness, see Todd F. Davis's "A Spiritual Topography: Northern Michigan in the Poetry of Jim Harrison." Remarkably, the paucity of published criticism regarding Harrison's work—despite his considerable popular and critical success—has neglected to explore his significant narrative examinations of the environment and its ethical interrelationship with humankind.

5. In an interview with *Salon Magazine*, Harrison further describes the process of becoming Dalva and her subsequent return during his writing of *The Road Home*. "I didn't have her—she had me," Harrison explains. "I actually dreamed her. She was on the porch in Santa Monica, longing for home. I even saw her naked in a dream, and it was quite overpowering. There's something

frightening about finding a woman who would take your heart." See also Harrison's own essay about writing in the voice of a woman, "First Person Female."

6. Harrison actually uses Claremont's statement in *The Road Home*, offering up himself—"an admittedly goofy poet"—as the object of deprecation. In a section of the novel narrated by Naomi, we are told that in the spring of 1986 Dalva sent her an essay "by some admittedly goofy poet she cared for that said that reality is an accretion of the perceptions of all creatures, not just us. The idea made my poor brain creak in expansion like a barn roof as the morning sun heats up" (314).

7. While it falls outside the scope of this chapter, in much of Harrison's work he clearly laments what we have done to the land and to the people who thrived upon it before its colonization. Such convictions clearly play a significant role in Dalva's grief; the past atrocities that her great grandfather witnessed are among the ghosts that haunt her. As with Gary Snyder, who writes in *Earth House Hold* (1968) that "something is always eating at the American heart like acid: it is the knowledge of what we have done to our continent, and the American Indian" (119), Harrison also sees our treatment of Native Americans as "our curse on the House of Atreus. They're our doom. The way we killed them is also what's killing us now. Greed" (Fergus 81). As Harrison reveals in *Just Before Dark* (1991), his interest in Native Americans and their many and diverse cultures is based on moral distinctions that he sadly believes many in our country simply are ignoring: "Native Americans are an obsession of mine, totally unshared by New York or Los Angeles for the average reason of moral vacuum" (22).

2 Writing Back through the Body: The Communion of Flesh and Spirit in the Work of Mary Swander

1. In *The Country of Language* (1999), Scott Russell Sanders explains that we "treat with care what we love, and we love only what we have truly learned to see, with all our senses alert" (24). Ironically, as Swander's own body shut down in certain ways, her senses became even more alert, and her dependence upon other forms and ways of living became much more significant. To survive, she had to be cognizant about her own body and the bodies (animals and plants) that might not only save her but sustain her as well.

2. In her acknowledgment—or better said, in her celebration—of the mysterious nature of the body, of its sacredness, Swander's vision seems similar to that of Annie Dillard's. In *Pilgrim at Tinker Creek* (1974), Dillard consistently works to fuse the mystical traditions of the spiritual world with the scientific traditions of the natural world. Dillard proclaims that physicists "are once again mystics" and that "all this means is that the physical world as we understand it now is more like the touch-and-go creek world I see than it is like the abiding world of which the mountains seem to speak" (204). Like Dillard, Swander progresses in her understanding of her own body and its connections to all other things by studying the natural world and the ways in which scientific and religious insights inform the manner in which we approach the natural world.

3. In *Writing from the Center* (1995), Sanders claims that "no matter where we live, the energy of creation flows in each of us, every second. We can feel it in heartbeat and dream and desire; we can sense it in everything that grows, from bacteria to beech trees, from babies to butterflies" (162).

4. In "Red Cabbage and Pears, Or How I Became a Pacifist," Swander furthers this notion by relating how she came to a position of pacifism through several influences, including her perspective that all living things are associated, that the very planet is an intricate web of life, and that harming one life in turn harms another. In her desire to farm organically—for her own health and the health of the planet—Swander explains that she "realized that we could spend our lives fighting cabbage worms and apple maggots. Or we can embrace a whole new harvest" (33).

3 Always Becoming: The Nature of Transcendence in the Poetry of Mary Oliver

1. Perhaps the most notable example of Oliver's precarious relationship with scholars and editors occurred when her work was omitted from the sixth and seventh editions of A. Poulin Jr., and Michael Waters's *Contemporary American Poetry*. After including her work in the fourth and fifth editions, Poulin and, after his death, Waters dropped Oliver's work from the anthology, perhaps reflecting the shifting currents of critical taste. What was the motivation or reasoning behind such an editorial move? Is Oliver's "religious" perspective— a combination of transcendental thought, Christianity, Buddhism, and eclectic Unitarianism—so at odds with the broader artistic and scholarly community that despite her obvious stature in the field of contemporary American poetry she is expendable? Or is her popularity, her ability to cross the border between serious artist and poet of the people, somehow a failing point for an academic industry that often celebrates texts that create distance between the popular audience and the more educated, artistic elite? Regardless, in 2006, Waters reinstated Oliver's poetry in the eighth edition of this influential anthology.

2. Vicki Graham demonstrates that although certain segments of feminist scholarship have sought to caution the reader to Oliver's use of nature in her poetry—suggesting that "her poems flirt dangerously with romantic assumptions about the close association of women with nature that many theorists claim put the woman writer at risk" (352)—such efforts have failed. "Twenty years of feminist, deconstructive, and linguistic theory have not weaned writers like Oliver, Marilynne Robinson, and Susan Griffin (to name just a few)," Graham writes, "from what skeptics might label a naïve belief in the possibility of intimate contact with the nonlinguistic world of nature and a confidence in the potential of language to represent that experience" (352).

3. Oliver writes that "Persons environmentally inclined have suggested that I am one of them. I don't argue with them, but it's not quite a fit. My work doesn't document any of the sane and learned arguments for saving, healing, and protecting the earth for our existence. What I write begins nor ends with the human world. Maybe I would be an environmentalist if I thought about it. But I don't. I don't think in terms of the all, the network of our needs and

our misdeeds, the interrelationship of our lives and the lives of all else. On the contrary, I am forever just going out for a walk and tripping over the root, or the petal, of some trivia, then seeing it as if in a second sight, as emblematic. By no means is this a unique way to live but is, rather, the path found by all who are mystically inclined" (*Winter Hours* 99). While Oliver would not claim that environmentalism or postmodern theory led her to such conclusions—her own affinity for philosophy, as previously mentioned, might best be described as a form of transcendentalism intertwined with Buddhist and Judeo-Christian mysticism—the same kind of work is accomplished in her poems.

4 Saints, Sinners, and the Dickensian Novel: The Ethics of Storytelling in John Irving's *The Cider House Rules*

1. In an interview with Alison Freeland, Irving underscores the significance of literary character in the act of storytelling: "What you remember about a novel is the emotional effect that the characters had on you. Long after the story, the plot, the intricacies of what happens, to whom, when—long after that stuff is out of your mind, out of memory, and you really need to read the book again to familiarize yourself with exactly how the story unfolds, a novel keeps working its magic on readers because of the emotional impact of characters that just can't be duplicated in a short story, even a short novel" (139).
2. In his review of *The Cider House Rules*, Christopher Lehmann-Haupt concurs with this thread of Harter and Thompson's argument, contending that the novelist's central point "is driven home with the sledgehammer effect that John Irving usually uses" (20).
3. In his essay "Against the Under Toad," collected in *Writing into the World: Essays, 1973–1987* (1991), Des Pres also stresses the intimate relationship between fiction and the world beyond in a moving passage of great ethical force: "Fiction speaks to us, touches our deepest fears and wishes, in so far as it articulates our embattled sense of being *in* the world, thereby confirming the self in its struggle to face and endure the besetting difficulties of a time and condition" (102–3).
4. While Irving attacks many avant-garde, postmodern writers, he avails himself nevertheless of some of the metafictional tools of postmodernity. In several instances, he employs metafiction to critique what he deems most vacuous and least admirable in contemporary fiction. Speaking about the minor character Helmbart who appears in both *The Water-Method Man* (1972) and *The 158-Pound Marriage* (1974), Jerome Klinkowitz contends that Helmbart's name is an "obvious play on the occasional duo-syllabic pronunciation of Donald Barthelme's last name," and like Barthelme and Gass, Helmbart is an advocate for "the new novel." Klinkowitz contends that "Irving's objection to Helmbart's work and his contrary method in his own establishes the central purposes of Irving's art: that fiction cannot be *just* about the act or theory of writing, but must incorporate the act or theory into a fiction that's still about life. His favorite writer is Charles Dickens, who balanced sentimentality with the attractive and persuasive powers of life itself" (36).

5. In an interesting but insightful coincidence during an interview conducted by *Image*, Irving echoes Massey's denouncement of categorization: "I have a horror of the instinct to categorize; I don't do it, and when I feel it's being done to me, I behave as perversely opposite to the offensive presumption as I can" (49).

6. Reflecting upon his own time spent in Europe as a young writer, Irving suggests that what was most significant about his days as an expatriate has little to do with location. Going so far as to suggest that Alaska or Tokyo would have been equally conducive to his maturation, he suggests, rather, that the dislocation accompanying any move into unfamiliar surroundings served as the catalyst for his transformation. "What I felt very strongly happen to me," Irving explains, "is that the European experience—again, it could have been the Tokyo experience, or I could have gone to Alaska, and I think Alaska would have become a kind of Vienna for me—I just needed to be someplace that removed me from looking with complacency at all the trivia of my surroundings—suddenly it made things not trivial anymore" (Miller 181). Irving's capacity for not overlooking the details of everyday existence, for taking on a perspective that elevates the mundane and the commonplace, allows him to use detail—much as Dickens did—to render ethical statements about the ways in which we approach the act of living. For a novelist like Irving who hopes to make his characters incredibly alive and indispensable to his readers—so much so that, as he explains in an interview with the *New England Review*, "what you remember about a novel is the emotional effect that the characters had on you" (139)—the gathering of detail and its placement within the narrative take on a level of importance not found in all forms of storytelling. For example, the minimalist school of fiction as well as the postmodernist metafictionists—both openly abhorred and denigrated on numerous occasions by Irving in essays and interviews—do not work toward what Irving calls "exuberance," the vitality of life somehow represented on the page. "Exuberance is unfashionable," Irving remarks in an interview with *Image*. "I point to the recent foolishness regarding 'minimalism' in the novel.... The idea of a 'minimalist' novel makes me gag. A novel is as much as you can bite off; if it's minimal, that says what you are" (49).

7. While Larch believes that he has a duty to perform abortions for the women who request his services during the course of *The Cider House Rules*, he does not argue for the ethical correctness of the procedure. In fact, as Larch explains to Homer Wells, "I'm not saying it's [abortion] *right*, you understand? I'm saying it's her choice—it's a woman's choice. She's got a right to have a choice, you understand?" (115).

8. Early in his life as an obstetrician, Larch realizes that much of the world wishes to categorize and dichotomize what he does. Larch instinctively fights such arbitrary definitions: "He was an obstetrician; he delivered babies into the world," Irving writes, "his colleagues called this 'the Lord's work.' And he was an abortionist; he delivered mothers, too. His colleagues called this 'the Devil's work,' but it was *all* the Lord's work to Wilbur Larch. As Mrs Maxwell observes in the novel: 'The true physician's soul cannot be too broad and gentle'" (75). Later, during his tenure at St Cloud's, the terms "Lord's work" and "Devil's work" prove helpful in distinguishing for Larch and his nurses between the kinds of procedures they are preparing to perform.

After serving as a physician during the First World War , moreover, Larch adamantly claims to have seen the genuine work of the Devil: "the Devil worked with shell and grenade fragments, with shrapnel and with the little, dirty bits of clothing carried with a missile into a wound. The Devil's work was gas bacillus infection, that scourge of the First World War—Wilbur Larch would never forget how it crackled to the touch" (76). Larch finds it difficult to understand how a nation could proudly support the Devil's work in war, yet outlaw the abortions he performs at the orphanage during peacetime. In a letter to his nurses sent from the military hospital where he works, Larch asks that his replacement at the orphanage, a doctor who refuses to perform abortions because he believes them to be immoral and unethical, be told that "the work at the orphanage is *all* the Lord's work—everything you do, you do *for* the orphans, you deliver *them*!" (76).

9. The narrative significance of the orphanage's nightly readings has been noted by several critics, including Debra Shostak, who observes that "Irving's debt to Dickens is repaid in a variety of ways—the bizarre or eccentric characters who populate his fictional terrain, the comic names, the homage in *The Cider House Rules* by way of numerous allusions to *David Copperfield* and *Great Expectations*, which are bibles to the orphan Homer Wells" (133).

10. Irving emphasizes the bond between Homer and Larch so that later in the novel we are not surprised by Homer's return to St Cloud's or his decision to perform an abortion. To achieve such an effect, Irving makes use of relational characterscape, a form of characterscape in which we come to understand better both characters within the same scene because of their interaction. In a dramatic sequence that includes the first father–son kiss shared by Homer and Larch, Irving depicts Homer saving a woman suffering from eclampsia, a condition that threatens the life of both the mother and the unborn child because of puerperal convulsions. Absent because he has gone to track down a cadaver that he plans to use in Homer's medical training, Larch upon his return discovers Homer asleep and the mother and infant in good health after the exhausting 30-hour ordeal. Proud of Homer's fine performance, Larch is moved to kiss Homer as he sleeps. At the scene's conclusion, we are told that Homer only feigns sleep while Larch kisses him: "Homer Wells felt his tears come silently; there were more tears than he remembered crying the last time he had cried....He cried because he had received his first fatherly kisses....If Homer Wells had received his first fatherly kisses, Dr. Larch had given the first kisses he had *ever* given—fatherly, or otherwise—since the day in the Portland boarding house when he caught the clap from Mrs. Eames....Oh God, thought Wilbur Larch, what will happen to me when Homer has to go?" (138–9).

11. For additional discussion about legalism and its dramatization in Irving's novel, see Bruce L. Rockwood's "Abortion Stories: Uncivil Discourse and *Cider House Rules*."

5 Curses and Blessings: Identity and Essentialism in the Work of Sherman Alexie

1. In *Formalism and Reader-Response Theory*, we discuss W. K. Wimsatt and Monroe C. Beardsley's *affective* and *intentional* fallacies, acknowledging the

potential benefits of viewing a literary work of art as both impersonal and ahistorical. We concede that the ultimate artistic success of a poem or short story cannot be based solely upon the author's personal experience. After all, how many atrociously written, utterly unartful books have been published mainly because the writer literally had the experience that was the principal subject of the book? At the same time, we can neither pretend to be nor wish to be, divorced from human feelings and tendencies, as critics. We live in a time in which the notion and dependability of the "authentic" has been seriously damaged. Some wonder if the authentic is merely a construction itself (that is, Baudrillard's simulacrum); others attempt to fool or deceive an audience about the degree or level of authenticity in a given work or experience; and still others (certainly the most popular position) seek the authentic continuously in talk shows, in reality television, in the world of celebrity nonfiction and memoir. Yet we cannot deny that there is a difference between physically doing something—the literal lived experience—and simply researching and reading about something. And it is a natural human proclivity to react more strongly to the storyteller who has literally lived the experience and then constructed the story based on that experience than to the storyteller who has merely imagined him- or herself into such settings. We acknowledge that there is a weakness to such an argument, but there is a weakness to Wimsatt and Beardsley's argument as well. This is an issue that cannot be settled with the pendulous swing of dichotomy, but rather, must be negotiated case by case.

2. For the first time in US history, the most recent census—taken in 2002—allowed individuals to claim more than one category, to expand the definition of culture and race. While this does not do away with essentialist notions of race (and the attendant racism that far too often follows), it does represent an official step forward, one that may lead to very different ways of thinking about how we define ourselves as people.

3. In *Playing Indian* (1998), Philip J. Deloria offers a real-world example of this kind of power-brokering. As he explains, "the quicksand dynamics of power link these two worlds (Indian and U.S.) in intimate and confusing ways, for the power that dominated Indians could, at the same time, be turned to their advantage" (178). Deloria uses the example of the newspaper *Indian Country Today*, which attacks the lack of Indian voices in the mainstream media, although it has been partially funded by the Gannett Foundation, a mainstream institution. Time and again, Alexie acknowledges the ways in which Indians can turn their marginalization into power—although this form of power often brings about negative consequences.

4. The way in which this desire for a purely essentialist perspective manifests itself outside of the oral tradition may be seen in the attacks on Alexie that involve a critique of his less-than-traditional settings, characters, and storylines. In an interview, Alexie claims that "most of our Indian literature is written by people whose lives are nothing like the Indians they're writing about. There's a lot of people pretending to be 'traditional,' all these academic professors living in university towns, who rarely spend any time on a reservation, writing all these 'traditional' books. Momaday—he's not a traditional man. And there's nothing wrong with that, I'm not either, but this adherence to the expected idea, the bear and all this imagery. I think it is

dangerous, and detrimental" ("Crossroads" 8). As Stephen F. Evans points out in "'Open Containers': Sherman Alexie's Drunken Indians," Alexie comes under attack from critics who claim that the "traditional" is the province of the Native American author. These critics argue that Alexie does great damage in not portraying a more "pure" or "positive" Indian experience, one akin to the work of Momaday or Silko. While we respect the work of authors like Momaday and Silko—writers whom these more traditional critics often praise and hold up as models for other Indian writers to follow—we would argue that critics like Gloria Bird, Louis Owens, and Elizabeth Cook-Lynn tread the borders of fundamentalism, perhaps even crossing over the line occasionally, in calling for a "role-model" literature, one that, as Alexie remarks, pretends to be "traditional." In an online posting, Alexie explains that his "mom is the drug and alcohol treatment counselor on the rez, so I'm quite aware of what's going on out there. There are two major cocaine and crack dealers on the rez now. They're Crips gang members. In every government housing village, crack vials are on the lawns. Fewer and fewer kids are going to college. Domestic violence incidents are rising. Property crime, almost unheard of during my years on the rez, has risen dramatically. My fiction doesn't even come close to how bad it can be, and how good it can be, on my reservation" ("Re: Alexie Article").

5. Interestingly, while most of Oliver's poetry has ignored the consumer complex that has grown increasingly pervasive and intrusive over the course of her life and career, she has recently published a poem whose title acknowledges such devastation in ways her other poems do not: "What Was Once the Largest Shopping Center in Northern Ohio Was Built Where There Had Been a Pond I Used to Visit Every Summer Afternoon" (*Why I Wake Early* 36).

6. For an in-depth study of the role of basketball in a tribal setting, see Larry Colton's *Counting Coup: A True Story of Basketball and Honor on the Little Big Horn* (2000).

6 "Our long national nightmare is over": Moral Repair and Jeffrey Eugenides's *The Virgin Suicides*

1. Walker also reminds us of the dangers of moral relativism, pointing out the ways in which communities evolve their own notions of morality, rather than relying on the findings of academics and philosophers: "Morality 'itself'—that which needs to be understood and reflectively tested—is always something people are actually doing together in their communities, societies, and ongoing relationships. It's not up to academic philosophers to discover it or make it up, even if it is, as I believe it is, a worthy task to try to understand it more deeply and to understand how it is open to criticism, refinement, and improvement. That task is not solely reserved to philosophers, and when philosophers assume that task they do not start in an epistemic position entirely different from anyone else.... Without already knowing a good deal about (what we call) moral reasoning, moral rules, moral responsibility, and so on, we wouldn't know where to begin or what

we are talking about. We're all in the same boat, epistemically, in this way" ("Morality in Practice" 175).

2. For Walker, the concept of moral repair involves an explicit pact that has been created by a community with shared value systems and a concerted desire for reconciliation. "Old forms of responsibility can be eroded or strengthened, and new ones established and enforced," she writes. "But senses of value and responsibility can only be shorn up, shifted, lost, or newly installed *by us*, that is, by many acts of many of us, or at least by enough of us at a particular place and time. We do this by doing what morality requires, by teaching our children and reminding each other of it. We also do this by the ways we respond to the doing of what is *not* morally acceptable. We show what we will 'stand for'" ("Moral Repair" 112).

3. Alexander employs the word *pollution* to describe the manner in which Watergate slowly made its way into the American consciousness. "Watergate had become a symbol of pollution," Alexander writes, "embodying a sense of evil and impurity" (158). Initial reports about the break-in in June 1972 were generally dismissed by the American public, which largely ignored the crisis until televised hearings ensued during the summer of 1973.

4. The identity of Deep Throat is, of course, no longer elusive. In May 2005, W. Mark Felt, the former Associate Director of the Federal Bureau of Investigation, confirmed to *Vanity Fair* magazine that he had acted as Bob Woodward's secret informant during the Watergate crisis. Woodward detailed his experiences with Felt in *The Secret Man: The Story of Watergate's Deep Throat* (2005).

5. In itself, the Lisbons' surname connotes powerful notions of immigration. As the capital of Portugal, Lisbon was the point of departure for numerous explorers in search of brave new worlds.

6. The Saturday Night Massacre occurred on October 20th, 1973, when President Nixon ordered Attorney General Elliot Richardson to fire special prosecutor Archibald Cox, who had subpoenaed copies of taped conversations from the Oval Office. After Richardson resigned in protest, Nixon ordered Deputy Attorney General William Ruckelshaus to fire Cox. Like Richardson, Ruckelshaus resigned in protest. At this juncture, the President ordered Solicitor General Robert Bork, who was acting head of the Justice Department, to fire Cox. Bork complied with the President's order after Richardson argued that Bork's resignation would leave the Justice Department in disarray at a critical moment in American constitutional history in terms of the separation of powers. It was also the death knell for the Nixon Administration, as evidenced by the three million letters of protest received by the White House during the subsequent weekend. For many Americans, the firing of Cox was the proverbial last straw, Alexander writes, because it "made them fear pollution of their ideals and themselves" (168).

7. While all four of the remaining Lisbon daughters attempt suicide on June 16th, only Mary survives the episode, despite trying to gas herself in the kitchen oven. She lives for more than a month, finally ingesting a lethal dose of sleeping pills in early August. Belatedly recognizing the ineffectiveness of her scheme to quarantine her daughters from the corrosive postwar world, Mrs. Lisbon allows Mary to take voice lessons from a neighbor, Mr. Jessup, only a few days before her death.

7 "What's Filipino? What's authentic? What's in the blood?": Alterity and Ethics in the Novels of Jessica Hagedorn

1. In *Empire* (2000), Michael Hardt and Antonio Negri explain this desire for universalizing capitalism as the product of a fundamental historical revision in the economic makeup of the world marketplace: "We believe that this shift makes perfectly clear and possible today the capitalistic project to bring together economic power and political power, to realize, in other words, a properly capitalistic order" (9). Simply put, globalization serves as the catalyst for new forms of Empire in a postcolonial and postimperialist world characterized by shifting modes of national and legalistic authority, as well as by radically divergent means of production and a concomitant escalation of international consumerism.

2. As Nerissa S. Balce remarks, the phrase finds its origins as "a pejorative used by Americans for Filipinos during the early 1900s" and "refers both to the elites who oppress the poor and to the poor themselves who have no recourse but to eat dog, considered a poor person's meal. The novel's title, then, implies both the contemporary and the historical representations of Filipinos. On the one hand, the elites and the poor are both dogeaters. On the other hand, the novel's reinscription of Philippine history recalls the racialized stereotype of the Filipino as backward and savage" (55).

3. Hagedorn's thinly veiled portrait of opposition leader Benigno Aquino Jr.'s assassination on August 21, 1983 contributes to the *roman á clef* flavor of *Dogeaters*, a novel that also makes particular reference to the public persona of First Lady Imelda Marcos as well as to numerous other Filipino historical figures.

4. In an April 1994 interview with Kay Bonetti, Hagedorn suggests that Joey's revolutionary conversion has the possibility of ambiguous outcomes: "I didn't want to deal with whether he would become the good revolutionary or not. I think there's been so much disillusionment that's occurred with the Left in the Philippines. And I could see that the point was that Joey is taught something. Then where he goes from there wasn't my concern anymore. It was going to be very ambiguous because he could turn into a really awful person once again. This new knowledge that he has about what's going on around him doesn't necessarily mean he's going to become a better person."

5. See Vincente L. Rafael's "Patronage and Pornography: Ideology and Spectatorship in the Early Marcos Years" for additional discussion about the *bomba* phenomenon.

6. In one instance, the First Lady even went as far as to coin an audacious, self-serving term—"Imeldific"—to account for her yen for pursuing an opulent lifestyle: "I was born ostentatious. They will list my name in the dictionary someday," she remarked in 1988. "They will use '*Imeldific*' to mean ostentatious extravagance" (quoted in Soukhanov 140). Journalist Michael Defensor later fashioned the term "Superma'am" to account for Imelda Marcos's outrageous, ego-driven desire for shoes, diamonds, and other finery (1).

7. On November 18, 1981, 26 construction workers were crushed during the collapse of one of the floors of a Manila cultural center commissioned by Imelda Marcos for an international film festival honoring her husband's ostensible love of cinema. In one of the most egregious historical examples of her remarkable indifference to the welfare of her people, the First Lady refused to acknowledge the workers' tragic demise. In *Dogeaters*, the callous Madame "orders the survivors to continue building; more cement is poured over dead bodies; they finish exactly three hours before the first film is scheduled to be shown" (130).

8. In Tagalog, *Kundiman* refers to a specific genre of Filipino love songs. In her interview with Bonetti, Hagedorn discusses the *Kundiman's* own intricate history of colonization and recalls that "there may have been a Spanish influence on it. We have little orchestras called *rondallas* and musicians play this banjo-like instrument called the *banduria*. When I finally went to Spain, I found out the Gypsies play it there, and the Spanish have claimed it. But actually maybe the Arabs brought it, the Moors. And so maybe that's how it came to the Philippines. Who knows?"

9. In *The Gangster of Love*, Hagedorn notes that in Tagalog the phrase *yo-yo* means "to return." Interestingly, *yo-yo* derives from *yau-yau*, which means "to cast out" (285). In this way, the phrase connotes the idea of coming as well as going, the perplexing double-bind that often afflicts the cultural attitudes of first-generation immigrants.

10. This phenomenon frequently takes on intergenerational overtones, especially regarding the ways in which Filipino Americans think about the connections between the Philippines and its colonial history. As Oscar V. Campomanes argues, "The signifiers 'Filipino' and 'Philippines' evoke colonialist meanings and cultural redactions which possess inordinate power to shape the fates of. . . Filipino peoples everywhere. These considerations," he adds, "overdetermine their dominant sense of nonbelonging in the United States, the Philippines, and other places" (151).

11. It is worth noting that the Riveras would be considered as "fourth-wave" immigrants in the parlance of Filipino immigrant terminology. According to Naomi De Castro's valuable documentary *In No One's Shadow: Filipinos in America* (1988), Filipino immigration has largely occurred in four distinct waves. The first wave involves pre-1906 immigration activity associated with the 1903 passage of the United States Government's Pensionado Act, which allowed Filipino students to continue their studies in American colleges and universities. The emergence of the "Sakada" system instigated the second wave of Filipino immigration in 1906. Sakadas functioned as plantation workers contracted to harvest the sugar and pineapple fields of Hawaii. The third wave followed the passage of the 1945 War Brides Act, which permitted veterans to bring their Filipino wives and children to the United States. Finally, the fourth wave and its massive influx of Filipino immigrants occurred following the passage of the Immigration Nationality Act of 1965.

8 "Everybody had a hard year": *The White Album* and the Beatles' Poetics of Apocalypse

1. The Beatles' alleged postmodernist tendencies are a matter of ongoing critical debate. While it is possible to argue—as Kenneth Womack has done in "The Beatles as Modernists"—that the Beatles work from a modernist position that posits a unified moral center, there is a growing certainty among Beatles scholars that frames the band as innovative postmodern visionaries. In such works as Henry W. Sullivan's *The Beatles with Lacan: Rock 'n' Roll as Requiem for the Modern Age* (1995), David Quantick's *Revolution: The Making of the Beatles' White Album* (2002), Devin McKinney's *Magic Circles: The Beatles in Dream and History* (2003), Ed Whitley's "The Postmodern *White Album*," and Jeffrey Roessner's "We All Want to Change the World: Postmodern Politics and the Beatles' *White Album*," the Beatles are essentially—indeed, *unflinchingly*—categorized in terms of an increasingly popular reading of the *White Album* as a series of arch parodies that emphasizes their postmodernity.

2. While it has become *de rigueur* among Beatles biographers to characterize *The White Album* as one of the group's more disconnected recording ventures—ground zero for their eventual disbandment—the reality of the work's production suggests otherwise. Having returned from their well-known spiritual sojourn with the Maharishi in Rishikesh, the Beatles assembled in May 1968 at Kinfauns, Harrison's Esher recording studio. Together, they created 23 demos in preparation for recording throughout the summer and fall months the 30 songs that comprise *The White Album*. The demos include "Cry Baby Cry"; "Child of Nature"; "The Continuing Story of Bungalow Bill"; "I'm So Tired"; "Yer Blues"; "Everybody's Got Something to Hide Except for Me and My Monkey"; "What's the New Mary Jane"; "Revolution"; "While My Guitar Gently Weeps"; "Circles"; "Sour Milk Sea"; "Not Guilty"; "Piggies"; "Julia"; "Blackbird"; "Rocky Raccoon"; "Back in the USSR"; "Honey Pie"; "Mother Nature's Son"; "Ob-La-Di, Ob-La-Da"; "Junk"; "Dear Prudence"; and "Sexy Sadie."

3. "Glass Onion," with its pointed allusion to Liverpool, evokes a wealth of intriguing semantic interpretations. The word Liverpool finds its origins in a twelfth-century pool that sat beside the town. It was a sluggish, dirty tidal inlet that joined the Mersey River just south of the Pier Head. The city's name has become synonymous with the delftware and porcelain manufactured in Liverpool in the eighteenth century, and, as an adjective, it has taken on similar meanings connoting filth and a cold, stubborn sensibility. "Liverpool weather," for example, is known for its dank and dirty winds, while hard, nearly inedible biscuits are called "Liverpool pantiles." And then there is the paradoxical "Liverpool kiss," which connotes a "blow delivered to the head or face"—a head-butt. In sharp contrast with Josh Rogan's nostalgic musings about the "cast-iron" shore in "The Skipper's Lament," the Beatles' Liverpool in "Glass Onion" exists as a downtrodden home for Lennon and McCartney's restless, corrosive urbanites—the characters who act as the songwriting duo's stock-in-trade. Like cast iron, they are a hard people, "insensible to fatigue; rigid, stern, unyielding" (*OED*).

4. McCartney's nostalgic contentment in "Mother Nature's Son" is brought into bold relief in the *Grey Album* (2003) by DJ Danger Mouse's controversial

"mash-up" of the Beatles' *White Album* with Jay-Z's hip-hop *Black Album* (2003). In spite of its notorious (and, quite frankly, illegal) origins, Danger Mouse's revisioning of "Mother Nature's Son" makes for one of the *Grey Album*'s finest tracks. By combining McCartney's sanguine acoustic guitar in "Mother Nature's Son" with Jay-Z's heartbreaking lyrics in "December 4th" about growing up in a world fraught with poverty and drugs, Danger Mouse succeeds in brilliantly contrasting McCartney's idyllic childhood memories with Jay-Z's difficult youth—especially in terms of the hip-hop star's disquieting relationship with his mother, Gloria Carter, whose strained memories are featured in a moving pair of narrative interludes. Danger Mouse's coalescence of "Mother Nature's Son" and "December 4th" posits an implicit commentary about the harshly divergent sociohistorical experiences among various segments of white and black culture, as well as a meaningful analysis of the ways in which we think and feel about the past. Boston's DJ BC offers a similar, humor-oriented reading of "Mother Nature's Son" in a mashup of the Beatles and the Beastie Boys entitled "Mother Nature's Rump."

5. McCartney's penchant for musical throwbacks is the stuff of pop legend. Additional examples include *Sgt. Pepper*'s "When I'm 64," Wings' "You Gave Me the Answer" and "Baby's Request," and the unreleased "Room with a View."

6. Fredric Jameson interprets the Beatles and the Rolling Stones as the "high-modernist moment" of punk and new wave rock. In the same breath, he locates the Beatles somewhere just beyond modernism's steady decline, yet nevertheless appears to acknowledge their incongruity with postmodernism's "inverted millenarianism" (1).

9 Finding Forgiveness, or Something Like It, in David Mamet's *House of Games*, *The Spanish Prisoner*, and *State and Main*

1. In *South of the Northeast Kingdom*, Mamet remarks that "there are those human senses that we all acknowledge, but which we cannot quantify. The girl at the stoplight turns as she feels your gaze. No conscious effort can bring about this result; it is a survival of a primal, an occult, powerful part of life. Similarly, there is a mystery in the evanescent. It surfaces, certainly, at birth and death, but it is present regularly, intermittently, just beyond, and different from a conscious knowledge" (xv–xvi).

2. As Myles Weber observes, "By appealing only to the rational mind, the 'problem play' fails to grip audience members at a deeper level of consciousness. At most, it instills in them a sense of superiority to those characters whose actions they recognize as morally repugnant" (136).

3. In this instance, we extrapolate the idea of rectangulation from the concept of triangulation, the psychological term that denotes the manner in which two members of a relationship become enmeshed to the detriment of the third person's interests and well-being. In *The Spanish Prisoner*, Mr Klein, Jimmy, and Susan work collectively to manipulate Joe, the highly vulnerable fourth corner of their rectangular relationship.

4. Mamet's intricate characterization of Jimmy and Susan demonstrates his concerted effort in his screenplays to create round characters who defy our inclinations to reduce the irreducible, to nullify their complexity, and to erase their otherness: "I always want everyone to be sympathetic to all the characters," Mamet notes. "Because when you aren't, what you are doing is writing a melodrama with good guys and bad guys. Drama is really about conflicting impulses in the individual. That is what *all* drama is about" ("Celebrating" 65).

5. In this instance, Mamet is clearly referencing his own dilemmas as a Pulitzer Prize-winning playwright attempting to work within Hollywood's ethically dubious system, while also striving to evade its myriad possibilities for self-corruption.

6. Ann's efforts in this regard find their origins in her attempts to entice her community into grappling with the nature and value of truth. As the motto for the *Waterford Sentinel* proclaims to its would-be readers: "You shall not bear false witness." Likewise, Ann's goals for establishing a working community theater are indicative of Mamet's own convictions about drama's capacity for involving audiences in a larger search for authenticity: "The theater is a most useful political tool; it's a place where we go to hear the truth," Mamet observes. "The difference with theater is that people go to participate in it as a community endeavor; they seek that by nature" ("I Just Kept Writing" 33).

7. In this way, Ann takes a leap of faith—a generous, albeit risky maneuver, given the brevity of their relationship—and affords Joe with the opportunity for embracing heroism: "If we are happy, we want someone to be for us and to whom we can be a hero," Mamet contends. "In misery, we strive to be or find a victim. In either case, we're searching for a partner to share our idea of home" (*Make-Believe Town* 115).

8. Writing for the *Village Voice*, Jessica Winter clearly disagrees with the notion that Joe can achieve alterity and yet remain complicit in the film's production: "The interlocking hijinks and homespun non sequiturs attempt homage to Sturges, but surely Preston would have inverted Mamet's scenario, in which our hero doesn't have to confess an inconvenient truth but gets Brownie-points for wanting to," she writes. "The narrative ends up a fatuous triumph of Machiavellian thought and action; *State and Main* is a Hollywood satire as cynical and thick-headed as its supposed targets."

10 Performing Empowerment: Revisiting Liberation Pedagogy in Eve Ensler's *The Vagina Monologues*

1. In addition to Ensler, a number of contemporary women writers have devoted their energies to the reclamation of the female sexual identity. Principal among these works are Holly Hughes's *Clit Notes: A Sapphic Sampler* (1996) and Inga Muscio's *Cunt: A Declaration of Independence* (1998).

2. In *A Pedagogy for Liberation: Dialogues on Transforming Education* (1987), Shor and Freire extend the latter's colonial metaphor to contemporary education, an arena that succeeds, they argue, in erecting its own "culture of silence." According to Shor and Freire, "The official pedagogy constructs [students] as

passive/aggressive characters. After years in dull transfer-of-knowledge class-es, in boring courses filled with sedating teacher-talk, many have become nonparticipants, waiting for the teacher to set the rules and start narrating what to memorize. These students are silent because they no longer expect education to include the joy of learning, moments of passion or inspiration or comedy, or even that education will speak to the real conditions of their lives" (122).

3. As with *The Vagina Monologues* and V-Day, Ensler's own liberation pedagogy is exemplified by her work on behalf of the Revolutionary Association of the Women of Afghanistan (RAWA). Her activism regarding the cultural tragedy of Afghanistan's gender apartheid underscores the nature of the liberation pedagogy that exists at the core of her aesthetic: "We have to address what's going on, that we are living in a paradigm of escalating violence—based, in my opinion, on corporate greed and the emerging corporate globalization of the world," Ensler remarks in a *Salon Magazine* interview concerning her RAWA activities. "Women are commodities within that structure: they are bodies, serving or not serving. I think we have to stop and say, 'Is this the par-adigm we want to keep living in? Is this the paradigm we want? Do we want to perish as a people?' "

4. In *Teaching to Transgress: Education as the Practice of Freedom* (1994), bell hooks accounts for the sexist elements in Freire's *The Pedagogy of the Oppressed*: "In talking with academic feminists (usually white women) who feel they must either dismiss or devalue the work of Freire because of sexism, I see clearly how our different responses are shaped by the standpoint that we bring to the work. I came to Freire thirsty, dying of thirst (in that way that the colo-nized, marginalized subject who is still unsure of how to break the hold of the status quo, who longs for change, is needy, is thirsty), and I found in his work (and the work of Malcolm X, Fanon, etc.) a way to quench that thirst. To have work that promotes one's liberation is such a powerful gift that it does not matter so much if the gift is flawed" (49–50).

5. Broadhurst further defines liminal performance in terms of its intentional mixing of linguistic and theatrical codes, eclectic style, playfulness, and self-conscious repetition among other traits (12–14). As the individual readings of Ensler's micro-narratives will demonstrate, *The Vagina Monologues* embraces nearly all of these elements in one form or another.

6. We are indebted to Judith Myers-Walls and Mayi Fonseca for enumerating and describing Freire's eight principles for a liberation pedagogy.

7. In her foreword to *The Vagina Monologues*, Gloria Steinem writes: "By the time feminists were putting CUNT POWER! On buttons and T-shirts as a way of reclaiming that devalued word, I could recognize the restoration of an ancient power. After all, the Indo-European word *cunt* was derived from the goddess Kali's title of Kunda or Cunti, and shares the same root as *kin* and *country*" (xiv).

8. Interestingly, Ensler signals the end of each performance of *The Vagina Monologues* by playing TLC's hit song about empowerment, "UnPretty." The song's lyrics pointedly illustrate its narrator's socially constructed desire to please her partner by conforming to his explicitly gendered expectations: "I used to be so cute to me / Just a little bit skinny / Why do I look to all these

things / To keep you happy / Maybe get rid of you / And then I'll get back to me."

11   How Do You Solve a Problem Like *Magnolia*?

1. Anderson describes his own writing experience with *Magnolia* as "an interesting study in a writer writing from his gut" (vii). Although *Magnolia* is a highly structured film—similar in its complexity to *Nashville* (1975) or *Short Cuts* (1993) by Robert Altman—for Anderson the "felt" quality of the film was of utmost importance. Anderson does not wish to highlight the cerebral aspects of his work here, but rather, as he states in the introduction to his screenplay, he wants to "trust the gut" (viii).

2. In *"Magnolia*: Masquerading as Soap Opera," Joanne Clarke Dillman argues that "this sequence foregrounds the constructed unity of the televisual world." "Doesn't this happen during Live Aid concerts and the Concert for New York City?" she asks. "The imagined community, linked through time and obliterating space, is only possible on TV (or now, on the Webcast)" (147). While we agree with Dillman that this "foregrounds the constructed unity" of the scene, we would not acquiesce to the notion that it must necessarily only represent a televisual world, a world of nonreality at the worst and at the best that of the simulacrum of which Jean Baudrillard speaks. Instead, we argue that for a generation that has been assimilated into the world through such devices as television or the Webcast, perhaps this moment of song shared by many disparate others in disparate places fits seamlessly with their emotional understanding of the world.

3. This notion correlates with Anderson's own resolve that movies can tell the truth or they can lie. "I'm a film geek," Anderson confesses in an interview with Chuck Stephens. "I was raised on movies. And there come these times in life where you just get to a spot when you feel like movies are betraying you.... and you resent movies for maybe taking away from the painful truth of what's happening to you—but that's exactly why those moments show up in movies. Those things 'do happen' " (205).

4. A. G. Harmon contends that "good artists, including Anderson, take advantage of the similarities between life and drama, and draw our attention to the strange things that appear in the sky of the silver screen" (116).

5. As the camera pans across the television audience during the taping of *What Do Kids Know?*, we see placards with verses from the book of Exodus. At this time, we are unsure what they mean: Is it simply the absurdist ranting of a contemporary prophet, the lunatic who consistently says the world will end but never knows the right date for our demise? Or is it Anderson's own foreshadowing of where the film is headed? Upon one's first viewing of this film, it is hard to imagine that anyone anticipates a rain of frogs on the San Fernando Valley.

Conclusion: Postmodern Humanism and the Ethical Future

1. As Jerry Aline Flieger warns, the instant gratification that we have come to desire in postmodern life threatens to engender an increasing sense of para-

noia among mass culture: "The transparency of our information-saturated global monad, in the age of instantaneous 'contact' and access, doubtless confers a paranoid modality to 'postmodern' life, giving us the feeling that we are watched everywhere, monitored and transcribed by a ubiquitous information bank. Much postmodern writing reflects this feeling of being under the gaze of an anonymous surveillance—the sense that the ever growing database which catalogues us all has its eye on us, tracking our social and economic history, sometimes for political reasons, sometimes to facilitate the new economic or cultural order (as in the credit rating system in the West)." Worse yet, Flieger writes, this paranoia points to "a bleak or even psychotic moment, leading to the effacement of the individual and the diminution of social contact" (87).

2. Smith argues that the dangers of a politically engendered nostalgia extend well beyond our futile dreams for an "archetypal paradise": "If nostalgia is universal, even a return to pre-industrial society won't help. We are convinced that whatever it is we long for wasn't actually there, that we are longing for something—community, stability, the feeling of being at home—that is unattainable anywhere. Thus, not only has industrialization obliterated agrarian society, but its accompanying theory of nostalgia has destabilized our individual and collective memories of our pre-industrial past" (522–3).

3. For McCarthy, this concept of re-orientation involves a revaluation of what it means to be an individual, a fully realized self: "Opening up the reductiveness of the signifier to an understanding of the complicities of desire and concept is a step to relocating the individual, as the subject of ethico-politico praxis, within the mutually supportive dynamics of modernity and postmodernity. If the pleasures of deconstruction have perverted the modernist spirit of equality, liberty and fraternity into degrading conditions of existence for the weaker sections of society, then reversing this process entails an awareness of the subject's dissolution, by stages, into signifier, difference, particle-quanta, and finally into that autonomous mathesis of number concealed beneath postmodern figural play."

References

Alexander, Jeffrey C. *The Meanings of Social Life: A Cultural Sociology*. Oxford: Oxford University Press, 2003.

Alexie, Sherman. *The Business of Fancydancing*. Brooklyn: Hanging Loose, 1992.

Alexie, Sherman. "Crossroads: A Conversation with Sherman Alexie." Interview with John Purdy. *Studies in American Indian Literatures* 9.4 (1997): 1–18.

Alexie, Sherman. *The Lone Ranger and Tonto Fistfight in Heaven*. New York: Atlantic Monthly, 1993.

Alexie, Sherman. "Re: Alexie Article." Online positing. 3 July 1997. <nativelitl@csd.uwm.edu.Ross1.>

Alexie, Sherman. *Ten Little Indians*. New York: Grove, 2003.

Alexie, Sherman. *The Toughest Indiana in the World*. New York: Atlantic Monthly, 2000.

Allen, William Rodney, ed. *Conversations with Kurt Vonnegut*. Jackson: University Press of Mississippi, 1988.

Altman, Robert, dir. *Nashville*. Paramount, 1975.

Altman, Robert, dir. *Short Cuts*. Fine Line, 1993.

Anderson, Paul Thomas, dir. *Boogie Nights*. New Line, 1997.

Anderson, Paul Thomas. Interview. *Magnolia: The Shooting Script*. 197–208.

Anderson, Paul Thomas, dir. *Magnolia*. New Line, 1999.

Anderson, Paul Thomas. *Magnolia: The Shooting Script*. New York: Newmarket, 2000.

Anderson, Paul Thomas, dir. *Sydney [Hard Eight]*. Sony, 1996.

Assoun, Paul-Laurent. "The Subject and the Other in Levinas and Lacan." Trans. Dianah Jackson and Denise Merkle. *Levinas and Lacan: The Missed Encounter*. Ed. Sarah Harasym. Albany: State University of New York Press, 1998. 79–101.

Balce, Nerissa S. "*Dogeaters*, by Jessica Hagedorn." *A Resource Guide to Asian American Literature*. Ed. Sau-ling Cynthia Wong and Stephen H. Sumida. New York: MLA, 2001. 54–65.

Balce, Nerissa S. "Imagining the Neocolony." *Hitting Critical Mass: A Journal of Asian American Cultural Criticism* 2 (1995). <ist-socrates.berkeley.edu/~critmass/v2n2/balce1.html.>

Baudrillard, Jean. "The Precession of Simulacra." *A Postmodern Reader*. Ed. Joseph Natoli and Linda Hutcheon. Albany: State University of New York Press, 1993. 342–75.

Baudrillard, Jean. *Simulations*. Trans. Paul Foss, Paul Patton, and Philip Beitchman. New York: Semiotext(e), 1983.

Beatles, The. *Abbey Road*. 1969. Parlophone, 1987.

Beatles, The. *The Beatles [The White Album]*. 1968. Parlophone, 1987.

Beatles, The. *The Beatles Anthology*. San Francisco: Chronicle, 2000.

Beatles, The. *Let It Be*. 1970. Parlophone, 1987.

Beatles, The. *Magical Mystery Tour*. 1967. Parlophone, 1987.

Beatles, The. *Past Masters, Volume 2*. Parlophone, 1987.

Beatles, The. *Please Please Me*. 1963. Parlophone, 1987.

Beatles, The. *Revolver*. 1966. Parlophone, 1987.

Beatles, The. *Rubber Soul*. 1965. Parlophone, 1987.

Beatles, The. *Sgt. Pepper's Lonely Hearts Club Band*. 1967. Parlophone, 1987.

Bell, Madison Smartt. "The Story of the Days of Creation." *Genesis: As It is Written: Contemporary Writers on Our First Stories*. Ed. David Rosenberg. New York: Harper Collins, 1996. 23–34.

Bernstein, Carl and Bob Woodward. *All the President's Men*. New York: Simon and Schuster, 1974.

Berry, Wendell. "Christianity and the Survival of Creation." *Sex, Economy, Freedom and Community*. New York: Pantheon, 1993. 93–116.

Berry, Wendell. *Life Is a Miracle: An Essay Against Modern Superstition*. Washington, DC: Counterpoint, 2000.

Berry, Wendell. "The Peace of Wild Things." *Collected Poems, 1957–1982*. San Francisco: North Point, 1984. 69.

Berry, Wendell. *Standing by Words*. San Francisco: North Point, 1983.

Bird, Gloria. "The Exaggeration of Despair in Sherman Alexie's *Reservation Blues*." *Wicazo Sa Review* 11.2 (1995): 47–52.

Björk. *Debut*. Elektra, 1993.

Bloom, Harold. *The Anxiety of Influence: A Theory of Poetry*. New York: Oxford University Press, 1973.

Branch, Michael P. "Sick of Being Sick of Nature." *Isotope: A Journal of Literary Nature and Science Writing* 3.1 (2005): 42–43.

Broadhurst, Susan. *Liminal Acts: A Critical Overview of Contemporary Performance and Theory*. London: Cassell, 1999.

Buell, Lawrence. *The Environmental Imagination: Thoreau, Nature Writing, and the Formation of American Culture*. Cambridge: Belknap, 1995.

Cahill, Michael. *A Nixon Man*. New York: St. Martin's Press, 1998.

Callicott, J. Baird. *Beyond the Land Ethic: More Essays in Environmental Philosophy*. Albany: State University of New York Press, 1999.

Campomanes, Oscar V. "Filipinos in the United States and Their Literature of Exile." *Asian American Writers*. Ed. Harold Bloom. Philadelphia: Chelsea House, 1998. 149–69.

Cassell, Eric J. *The Nature of Suffering and the Goals of Medicine*. Oxford: Oxford University Press, 1991.

Chess, Stella and Jane Whitbread. *Daughters: From Infancy to Independence*. New York: Doubleday, 1978.

Christensen, Laird. "The Pragmatic Mysticism of Mary Oliver." *Ecopoetry: A Critical Introduction*. Ed. J. Scott Bryson. Salt Lake City: University of Utah Press, 2002. 135–52.

Cixous, Hélène. "The Laugh of the Medusa." *Feminisms: An Anthology of Literary Theory and Criticism*. Ed. Robyn R. Warhol and Diane Price Herndl. New Brunswick: Rutgers University Press, 1991. 334–49.

Coles, Robert. *The Call of Stories: Teaching and the Moral Imagination*. Boston: Houghton Mifflin, 1989.

Colleran, Jeanne and Jenny S. Spencer, eds. Introduction. *Staging Resistance: Essays on Political Theater*. Ann Arbor: University of Michigan Press, 1998. 1–10.

Colton, Larry. *Counting Coup: A True Story of Basketball and Honor on the Little Big Horn*. New York: Warner, 2000.

Cook-Lynn, Elizabeth. "American Indiana Intellectualism and the New Indian Story." *Natives and Academics: Researching and Writing about American Indians.* Ed. Devon A. Mihesuah. Lincoln: University of Nebraska Press, 1998. 111–38.

Corker, David. "Otherness, the Other, and Alterity." *Knots.* 2003. <www.uea. ac.uk/eas/people/corker/knots/otherness.shtml.>

Davis, Todd F. *Kurt Vonnegut's Crusade, Or, How a Postmodern Harlequin Preached a New Kind of Humanism.* Albany: State University of New York Press, 2006.

Davis, Todd F. *Some Heaven: Poems.* East Lansing: Michigan State University Press, 2006.

Davis, Todd F. "A Spiritual Topography: Northern Michigan in the Poetry of Jim Harrison." *Midwest Quarterly* 42.1 (2000): 94–104.

Davis, Todd F. and Kenneth Womack. *Formalist Criticism and Reader-Response Theory.* New York: Palgrave, 2002.

De Castro, Naomi, dir. *In No One's Shadow: Filipinos in America.* CrossCurrent Media, 1988.

Defensor, Michael. "Imeldific Milestones." *Asiaweek* 31 December 1999: 1.

DeGiglio-Bellemare, Mario. "*Magnolia* and the Signs of the Times: A Theological Reflection." *The Journal of Religion and Film* 4.2 (2000). <www.unomaha.edu/jrf/magnolia.htm.>

Dei, George. "The Women of a Ghanaian Village: A Study of Social Change." *African Studies Review* 37.2 (1994): 121–45.

Deloria, Philip J. *Playing Indian.* New Haven: Yale University Press, 1998.

DeMott, Benjamin. Review of *The Cider House Rules,* by John Irving. *New York Times Book Review* 26 May 1985: 1, 25.

Des Pres, Terrence. "Against the Under Toad: The Novels of John Irving." *Writing into the World: Essays, 1973–1987.* New York: Viking, 1991. 97–103.

Didion, Joan. *The White Album.* New York: Simon and Schuster, 1968.

Dillard, Annie. *Holy the Firm.* New York: Harper & Row, 1977.

Dillard, Annie. *Pilgrim at Tinker Creek.* New York: Harper & Row, 1974.

Dillman, Joanne Clarke. "*Magnolia*: Masquerading as Soap Opera." *Journal of Popular Film & Television* 33.3 (2005): 142–50.

DJ BC. "Mother Nature's Rump." <www.djbc.net/beastles.>

DJ Danger Mouse. *The Grey Album.* 2004.

Dowlding, William J. *Beatlesongs.* New York: Simon and Schuster, 1989.

Duff, Kat. *The Alchemy of Illness.* New York: Bell Tower, 1993.

Duncan, Robert. *Roots and Branches.* New York: Norton, 1969.

Dunn, Stephen. *New and Selected Poems: 1974–1994.* New York: Norton, 1994.

Dunn, Stephen. "Personal." *Riffs & Reciprocities: Prose Pairs.* New York: Norton, 1998. 73.

Dylan, Bob. *Highway 61 Revisited.* Columbia, 1965.

Eagleton, Terry. *After Theory.* New York: Basic, 2003.

Ebert, Roger. Review of *All the President's Men. Chicago Sun-Times* 1 January 1976. <rogerebert.suntimes.com/apps/pbcs.dll/article?AID=/19760101/REVIEWS/601010301/1023.>

Ebert, Roger. Review of *Magnolia. Chicago Sun-Times.* 7 January 2000 <rogerebert.suntimes.com/-apps/pbcs.dll/article?AID=/20000107/REVIEWS/1070303/1023.>

Eggers, Dave. *A Heartbreaking Work of Staggering Genius.* New York: Simon and Schuster, 2000.

Elder, John. *Imagining the Earth: Poetry and the Vision of Nature*. Urbana: University of Illinois Press, 1985.

Elder, John. *Reading the Mountains of Home*. Cambridge: Harvard University Press, 1998.

Ellsworth, Elizabeth. "Why Doesn't This Feel Empowering?: Working through the Repressive Myths of Critical Pedagogy." *Teaching for Change: Addressing Issues of Difference in the College Classroom*. Ed. Kathryn Geismar and Guitele Nicoleau. Cambridge: Harvard Educational Review, 1993. 43–70.

Emerson, Ralph Waldo. "Nature." *Selections from Ralph Waldo Emerson*. Ed. Stephen E. Whicher. Boston: Houghton Mifflin, 1960. 21–56.

Ensler, Eve. "Eve Ensler: 'Afghanistan Is Everywhere.'" Interview with Janelle Brown. *Salon Magazine* 26 November 2001. <www.salon.com.people/feature/2001/11/26/ensler/index_np.html.>

Ensler, Eve. Introduction. Ensler, *The Vagina Monologues: The V-Day Edition*. xxiii–xxxvi.

Ensler, Eve. *The Vagina Monologues: The V-Day Edition*. New York: Villard, 2001.

Eugenides, Jeffrey. *The Virgin Suicides*. New York: Farrar Straus Giroux, 1993.

Evans, Stephen F. "'Open Containers': Sherman Alexie's Drunken Indians." *American Indian Quarterly* 25.1 (2001): 46–72.

Everett, Walter. *The Beatles as Musicians: Revolver through the Anthology*. Oxford: Oxford University Press, 1999.

Fein, Esther B. "Costly Pleasures." *New York Times Book Review* 26 May 1985: 25.

Fergus, Jim. "Jim Harrison: Today's Hemingway?" *MD* (May 1985): 116, 118–9, 244–6.

Fleming, Andrew, dir. *Dick*. Sony, 1999.

Flieger, Jerry Aline. "Postmodern Perspective: The Paranoid Eye." *New Literary History* 28.1 (1997): 87–109.

Forte, Jeanie. "Focus on the Body: Pain, Praxis, and Pleasure in Feminist Performance." *Critical Theory and Performance*. Ed. Janelle G. Reinelt and Joseph R. Roach. Ann Arbor: University of Michigan Press, 1992. 248–62.

Fowles, John. *The Tree*. New York: Ecco, 1983.

Frank, Arthur W. *The Wounded Storyteller: Body, Illness, and Ethics*. Chicago: University of Chicago Press, 1995.

Freire, Paulo. *The Pedagogy of the Oppressed: Thirtieth-Anniversary Edition*. 1970. Trans. Myra Bergman Ramos. New York: Continuum, 2000.

Graham, Vicki. "'Into the body of another': Mary Oliver and the Poetics of Becoming Other." *Papers on Language and Literature* 30.4 (1994): 352–72.

Hagedorn, Jessica. *Dogeaters*. 1990. New York: Penguin, 1991.

Hagedorn, Jessica. *The Gangster of Love*. 1996. New York: Penguin, 1997.

Hagedorn, Jessica. "An Interview with Jessica Hagedorn." April 1994. Interview with Kay Bonetti. <missouri-review.org/interviews/hagedorn.html.>

Haines, John. *Fables and Distances: New and Selected Essays*. Saint Paul: Graywolf, 1996.

Halpern, Daniel and Dan Frank, eds. *The Nature Reader*. Hopewell: Ecco, 1996.

Han, Haewon. "Prospects for Our Youth." *Yisei Magazine* 6 (1992). <www.hcs.harvard.edu/~yisei/backissues/fall_92/yf92_40.html.>

Hardt, Michael and Antonio Negri. *Empire*. Cambridge: Harvard University Press, 2000.

Harmon, A. G. "Ordered Chaos: Three Films by Paul Thomas Anderson." *Image: A Journal of the Arts & Religion* 27 (2000): 107–16.

Harpham, Geoffrey Galt. *Shadows of Ethics: Criticism and the Just Society.* Durham: Duke University Press, 1999.

Harris, Kathleen Mullan. "The Health Status and Risk Behaviors of Adolescents in Immigrant Families." *Children of Immigrants: Health, Adjustment, and Public Assistance.* Ed. Donald J. Hernandez. Washington, DC: National Academy, 1999. 286–347.

Harrison, Jim. *After Ikkyü and Other Poems.* Boston: Shambhala, 1996.

Harrison, Jim. *Dalva.* New York: Dutton, 1988.

Harrison, Jim. "First Person Female." *The New York Times Magazine* 16 May 1999: 99–101.

Harrison, Jim. Interview with Eleanor Wachtel. *Brick* 63 (1999): 18–26.

Harrison, Jim. Interview with Kay Bonetti. *Missouri Review* 8.3 (1985): 63–86.

Harrison, Jim. *Just Before Dark.* Livingston, MO: Clark City, 1991.

Harrison, Jim. *Legends of the Fall.* New York: Delta, 1979.

Harrison, Jim. "The Man Whose Soul Is Not for Sale: Jim Harrison." Interview. *Rendezvous: Idaho State University Journal of Arts and Letters* 21.1 (1985): 26–42.

Harrison, Jim. "Passacaglia on Getting Lost." *The Nature Reader.* Ed. Daniel Halpern and Dan Frank. Hopewell: Ecco, 1996. 214–19.

Harrison, Jim. "Poetry as Survival." *Antæus* 64–65 (1990): 370–80.

Harrison, Jim. *The Road Home.* New York: Atlantic Monthly, 1998.

Harrison, Jim. *Sundog.* New York: Dutton, 1984.

Harrison, Jim. *Warlock.* New York: Delta, 1981.

Harrison, Jim. *Wolf.* New York: Delta, 1971.

Harrison, Jim. *The Woman Lit by Fireflies.* Boston: Houghton Mifflin, 1990.

Harter, Carol C. and James R. Thompson. *John Irving.* Boston: Twayne, 1986.

Harvey, David. *Spaces of Capital: Towards a Critical Geography.* New York: Routledge, 2001.

Hawksley, Humphrey. "Stark Reality of the American Dream." 18 August 2005. <news.bbc.co.uk/1/hi/programmes/from_our_own_correspondent/4159974.stm.>

Heaney, Tom. "Issues in Freirean Pedagogy." *Thresholds in Education* 20 June 1995. <nlu.nl.edu/ace/Resources/Documents/FreireIssues.html.>

Heat-Moon, William Least. *PrairyErth: A Deep Map.* Boston: Houghton Mifflin, 1991.

Hochschild, Jennifer L. *Facing up to the American Dream: Race, Class, and the Soul of the Nation.* Princeton: Princeton University Press, 1995.

hooks, bell. *Teaching to Transgress: Education as the Practice of Freedom.* New York: Routledge, 1994.

Hughes, Holly. *Clit Notes: A Sapphic Sampler.* New York: Grove, 1996.

Irving, John. *Cider House Rules.* New York: Morrow, 1985.

Irving, John. "A Conversation with John Irving." *Image* 2 (1992): 45–57.

Irving, John. "A Conversation with John Irving." Interview with Alison Freeland. *New England Review* 18 (1997): 135–42.

Irving, John. *The Hotel New Hampshire.* New York: Dutton, 1981.

Irving, John. "An Interview with John Irving." *Anything Can Happen: Interviews with Contemporary American Novelists.* Ed. Tom LeClair and Larry McCaffery. Urbana: University of Illinois Press, 1988. 176–98.

Irving, John. "The King of the Novel." *Trying to Save Piggy Sneed*. By Irving. New York: Arcade, 1996. 347–81.

Irving, John. *A Prayer for Owen Meany*. New York: Morrow, 1989.

Irving, John. *Three by Irving: Setting Free the Bears, The Water-Method Man*, [and] *The 158-Pound Marriage*. 1969, 1972, 1974. New York: Random House, 1980.

Irving, John. *A Widow for One Year*. New York: Random House, 1998.

Irving, John. *The World According to Garp*. New York: Dutton, 1978.

Jameson, Fredric R. *Postmodernism or, the Cultural Logic of Late Capitalism*. Durham: Duke University Press, 1991.

Jay-Z. *The Black Album*. Def Jam, 2003.

Johnson, Mark. " 'Keep Looking': Mary Oliver's Emersonian Project." *The Massachusetts Review* 46.1 (2005): 78–98.

Kane, Leslie, ed. *David Mamet in Conversation*. Ann Arbor: University of Michigan Press, 2001.

Kane, Leslie, ed. *Weasels and Wisemen: Ethics and Ethnicity in the Work of David Mamet*. New York: Palgrave, 1999.

Kempley, Rita. "Flower Power: Cruise and Company in a Heady *Magnolia*." *The Washington Post* 7 January 2000: C1.

Kinnell, Galway. *Selected Poems*. Boston: Houghton Mifflin, 1982.

Kirby, David. "Theory in Chaos." *The Christian Science Monitor* 27 January 2004: 11.

Klinkowitz, Jerome. *Literary Subversions: New American Fiction and the Practice of Criticism*. Carbondale: Southern Illinois University Press, 1985.

Kushner, Tony. "In Praise of Contradiction and Conundrum." *Theater* 31.3 (2001): 62–4.

Lee, Li-Young. Interview with Ilya Kaminsky and Katherine Towler. *The Sun* 356 (2005): 4–9.

Lee, Rachel C. *The Americans of Asian American Literature: Gendered Fictions of Nation and Transnation*. Princeton: Princeton University Press, 1999.

Lehmann-Haupt, Christopher. Review of *The Cider House Rules*, by John Irving. *New York Times* 20 May 1985: 20.

Levinas, Emmanuel. *Alterity and Transcendence*. Trans. Michael B. Smith. New York: Columbia University Press, 1999.

Levinas, Emmanuel. *Otherwise than Being: or Beyond Essence*. Trans. Alphonso Lingis. Pittsburgh: Duquesne University Press, 1998.

Levinas, Emmanuel. *Totality and Infinity*. Trans. Alphonso Lingis. Pittsburgh: Duquesne University Press, 2003.

Lopez, Barry. *Crossing Open Ground*. New York: Scribner's, 1988.

Lyotard, Jean-François. *The Postmodern Condition: A Report on Knowledge*. Trans. Geoff Bennington and Brian Massumi. Minneapolis: University of Minnesota Press, 1984.

MacDonald, Ian. *Revolution in the Head: The Beatles' Records and the Sixties*. New York: Henry Holt, 1994.

Mairs, Nancy. *Carnal Acts*. New York: Harper Collins, 1990.

Mairs, Nancy. *Plain Text*. Tucson: University of Arizona Press, 1986.

Mamet, David. "Celebrating the Capacity for Self-Knowledge." Interview with Henry I. Schvey. Kane. 60–71.

Mamet, David, dir. *Heist*. Warner Brothers, 2001.

Mamet, David, dir. *House of Games*. Orion, 1987.

Mamet, David. "I Just Kept Writing." Interview with Steven Dzielak Kane 31–8.

Mamet, David. *Make-Believe Town: Essays and Remembrances*. Boston: Little, Brown and Company, 1996.

Mamet, David. *South of the Northeast Kingdom*. Washington, DC: National Geographic, 2002.

Mamet, David, dir. *The Spanish Prisoner*. Sony, 1997.

Mamet, David, dir. *State and Main*. New Line, 2000.

Martone, Michael. *Seeing Eye*. Cambridge: Zoland, 1995.

Maslin, Janet. "Tangled Lives on the Cusp of the Millennium." *The New York Times* 17 December 1999: E1, E15.

Massey, Irving. *Find You the Virtue: Ethics, Image, and Desire in Literature*. Lanham: George Mason University Press, 1987.

Mathews, Freya. "Value in Nature and Meaning in Life." *Environmental Ethics*. Ed. Robert Elliot. Oxford: Oxford University Press, 1995. 142–54.

McCarthy, Paul. "Postmodern Pleasure and Perversity: Scientism and Sadism." *Postmodern Culture* 3.2 (1992). <muse.jhu.edu/journals/postmodern _culture.>

McClintock, James I. *Nature's Kindred Spirits: Aldo Leopold, Joseph Wood Krutch, Edward Abbey, Annie Dillard, and Gary Snyder*. Madison: University of Wisconsin Press, 1994.

McGinn, Colin. *Ethics, Evil, and Fiction*. Oxford: Clarendon, 1997.

McKinney, Devin. *Magic Circles: The Beatles in Dream and History*. Cambridge: Harvard University Press, 2003.

McLaren, Peter. *Che Guevara, Paulo Freire, and the Pedagogy of Revolution*. Lanham: Rowman and Littlefield, 2000.

Mendible, Myra. "Desiring Images: Representation and Spectacle in *Dogeaters*." *Critique* 43 (2002): 289–304.

Miles, Jonathan. "Jim Harrison: The Salon Interview." *Salon Magazine* 2 December 1998. <http://www.salonmagazine.com/books/int/1998/12cov_02intb.html.>

Miller, Gabriel. *John Irving*. New York: Ungar, 1982.

Mitchell, Stephen. *Genesis: A New Translation of the Classic Biblical Stories*. New York: Harper Collins, 1996.

Morris, Wesley. "*Magnolia* in Full Bloom." *San Francisco Examiner* 7 January 2000: C1.

Murdoch, Iris. *The Sovereignty of Good*. 1970. London: Ark, 1985.

Muscio, Inga. *Cunt: A Declaration of Independence*. Seattle: Seal, 1998.

Myers-Walls, Judith and Mayi Fonseca. "Liberation Pedagogy: A Process to Empower Students." Child Development and Family Studies Departmental Colloquium, Purdue University, March 1991.

Norris, Kathleen. *Amazing Grace: A Vocabulary of Faith*. New York: Riverhead, 1998.

Norris, Kathleen. *Dakota: A Spiritual Geography*. Boston: Houghton Mifflin, 1993.

Nussbaum, Martha C. *Poetic Justice: The Literary Imagination and Public Life*. Boston: Beacon, 1995.

Obel, Karen. "The Story of V-Day and the College Initiative." Ensler, *The Vagina Monologues: The V-Day Edition*, 2001. 129–71.

Oelschlaeger, Max. *The Idea of Wilderness: From Prehistory to the Age of Ecology*. New Haven: Yale University Press, 1991.

Oliver, Mary. *Blue Pastures*. New York: Harcourt Brace, 1995.

Oliver, Mary. *Long Life: Essays and Other Writings*. Cambridge: Da Capo, 2004.

Oliver, Mary. *New and Selected Poems, Volume One*. Boston: Beacon, 1992.

Oliver, Mary. *New and Selected Poems, Volume Two.* Boston: Beacon, 2005.

Oliver, Mary. *Twelve Moons.* Boston: Little, Brown and Company, 1979.

Oliver, Mary. *Why I Wake Early: New Poems.* Boston: Beacon, 2004.

Oliver, Mary. *Winter Hours: Prose, Prose Poems, and Poems.* Boston: Houghton Mifflin, 1999.

O'Reilley, Mary Rose. *The Barn at the End of the World: The Apprenticeship of a Quaker, Buddhist Shepherd.* Minneapolis: Milkweed, 2000.

O'Russell, David. *Three Kings.* Warner, 1999.

Owens, Louis. "Through an Amber Glass: Chief Doom and the Native American Novel Today." *Mixedblood Messages: Literature, Film, Family, Place.* Norman: University of Oklahoma Press, 1998. 57–82.

Oxford English Dictionary. <dictionary.oed.com.>

Pakula, Alan J., dir. *All the President's Men.* Warner Brothers, 1976.

Pankey, Eric. "Santo Spirito." *The Late Romances: Poems.* New York: Knopf, 1997. 43.

Pollack, Alan W. "Alan W. Pollack's 'Notes On' Series." 2000. <www.recmusic beatles.com/public/files/awp/awp.html.>

Poulin, A., Jr., ed. *Contemporary American Poetry.* 6th ed. Boston: Houghton Mifflin, 1996.

Poulin, A., Jr. and Michael Waters, eds. *Contemporary American Poetry.* 7th ed. Boston: Houghton Mifflin, 2001.

Poulin, A., Jr. and Michael Waters, eds. *Contemporary American Poetry.* 8th ed. Boston: Houghton Mifflin, 2006.

Quantick, David. *Revolution: The Making of the Beatles' White Album.* Chicago: Chicago Review, 2002.

Quigley, Peter. "Rethinking Resistance: Environmentalism, Literature, and Poststructural Theory." *Postmodern Environmental Ethics.* Ed. Max Oelschlaeger. Albany: State University of New York Press, 1995. 173–91.

Rafael, Vincente L. "Patronage and Pornography: Ideology and Spectatorship in the Early Marcos Years." *Comparative Studies in Society and History* 32 (1990): 282–304.

Reilly, Edward C. *Jim Harrison.* New York: Twayne, 1996.

Rich, Adrienne. *Blood, Bread, and Poetry: Selected Prose 1979–1985.* London: Virago, 1987.

Rich, Adrienne. *Of Woman Born: Motherhood as Experience and Institution.* New York: Norton, 1976.

Riley, Tim. *Tell Me Why: A Beatles Commentary.* New York: Knopf, 1988.

Roberson, William H. " 'A Good Day to Live': The Prose Works of Jim Harrison." *The Great Lakes Review: A Journal of Midwest Culture* 8.2–9.1 (1982–83): 29–37.

Rockwood, Bruce L., ed. "Abortion Stories: Uncivil Discourse and *Cider House Rules.*" *Law and Literature Perspectives.* New York: Lang, 1996. 289–340.

Roemer, Michael. *Telling Stories: Postmodernism and the Invalidation of Traditional Narrative.* Lanham: Rowman and Littlefield, 1995.

Roessner, Jeffrey. "We All Want to Change the World: Postmodern Politics and the Beatles' *White Album.*" *Reading the Beatles: Cultural Studies, Literary Criticism, and the Fab Four.* Ed. Kenneth Womack and Todd F. Davis. New York: State University of New York Press, 2006. 147–58.

Rogan, Josh [John Haines]. "The Skipper's Lament." <www.lulu.com/Josh-Rogan.>

Rogers, Pattiann. *The Dream of the Marsh Wren: Writing as Reciprocal Creation.* Minneapolis: Milkweed, 1999.

Rohrkemper, John. " 'Natty Bummpo Wants Tobacco': Jim Harrison's Wilderness." *The Great Lakes Review: A Journal of Midwest Culture* 8.2–9.1 (1982–83): 20–28.

Rosenberg, Brian. *Little Dorrit's Shadows: Character and Contradiction in Dickens.* Columbia: University of Missouri Press, 1996.

Ruddick, Lisa. "The Near Enemy of the Humanities Is Professionalism." *The Chronicle of Higher Education* 23 November 2001: B7–9.

Sanders, Scott Russell. *The Country of Language.* Minneapolis: Milkweed, 1999.

Sanders, Scott Russell. *Hunting for Hope: A Father's Journeys.* Boston: Beacon, 1998.

Sanders, Scott Russell. *Writing from the Center.* Bloomington: Indiana University Press, 1995.

San Juan, E., Jr. "Transforming Identity in Postcolonial Narrative: An Approach to the Novels of Jessica Hagedorn." *Post-Identity* 1 (1998): 5–28.

Sassen, Saskia. *Losing Control?: Sovereignty in an Age of Globalization.* New York: Columbia University Press, 1996.

Savage, Scott. *A Plain Life: Walking My Belief.* New York: Ballantine, 2000.

Shor, Ira and Paulo Freire. *A Pedagogy for Liberation: Dialogues on Transforming Education.* Westport: Bergin and Garvey, 1987.

Shostak, Debra. "The Family Romances of John Irving." *Essays in Literature* 21 (1994): 129–45.

Smith, Kimberly K. "Mere Nostalgia: Notes on a Progressive Paratheory." *Rhetoric & Public Affairs* 3.4 (2000): 505–27.

Snyder, Gary. *Earth House Hold.* New York: New Directions, 1968.

Soukhanov, Anne H. "Word Watch." *The Atlantic* 266 (1990): 140.

Steinem, Gloria. Foreword. Ensler, *The Vagina Monologues: The V-Day Edition,* 2001. ix–xix.

Stevens, Wallace. "The Motive for Metaphor." *The Collected Poems of Wallace Stevens.* New York: Vintage, 1954. 288.

Stocking, Kathleen. *Letters from the Leelanau: Essays of People and Place.* Ann Arbor: University of Michigan Press, 1990.

Stone, Oliver, dir. *Nixon.* Cinergi, 1995.

Strand, Mark. *The Weather of Words: Poetic Invention.* New York: Knopf, 2000.

Sullivan, Henry W. *The Beatles with Lacan: Rock 'n' Roll as Requiem for the Modern Age.* New York: Lang, 1995.

Swander, Mary. A conversation with Todd F. Davis. 15 November 2003.

Swander, Mary. *Crossing the Borders of the Known World."* Interview with Todd F. Davis. *Interdisciplinary Literary Studies* 3.2 (2002): 123–32.

Swander, Mary. *The Desert Pilgrim: En Route to Mysticism and Miracles.* New York: Viking, 2003.

Swander, Mary. *Driving the Body Back: Poems.* New York: Knopf, 1986.

Swander, Mary. *Heaven-and-Earth House: Poems.* New York: Knopf, 1994.

Swander, Mary. *Out of This World: A Woman's Life among the Amish.* New York: Viking, 1995.

Swander, Mary. "Red Cabbage and Pears, Or How I Became a Pacifist." *Living With Topsoil: Tending Spirits, Cherishing Land.* Ed. Steve Semken. North Liberty: Ice Cube, 2004.

Swander, Mary. *Succession: Poems.* Athens: University of Georgia Press, 1979.

Taylor, Charles. Review of *Magnolia. Salon Magazine* 17 December 1999. <www.salon.com/ent/movies/review/1999/12/17/magnolia/index.html.>

Thomas, Lewis. *The Lives of a Cell: Notes of a Biology Watcher.* New York: Viking, 1974.

TLC. "UnPretty." *FanMail.* La Face, 1999.

V-Day. *V-Day: Until the Violence Stops.* 2002. <www.v-day.org.>

Volf, Miroslav. *Exclusion and Embrace: A Theological Exploration of Identity, Otherness, and Reconciliation.* Nashville: Abingdon, 1996.

Vonnegut, Kurt. *God Bless You, Mr. Rosewater.* New York: Dell, 1965.

Von Trier, Lars. *Breaking the Waves.* Argus, 1996.

Walker, Margaret Urban. "Morality in Practice: A Response to Claudia Card and Lorraine Code." *Hypatia* 17.1 (2002): 174–82.

Walker, Margaret Urban. "Moral Repair and Its Limits." *Mapping the Ethical Turn: A Reader in Ethics, Culture, and Literary Theory.* Ed. Todd F. Davis and Kenneth Womack. Charlottesville: U of Virginia P, 2001. 110–27.

Weber, Myles. "David Mamet in Theory and Practice." *New England Review* 21 (2000): 136–42.

White, Jonathan. *Talking on the Water.* New York: Random House, 1994.

Whitley, Ed. "The Postmodern *White Album.*" *The Beatles, Popular Music, and Society.* Ed. Ian Inglis. New York: St. Martin's, 2000. 105–25.

Whitman, Walt. "*Song of Myself.*" *Leaves of Grass.* Ed. Sculley Bradley and Harold W. Blodgett. New York: Norton, 1973. 28–89.

Williams, Bernard. *Ethics and the Limits of Philosophy.* Cambridge: Harward UP, 1985.

Wings. *Back to the Egg.* Columbia, 1979.

Wings. *Venus and Mars.* Capitol, 1975.

Winter, Jessica. "Day for Naught." *The Village Voice* 20–26 December 2000. <www.village-voice.com/issues/0051/winter.php.>

Womack, Kenneth. "The Beatles as Modernists." *Music and Literary Modernism: Critical Essays and Comparative Studies.* Ed. Robert McParland. Forthcoming, Cambridge Scholars Press.

Womack, Kenneth. "The Great Traveling Medicine Show." 2004.

Woodward, Bob. *The Secret Man: The Story of Watergate's Deep Throat.* New York: Simon and Schuster, 2005.

Wright, James. *Above the River: The Complete Poems.* New York: Farrar Straus Giroux, 1990.

Zacharek, Stephanie. Review of *Dick. Salon Magazine* 4 August 1999. <www.salon.com/ent/movies/review/1999/08/04/dick/index.html?CP=SAL&DN=110.>

Index

Printed and bound by CPI Group (UK) Ltd, Croydon, CR0 4YY